Planning Care in Mental Health Nursing

Planning Care in Mental Health Nursing

Edited by
Robert Tummey

First published 2005 by
PALGRAVE MACMILLAN
Houndmills, Basingstoke, Hampshire RG21 6XS and
175 Fifth Avenue, New York, N.Y. 10010
Companies and representatives throughout the world.

PALGRAVE MACMILLAN is the global academic imprint of the Palgrave
Macmillan division of St. Martin's Press, LLC and of Palgrave Macmillan Ltd.
Macmillan® is a registered trademark in the United States, United Kingdom
and other countries. Palgrave is a registered trademark in the European
Union and other countries.

ISBN 1–4039–1526–1 paperback

This book is printed on paper suitable for recycling and made from fully
managed and sustained forest sources.

A catalogue record for this book is available from the British Library.

10   9   8   7   6   5   4   3   2   1
14 13 12 11 10 09 08 07 06 05

Printed in China.

Dedicated to the memory of my father
Robert John Tummey
And the living inspiration of Francesca,
Hannah and Rhys

Contents

Preface

This book will specifically address the systems, focus and delivery of planned care within mental health nursing. The intention being to create a platform for the exploration of planning care based on the variety of settings now established within mental health nursing practice. A great deal of progress has been made within mental health, to the point that many services are unrecognisable from that of ten years ago. With this change and emphasis on community care brings the need to mark the position and determine the progress made.

Within mental health nursing there has been a revolution of ideas and it is now for the resourceful, accountable practitioner to sift through and define their own position. For me, this book combines the effort of practitioners who have sifted, toiled and grasped knowledge their specific fields of expertise to give inspiration and encouragement to service users, carers and colleagues alike. The idea for creating such a platform for good practice is a result of the re-organisation of mental health services and the need to re-establish nursing within them. This book is dedicated to every practicing mental health nurse and those who are undergoing nurse education. It is not based on mental health problems, but aimed at the specific settings and interventions with which nurses practice, function and unite with the people who require their input. It is an overview of the whole process of planning care from assessment through to delivery, whilst taking into consideration that the service user is unique and individual.

Under each heading, a wide range of diagnostic presentations are explored. However, it is the individual, their social environment, clinical setting and intervention delivery within new structures that provides the greatest challenge for nurses. With the hope of planning care that overrides the containment of illness, and focuses on holistic health, advocacy and partnership.

Bob Tummey

Acknowledgements

I would like to offer my sincere thanks to a number of people who have assisted in making this book a reality. For acceptance of the concept and support throughout the process I thank the team at Palgrave, including Jon Reed, Magenta Lampson and Jo Digby. For continued managerial support and encouragement I thank Natalie Mills and Roger Minett. My gratitude goes to all contributors for sharing their academic and clinical expertise. And finally, I thank the reviewers for their useful advice and influential comments.

Notes on the Contributors

Nancy Bunch BSc (Hons) Health Studies, Cert.Ed, Dip.N, RMN. Lecturer Practitioner at the University of Plymouth and Somerset Partnership NHS Trust.

Michael Coffey MSc, BSc (Hons), RMN, RGN. Lecturer in Community Mental Health Nursing at University of Wales, Swansea.

Mike Fleet MSc. (Lond), PGCE, BSc, DipThorn, RMN, RGN. Senior Lecturer in Mental Health at University of Teesside and honorary practitioner in Assertive Outreach, Tees & North Yorkshire NHS Trust.

Dean-David Holyoake PhD, MSc, PGDip.N, BA, BSc (Hons), Dip.CPC, Dip.ChildPsychol, RMN. Clinical Nurse Specialist in Child & Adolescent Mental Health at New Phase Wing of Priory Healthcare, Birmingham.

Clare Hopkins MSc, PGCert. Systemic Practice, RMN. Primary Care Mental Health Worker, Gateshead Primary Care Trust and former Senior Lecturer in Mental Health Nursing at Northumbria University, Newcastle upon Tyne.

Barbara Jones BSN, RN. Nurse Clinician Analyst, UMASS Medical School, Newborn Screening Program, Jamaica Plain, Massachusetts, USA. Also carer for two adult sons diagnosed as suffering from mental illness.

Trevor Lowe MPhil (Psychology), PGCEA, BSc (Hons), RMN. Nurse Consultant in Psychosocial Interventions at Slough Community Mental Health Centre and former Lecturer Practitioner for Acute Admissions at Slough. Also, Honorary Lecturer at the Institute of Psychiatry, London.

Roger Minett MA, BA (Hons), CertEd (FE), RMN, RGN. Associate Head of Nursing at Coventry University.

Members of North East Warwickshire User Involvement Project.

Stephen Niemiec PGDipA, BA (Hons), RPN, RMN. Nurse Consultant in Crisis Resolution at Newcastle and North Tyneside Crisis Assessment and Treatment Service, Newcastle upon Tyne and Associate Director of Nursing for 3NNN Mental Health Trust.

Mark Rayne MA, RMN. Project Manager for Early Intervention in Psychosis at NIMHE West Midlands Development Centre and former Clinical Lead for Early Intervention in Psychosis, Walsall Teaching Primary Care NHS Trust.

Dave Roberts MSc, RMN, RGN. Programme Lead in Cancer Care at Oxford-Brookes University and Honorary Clinical Specialist in Psycho-Oncology, Oxford Radcliffe NHS Trust.

Jayne Sayers MSc, BSc (Hons), DipASS, CertEd, Cert.Health, RMN. Senior Lecturer in Older Adult Mental Health at the University of Central England in Birmingham and Honorary Lecturer in Mental Health at the University of Birmingham.

Maureen Smojkis MSc, BSc (Hons), DipSN, RMN. Lecturer in Counselling and Programme Co-ordinator for MA in Solution-Focused Brief Therapy at University of Birmingham and Associate Psychological Counsellor for Psychology Department, Northern Birmingham NHS Trust.

William Spence MEd, BSc (Hons), RMN, DipPSN Principal Lecturer in Mental Health at Oxford-Brookes University, Oxford and Honorary Community Mental Health Nurse, Oxford.

Robert Tummey MSc, PGCE, Dip Psych, ENB660, RMN. Senior Lecturer in Mental Health Nursing at Coventry University and Honorary Clinical Nurse Psychotherapist at Psychological Therapies Department, Coventry Primary Care Trust.

Malcolm Watts MA, PGCert, Cert.Health.Ed, Cert.SystemicTher, RGN, RMN. Lecturer Practitioner in Co-Morbidity (Mental Health & Substance Misuse) at Coventry University and South Warwickshire Primary Care Trust.

Linda Whitehead BSc, RMN, DipN (Lond). Clinical Nurse Specialist in Liaison Mental Health Nursing, Department of Psychological Medicine, John Radcliffe Hospital, Oxford.

Tom Williams MA (Distn), UKCP Registered Systemic/Family Therapist, Cert.Couns, RMN. Senior Clinical Nurse Therapist, Regional (Adult) Eating Disorder Service, Newcastle, North Tyneside and Northumberland Mental Health NHS Trust.

Introduction

Robert Tummey

This book is a celebration of the work and involvement that nurses deliver across the United Kingdom (UK). From the first concept of the book, the contributors and myself have been committed in providing the informed and valuable text you are about to read. It offers a comprehensive overview of the subject of planning care, detailing the explicit and specialised nature of the profession.

Each specific and specialised area is detailed to demonstrate the transferable skills within, not only for their service, but the wider delivery of mental health nursing. Indeed, for the chapters included, the task of informing and educating has been completed admirably. Various books discuss aspects of role, identity and therapeutic delivery. Some detail the interventions, some the illnesses, some the evidence, some the service. This book attempts to explore the core business of care through the process of mental health nursing within each working environment. It is the essential skill of caring in a professional way that has a unique place in the status of nursing.

It is my conviction that good nursing is spread through good education, role modelling and word of mouth. Those prepared to offer themselves to assist others in distress within the nursing partnership require acknowledgement. This I believe is overdue. Whether working within a hospital ward, a client's home, a mental health unit, a surgery, a health centre etc, all are part of the community. They are resources at the heart of care, but nevertheless in the community. This book is for all nurses, educators, mentors, users, carers and staff that have anything to do with the experience of care for people in mental health services.

Drawing from the Bigger Picture

From the first time I learnt to write a care plan I felt a sense of responsibility to the client and achievement as a professional. However, I was unsure how it all fitted together. Where did it fit into the experience and life of the client? How were their ongoing needs to be met? What was the bigger picture? There was a sense that the small piece of important work completed with the client was placed in isolation to the immediacy of service provision and requirement. Something was missing. This unfolded as my lack of understanding for the wider context; the bigger picture, the holism spoken of and the grand scheme. This is where the efforts of the client and I needed to be placed. To have an overview of or insight into the progressive nature of care and the various pathways open to the client. To articulate knowledge and awareness that the client is not isolated to a set of goals within their current context. To demonstrate competency in the role of mental health nurse and recognise the process involved. This was to acknowledge the point at which I had contact with the client and where that contact would or could be heading.

A text that could allow navigation of this would be one I wish to own, read and endorse. Navigating the understanding of what makes a good nurse can be a dilemma. One of the key instruments that can be developed is the use of self. To create a space for the interaction to take place and offer an opportunity to make sense of its intention.

The art and science of nursing care of the whole person is advocated and demonstrated throughout this text. Progress, perseverance and determination ensure this profession will conform to protocol, but also confirm alliance with the client.

Working at the Care-face

Ready with the intention to commit to the book, I identified the many clinical settings and set about acquiring the contributions from those areas. The contributors represent an array of mental health nursing knowledge. It was a consideration from the outset that combining the informed wisdom of practitioners and academics could create diverse viewpoint. Therefore, for the purpose of imparting the specific developmental nature of planning care, I opted for a universal format for each chapter that helps create uniformity. To ensure the book remained relevant, to the point and covered all necessary aspects I developed the template you can see for each.

The use of language is important and can either include or exclude its participants (Crawford *et al.*, 1998). Therefore, the terms used are identified as specific to each setting. For instance, although a number of people receiving mental health services prefer the title service user, this may not be appropriate or applicable for identifying someone receiving primary care. The terms patient and client are therefore inserted where the contributor feels this is necessary. You will find as you explore each chapter that the format is the same throughout, except for the stakeholders. Their approach and message is rather different and needs to inform through individuality.

The sections are easily accessible and enable the reader to find information across the services: whether exploring the assessment process for Older Adults and the difference with Rehab' and Recovery; identifying the referral process for Child and Adolescent Mental Health Services (CAMHS) and connection with Early Intervention; or comparing the time frame of involvement for two or more services etc.

Thus a reference point is established for gaining further understanding of the work of other mental health nurses within their own specialised clinical setting. I am aware that this does not include the practices of other disciplines and make no apologies for this. Mental health nurses are establishing an identity within a fast moving, evolving health service. It is the client, patient, service user who is central to the provision of care. It has been my intention to focus on the nurse who will be providing said care, the people who Barker (1999) terms the foot soldiers, working at the 'care-face'.

Unfolding the Stages

The introduction gives an overview and explanation of the main concepts for each given area. This allows a first insight into the various settings. The prevalence and population is in place to offer a contextual platform with which the nursing is delivered. A brief indication of the statistics involved for the people seen unfolds this stage of understanding. How many and who are they? Then we move to the start of the whole health machine. A discussion is offered for the process of referral. Again, a number of aspects are described to inform the reader of where the referrals come from. It establishes how the prospect of a referral is considered and the criteria used.

Next in the chapter sequence is an exploration of the various theoretical frameworks in use across the settings. Once a referral has been made, what is the theoretical context in which the client or potential client is viewed? These answers are an interesting read for the diversity of adoption from a number of theoreticians. The theories used are not all nurse-based, but rather research-orientated, Government led, theoretically influenced, across discipline and clinically adapted. Some may appear duplicated in their presentation. However, I have attempted to remain consistent with each chapter by retaining original emphasis. This is for the main purpose of acknowledging the distinct and explicit use of a model or philosophy for each area, models such as cognitive behavioural therapy (CBT) or medication management. However, where there is a clear repetition, I have referred the reader to the same information provided in another chapter, one with a more comprehensive view.

The principles and skills required for effective working with the specific client group and the delivery of the care plan are detailed. A look at the necessary aspects for the role undertaken in each setting is achieved through the identification of principles. Once gained or developed, these assist the professional to further their useful influence and offer genuineness that the client can acknowledge. If not possessed, the difficulties will be evident for themselves.

Assessment then forms a major contribution from approach used to risk priorities for the client group. A framework of understanding is thus produced as a foundation for the development of an agreeable plan of care. This leads into the dominant section for care planning. How is this determined? How is it then applied? What are the additional concerns? All these are explained individually. The case examples illustrate the realities of involvement. Most are quite simple in their explanation and may only cover one aspect of service delivery. This is mainly true of the latter chapters, attempting to discuss whole services rather than functionalised teams. It is therefore intentional that they narrow their focus, as the major issues described can be transferred into additional settings such as community or health centre.

The End of the Beginning

Before ending the introduction, I must acknowledge the stakeholders. In the age of service user and carer involvement, I believe it only fitting that we consider their voices in the context of our work. To gain understanding of what it is like to receive services, professional assistance and attempts at respite and so on. What is the experience of having a care plan written with you or for you? How does this affect the loved one you care for? How are our actions perceived and tolerated?

I feel that the two chapters have done some justice to the many people unable to have their thoughts considered in professional text. The explanations and insights provided are enlightening, honest and guidance for mental health nursing to embrace. I would like to thank them for their contribution, which is worthy of separate acknowledgement.

I trust that you will gain something from the reading of this book. I trust that it will inform elements of your practice. Most of all I trust that you will ensure the individual nature of planning care is intimately achieved with an eye on the bigger picture.

References

Barker, P. (1999) *The Philosophy and Practice of Psychiatric Nursing*, London: Churchill Livingstone.
Crawford, P., Brown, B. and Nolan, P. (1998) *Communicating Care: the language of nursing*, Cheltenham: Stanley Thornes Ltd.

PART 1

The Stakeholders

CHAPTER 1

Partnership with the Service User

Roger Minett with Members of the North East Warwickshire User Involvement Project

Madpersons as empowered consumers of services and madpersons as equal citizens are two quite different propositions. (Campbell, 1996: p. 224)

Introduction

This chapter will begin with a brief introduction to user involvement in mental health as it has emerged in the UK. The concept of partnership for care planning in mental health care between workers and service users will be explored and who the partners might be. Also, exploring issues of partnership working and what this actually means. Then, three brief accounts of personal experience will attempt to illustrate the service user perspective on the planning of care. These highlight what can be learnt from experience, thereby, leading on to the examination of partnership working, by looking at what is beneficial and what are the barriers. Some personal thoughts conclude the chapter identifying the attitudes and skills necessary for partnerships to work.

Service User Involvement

Within the NHS there has been an increasing impetus to develop and involve service users and the public in mental health. Numerous policy documents make reference to user involvement (DoH, 1994a, 1997, 1998, 1999b, 2001a). In mental health, service user involvement has been made mandatory by the publication of the Patients Charter for Mental Health (NHS Executive, 1997) and the National Service Framework for Mental Health (DoH, 1999c).

At the same time user involvement in mental health has proliferated. The beginning of the current user movement, according to Campbell (1996), can be traced to an international conference in Brighton in 1985. He suggests that

---

Box 1.1   Examples of user involvement

Clinical Practice, Commissioning, Auditing, Researching, Recruiting and Training Staff (Bhui *et al.*, 1998; Hostick, 1998; Maza, 1996; McClelland, 1998; Rose *et al.*, 1998; Ramon, 2001; Truman and Slade, 1999; Wolf, 2001; Town *et al.*, 1991).

---

at this conference evidence of such movements from other countries was revealed and highlighted the fragmented and underdeveloped nature of user activity in this country. He points out that the user movement has flourished since that time and cites a number of influencing factors. For example, the increasing awareness of civil rights in the 1970s and 1980s amongst those with mental illness and the policy of de-institutionalisation. This meant that the mentally ill were now in a better position to campaign and assert themselves against the hitherto monolithic professions in psychiatry. The growth and development of user participation and empowerment was also encouraged by the political climate of the 1980s and 1990s in which the New Right ideology emphasised self-help, minimal state intervention and consumerism (Fraher and Limpinnian, 1999).

Now, there are numerous examples of user involvement in many aspects of service development and delivery (see Box 1.1). Indeed, three authors of this chapter are current service users and have been involved in a number of these activities. However, there is none more important than in planning one's own care.

Apart from the need to comply with government policy and guidelines there are a number of benefits to professionals in user involvement. Campbell and Lindow (1997) suggest a number of these, including:

(i) It improves job satisfaction.
(ii) It may even improve clinical outcomes.
(iii) Services are unlikely to improve unless service users experiences and knowledge are taken into account.

There are further rationale for involving service users in their own care and the decision making process. *They are expert in their own illness.* This concept of 'expertness' is relatively new within health care, as hitherto, professionals have seen themselves as the experts. However, initiatives in chronic disease management are now aimed at encouraging professionals to regard users as experts in their own illness (DoH, 2001b).

Interestingly, there have been concerns raised with the concept of user involvement. For example, Pattison (2001) questions whether it is idealistic and wishful thinking, rather than reality. A number of current or former service users have written about their own involvement in mental health services and have accused agencies of tokenism (Read, 2001; Trivedi, 2001). Similarly, the user perspective may be ignored or disregarded by professionals who consider that they know best (Perkins and Repper, 1998) and if service users are articulate and authoritative they are often accused of being untypical and unrepresentative (Crepaz-Keay, 1996). The balance of power between service users and professionals is unequal and assertive or knowledgeable users may be threatening. Thus, there may be a reluctance to accept users as equals and dismiss the ideas and issues important to them (Campbell, 1996; Bowl, 1996; Perkins and Repper, 1998; Pattison, 2001).

Partnerships with Professionals

Partnership between service users and professionals has been highlighted in a number of government documents (DoH, 1994a, 1999a, b). It appears to be regarded as an essential ingredient for mental health services. For the purposes of this discussion, the emphasis will be on partnership at the individual level. A concept also recognised in the mental health nursing review (Butterworth and Rushworth, 1995), which asserted that all people who use services should engage in a new partnership with nurses in the delivery of care.

Trivedi (1996) suggests that there are a number of advantages to working in partnership, that include:

- Improved communication.
- Improved awareness of users needs.
- Active participation from users of services.
- Improved service provision.
- Service providers doing their jobs in a better and more collaborative way.

However, Bassett (2000) reminds us that mental health services do not have a good record for co-operation or collaboration, especially with service users, where partnership may be a worthwhile aspiration, but there should be an increase in co-operation first. In a research study of perceptions of hospital care, Sharma and Carson (1996) found that patients and staff had differing perceptions of the value of various aspects of their stay in hospital. They concluded that, in attempting to move towards a closer partnership with their patients, mental health nurses needed to be aware that there may be differences in how they and their patients perceive care. Alas, before partnerships can be developed, these differences need to be explored.

The Care Programme Approach

The Care Programme Approach (CPA) (DoH, 1990) requires professional workers to develop a package of care that is agreed in partnership with users and carers. One of the purposes is to improve quality of care offered and subsequently the person's quality of life. CPA was developed in 1990 because the government were concerned about follow-up care for people leaving psychiatric hospitals. It contained four key elements:

- Assessment of health and social needs.
- An agreed plan of care and treatment.
- Allocation of a key worker.
- Regular reviews of and, as appropriate, changes to the care plans.

(DoH, 1990)

The government did not prescribe how it would work, and left it to individual authorities to interpret, implement and develop specific procedures. They did emphasise elements of good practice and gave some guidelines. One of which was that service users should be fully involved in the development of their own care plans. Subsequent guidelines on how the CPA should be implemented were issued, emphasising the need for user and carer involvement (DoH, 1994b, 1995). Despite these guidelines early research commissioned by the DoH found evidence of only minimal involvement of users and carers (North *et al.*, 1993). Government has since reviewed the CPA policy and made some changes, but the imperative to involve service users and their carers remains (DoH, 1999a). Local authorities however were once again left to develop their own procedures and there is a good deal of evidence, from both the literature and the personal experience outlined below that:

- Users are not involved with their care plans.
- Indeed some did not know of their existence.
- Many do not know who their key worker is.
- They lack knowledge regarding their care.
- Are unfamiliar with their treatment programmes.
- Did not know the date of their review.
- Did not have a written copy of the care plan.

(Wolfe *et al.*, 1997; McDermott, 1998; Rose, 2001)

Therefore, far from partnership working, it seems that as far as care planning is concerned the user is being constantly marginalised. Rose suggests this is,

> almost a dereliction of duty to keep such a document from the user whose life it so directly affects. (Rose, 2001: p. 48)

The initiatives on user involvement, partnership working and CPA are welcome. However, there are a number of issues for exploration. These include, *Defining what the term partnership means? What is wanted and expected from the partnership? How to develop relationships for effective partnership working? What happens when the partnership breaks down or one of the partners moves on? What happens when there is disagreement?* We will explore these questions further after some examples of personal experience.

Service Users Experiences of Care Planning

Personal Experience 1: Julie

Personal History

My name is Julie and I have been a service user now for 16 years. I married when I was 18 years old and my illness started around my first pregnancy. Flash backs about my traumatic past were the start. I was in Germany with my husband at the time. On return to live in England I was very ill but no one could tell me what was wrong or diagnose the problem, until I finally got to see a psychiatrist.

Mental Health History

I have seen several psychiatrists over the years, each one going over the same things time and time again. In this time I have had a number of diagnoses from different psychiatrists including, schizophrenia, mania, psychosis and personality disorder. I don't really know what any of these terms mean and haven't had them explained to me. It always felt that no one had time to listen to me or understand what was going on inside me.

I was a 'revolving door patient', always in and out of hospital until the last two years in which I have managed to keep out of hospital even in periods of crisis (illness). In the past I have had a number of key workers from the mental health team, the shortest being four months and the longest two years. I had never, until recently, been involved in planning my own care or been party to the process of CPA. I now know about CPA because I am part of a user involvement, training group.

Current Experience

I now have a wonderful psychiatrist who I see when I have periods of crisis. This could be up to twice per week when I am unwell or two to four monthly when I am well. The most important point for me is that I can choose how often I see him. My current psychiatrist listens and is prepared to talk about anything, including symptoms and personal problems. He has developed a management plan in conjunction with myself that I have agreed, which I follow when I am feeling unwell. I keep a copy of it. I like the plan because it allows me to retain control of my illness and myself in periods of crisis (illness). I also have a care plan written with my community nurse. I believe I have this because I asked for it.

I am now busy with various user involvement projects. This involvement has given me so much more self-confidence and knowledge of what services should be like. I now feel more able to assert myself and ask for and be involved in my own care plans.

Notes: [Editor: Within Julie's road to recovery, she has found confidence and inclusion. Information and relationships have been the main factors for a more assured and empowered outcome.]

Personal Experience 2: Anita

Personal History

My first breakdown was at the age of 28 years in 1986. I was run down, trying to balance work with the running of the home and dealing with my two children alone. My husband worked nights and each time we saw each other we argued. He had threatened to divorce me, to put me in hospital and take the children. This was all too much in one day.

When the Doctor was called he asked if I would like to go to hospital for some rest. I said yes, thinking I was going to a general hospital. However, I ended up in a psychiatric unit where I did 'flip my lid'. Following that initial admission I was in and out of hospital like a 'YoYo'. A result of arguments with family, a divorce, losing countless jobs, being made redundant, children misbehaving and a new relationship that did not work.

Mental Health History

I was not offered any choice in treatment at all. I did not know care plans existed. Every time I have been in hospital under a section of the Mental Health Act (1983), I have appealed and been discharged. No one ever sat and discussed my care or what had happened to me. This was always done with other people such as relatives, or even the police. I was just seated in a side room or frog marched and injected. It felt like there was nothing I could do except sit quiet until a week later when I saw the consultant psychiatrist. If I disagreed with him, it would be another week and then another until my tribunal came. That's when I would have my say. But it's three months later and that's a long time sitting behind locked doors for a domestic argument.

I've been given various medications that have not helped. With some I have felt too tired to work. So in order to keep the mortgage paid I've stopped the medications and worked. The trouble is I haven't coped with working in the local community because of stigma. So, I've ended up back in hospital, losing jobs and back on medication with lots of side effects.

Over roughly 16 years of being in and out of the system I have been diagnosed with schizophrenia, seasonal affective disorder and now bi polar disorder.

Current Experience

In last 12 months things have changed for me. I have a new psychiatrist, new medication I have been supported by a new group of staff in the community called the recovery team and joined a user involvement group that helps keep me occupied. It has not been the medication that has stopped me from relapsing. I would put this down to the recovery team and the other changes in my life. I have changed my way of thinking, how I deal with situations and problems. I've changed my diet and now have lots of people to talk to. Just going for a cup of coffee with a member of the team is all I've needed in times where an argument may have upset the balance of my routine. Having someone to listen to me has been really important. It's only since I accessed the recovery team that I have changed for the better.

However, it wasn't until I was involved with the User Involvement Project that I knew care plans existed. On my last admission to hospital in 2002 I asked for my care plan and to be involved in writing it myself. I was given a blank copy of one, some notepaper and asked if I would like to write my own.

I now have the recovery team and access to day services if I want them. The user involvement project, have been a help I haven't had before. All I've had are four walls, isolation, being locked behind closed doors and medication. I have CPA, a care co-ordinator and a copy of my care plan. Things are so much better now.

Notes: [Editor: Anita gives a troubled account of her initial experience of Mental Health Services. She has since found a momentum and appears to embrace the new knowledge and support offered. Involvement, recognition and progression are the foundations for her story.

Interestingly and sadly, since this account has been written, Anita has been admitted to hospital under a section of the Mental Health Act (1983). The recovery team were not involved and her Community Mental Health Nurse was on holiday. Few of her wishes were taken into account and advanced directives were ignored. She now feels there is little partnership in the process of care.]

Personal Experience 3: Sheila

Current Experience

I have been using mental health services for approximately four and a half years now. Although, having had several hospital admissions, I have never seen a care plan whilst in hospital. Following a period of illness two years ago and what I thought was unsatisfactory 'after care', I asked for a care plan. Although I had a really good working relationship with my community mental health nurse (CMHN) I had never been given a care plan or asked what care I wanted. I subsequently received a care plan that had already been written up by the CMHN and was asked to sign it.

I have since been involved in a number of user involvement initiatives within my locality and attended the Wellness Recovery Action Plan (WRAP) training. As a result of this I then drew up my own care plan, including the following points:

- The signs and symptoms I experience when my health or well-being deteriorates.
- Medication that I would and would not take.
- The people I listen to, take notice of and who I would like to advocate on my behalf.
- Instructions about when services could take over responsibility for me.

This care plan was accepted by my psychiatrist and CMHN and included in my notes. On my last admission, just this year, I was asked to comment upon a revised information leaflet to be given to all patients on admission. The leaflets stated that all patients had care plans that were written with them. However, in fact, I had never seen one or even been asked to give an opinion on my own. Other patients had the same experience as me.

Since that admission I have had a new CMHN who immediately sat down with me to re-write my care plan in partnership with me. I have felt fully consulted and an equal partner in this process. He has accepted my own care plan and told me he will work with it.

I still know other service users who have never seen a copy of their care plan and are unsure if they have one.

Notes: [Editor: Sheila gives an interesting account of her experience and how she was able to assert her needs within her own care. She takes responsibility for this and requires an equality that should be afforded to all service users.]

What can be learnt from these experiences?

Who are the Partners?
The partners should be everyone and anyone who is involved in the person's care. This includes psychiatrists, social workers, nurses, voluntary workers, family or other carers and groups such as the user involvement project that we are part of. Agencies like job centres, the church or any other significant people may also be partners. There may be one key partner or key worker to develop a closer working relationship, but what is important is that there is agreement on who are the partners.

What is Expected from the Partnership?
Partnership is working together in planning care and in making decisions that affect loved ones and the user. Expectation for the partners includes:

- Having trust.
- Support when decisions cannot be made.

- Advocacy.
- Take account of wishes or desires.

This may mean ensuring the use of advanced directives or pre-arranged procedures that are agreed in a care plan.

What is needed is choice about the types of treatment that are offered and a chance to refuse medication or even hospitalisation. A chance to take a risk and share in the decision making process is necessary. Maintaining control of one's life should be attempted, even when a conflict occurs with others. Sometimes, decisions will need to be taken by others, but an important factor is to have the opportunity to maintain some control over life decisions.

The example of Anita illustrates that her current 'wellness' is fragile but through alternate methods and good relationships with her current workers (the recovery team), she is coping. However should she become very 'ill' again and her psychiatrist wish to apply the Mental Health Act:

- Will the recovery team advocate on her behalf?
- Will she be given the opportunity to try other coping strategies?
- Will partnerships with current carers, workers and supporters break down?
- Will her partners have the chance to support her?

> **?** *Point of Reflection*: It is difficult to answer these questions. However, it is worth considering whether these are achieved in services you are familiar with?

Information about care should be shared, including diagnosis, treatment and side effects of treatment, thus allowing an opportunity to discuss alternatives to treatment and incorporate planning. The personal account of Sheila discusses this, having attended training with WRAP Plan methods of coping. Service Users need and want to be involved in care planning, in a meaningful way as an equal partner. In all three personal accounts, the absence of information and explanation is startling. None were informed about their care and treatment and until recently they have all felt excluded from the care planning process.

What Happens When the Partnership Breaks Down or a Partner Moves On?

As in all partnerships and relationships there can be times when a break down or changes occur. Professional workers often move onto other jobs for example, but what is important, is that any new workers respect and honour agreements and contracts already in place. Advanced directives and care or management plans should be agreed with current care co-ordinators. However, these may be on shaky ground, as they have never been put to the test. Anita explained in her personal account, that it took a long time to get life back on track and it can be easily derailed when her routine is upset. Any new partners need to be cognisant of this and prepared to support the way that the current plans are. It is a requirement that the agreed care plan is adhered to when the CMHN or other partner is on holiday or leave.

Ideally, there should be full consultation about new staff if they are going to be care co-ordinators. It would be useful to meet beforehand and be assured by them that they will continue to work with agreed care plans or advanced directives before they take on that role.

What Happens When There is a Disagreement with Professional Partners?
This is a fundamental question.

- What rights do service users have in a situation where there is disagreement?
- Will the partnership be equal?
- Will the professional worker invoke legal, managerial or resource imperatives to take away decision making?
- Will risks be taken?

It is respected that professionals have a duty of care and that there may be times when the service user may not act in their own best interest. However, with advanced directives for periods of illness, it is imperative they are given a chance to work before radical or draconian treatment regimes are put into place or prescribed.

Service users have a right to ask for changes to care co-ordinators, including the psychiatrist. However, we suspect that the majority of service users would neither have the confidence to assert themselves in this way or the knowledge of how to go about it. Indeed this level of assertiveness can instil certain hostility amongst some staff. To question professional opinion or ask for changes to them may be regarded as manipulative and knowledgeable, and assertive service users are often seen as threatening.

Barriers to Developing Effective Partnerships When Planning Care?
There are numerous barriers to partnership-working. Lack of resources, negative or stereotypical images of service users and most importantly, the unequal relationships where one person may have power over another. There are also institutional barriers such as the need for form filling or adhering to procedural directives as well as boundary disputes between organisations.

The rhetoric on partnership, articulated in mental health policy is difficult to achieve with professions who may be constrained by a duty of care. Partnership is also difficult in the current climate. Whilst social inclusion has an importance, the developments of policies such as compulsory treatment orders are anathema to service users and professionals alike (Basset, 2000). The contradictions are pointed out by Pilgrim and Waldron (1998) who state:

> Consumerism emphasises personal choice and the user movement emphasises citizenship. Both of these are contradicted or negated by the powers delegated to service professionals' under mental health legislation. (p. 100)

Trivedi (1996) outlines a number of barriers or problems for nurses practising in partnership with service users. Nurses are being placed in contradictory roles of carers and agents of social control. There may be other barriers to effective partnership working for nurses including; being anxious about accountability, a reluctance to cast off security of professional status and the idea that if nurses are critical of services and supportive of users this may pose risks to their roles. The service user/professional partnership is not an equal partnership as there are times when professionals may act independently and against the wishes or knowledge of the user.

There is still a long way to go before partnership can be a reality in the lives of service users, rather than a much-used word in leaflets and reports (Bassett, 2000).

What Works in Forming Effective Partnerships in Order to Plan Care?

For partnership working to become a reality there needs to be effective collaboration from the service side and user. This entails developing a trusting relationship within which there is mutual respect. We believe that to develop this approach, the following points are essential:

- A need for active listening to each other (free from note-taking).
- To have information shared.
- To receive appropriate and applicable feedback.
- To be accepted as a person and not a diagnosis.
- To be acknowledged as an expert and not a participant.
- Recognition of a valid contribution.
- To be involved in the care plan.
- To receive the time, energy and commitment necessary for care.
- Equality in partnerships.
- To have the option of choice in the selection of a care co-ordinator.

 Point of Reflection: Is it possible to maintain a therapeutic, equal partnership with someone who has treated you against your will?

Conclusion

If the care planning process is to be effective and the concepts of partnership working aspired to, then nurses and other professionals need to accept service users as equals. Preconceived ideas will need to be cast off. There will always be a duty of care and a legal responsibility. This is accepted. However, it should be equally important and an expectation that there is a respect for the views, needs and wishes of the service user.

📖 Suggested Further Reading

Read, J and Reynolds, J. (Eds) (1996) *Speaking Our Mind: An Anthology*, Houndmills: MacMillan Press.

This is an excellent text that is written by service users. It gives opinion on a number of key issues and is an informative contribution to the mental health debate. Chapter 6 is of particular relevance to the issues discussed here.

References

Basset, T. (2000) Is partnership possible?, *Openmind*, 104, Jul./Aug.: 12–13.

Bhui, K., Aubin, A. and Strathdee, G. (1998) Making a reality of user involvement in community mental health services, *Psychiatric Bulletin*, 22: 8–11.

Bowl, R. (1996) Involving service users in mental health services: Social Services Departments and the National Health Service and Community Care Act 1990, *Journal of Mental Health*, 5, 3: 287–303.

Butterworth, T. and Rushworth, D. (1995) Working in partnership with people who use services: reaffirming the foundations for mental health nursing, *International Journal of Nursing Studies*, 32, 4: 373–85.

Campbell, P. (1996) The history of the user movement in the United Kingdom, in Heller, T., Reynolds, J., Gomm, R., Muston, R. and Pattison, S. (eds) *Mental Health Matters*, Houndmills: Macmillan Press.

Campbell, P. and Lindow, V. (1997) Changing practice: mental health nursing and user empowerment, *RCN Learning Materials On Mental Health*, Royal College of Nursing.

Crepaz-Keay, D. (1996) Who do you represent, in Read, J. and Reynolds, J. (eds) Speaking *Our Minds An Anthology*, Houndmills: Macmillan Press, pp. 184–6.

Department of Health (1990) *The Care Programme Approach*, HC(90) 23/LASSL (90) 11, London: DoH.

Department of Health (1994a) *Working in Partnership: A Collaborative Approach to Care*, London: HMSO.

Department of Health (1994b) *The Health of the Nation Key Area Handbook: Mental Illness*, Heywood: BAPS Health Publication Unit.

Department of Health (1995) *Building Bridges: a Guide to Arrangements for Inter-agency Working for the Care and Protection of Severely Mentally Ill People*, London: DoH.

Department of Health (1997) *The New NHS Modern and Dependable*, London: HMSO.

Department of Health (1998) *Modernising Mental Health Services: Safe, Sound and Supportive*, London: HMSO.

Department of Health (1999a) *Effective Care Co-Ordination in Mental Health Services: Modernising the Care Programme Approach, NHS Executive*, London: HMSO.

Department of Health (1999b) *Patient and Public Involvement in the New NHS*, London: HMSO.

Department of Health (1999c) *A National Service Framework for Mental Health*, London: HMSO.

Department of Health (2001a) *Involving Patients and the Public in HealthCare*, London: HMSO.

Department of Health (2001b) *The Expert Patient: A New Approach to Chronic Disease Management for the 21st Century*, London: HMSO.

Fraher, A. and Limpinnian, M. (1999) User empowerment within mental health nursing, in Wilkinson, G. and Miers, M. (eds) (1999) *Power and Nursing Practice*, Houndmills: Macmillan Press.

Hostick, T. (1998) Developing user involvement in mental health services, *Journal of Psychiatric and Mental Health Nursing*, 5: 439–44.

Maza, G. (1996) Structuring effective user involvement, in Heller, T., Reynolds, J., Gomm, R., Muston, R., and Pattison, S. (eds) *Mental Health Matters*, Houndmills: Macmillan Press.

McClelland, F. (1998) Monitoring Our Services Ourselves, *Mental Health Care*, 1, 8: 272–4.

McDermott, G. (1998) The care programme approach: a patient perspective, *Nursing Times Research*, 3, 1: 47–63.

NHS Executive (1997) *The Patients Charter – Mental Health Services*, Leeds: NHS Executive.

North, C., Ritchie, J. and Ward, K. (1993) *Factors Influencing the Implementation of the Care Programme Approach*, London: HMSO.

Pattison, S. (2001) User involvement and participation in the NHS: a personal perspective, in Heller, T. (ed.), *Working for Health*, London: Sage, pp. 196–205.

Perkins, R. and Repper, J. (1998) *Dilemmas in Community Mental Health Practice: Choice or Control*, Oxon: Radcliffe Medical Press.

Pilgrim, D. and Waldron, L. (1998) User involvement in mental health service development: How far can it go? *Journal of Mental Health*, 7, 1: 95–104.

Ramon, S. (2001) Participative mental health research: users and professional researchers working together, *Mental Health Care*, 3, 7: 224–8.

Read, J. (2001) Involving to empower, *Mental Health Today*, Dec. 2001: 18–20.

Rose, D. (2001) Users Voices: *The Perspectives of Mental Health Service Users on Community and Hospital Care*, The Sainsbury Centre for Mental Health.

Rose, D., Ford, R., Gawith, L., Lindley, P. and the KCW UFM User Group (1998) *In Our Experience User – Focused Monitoring of Mental Health Services in Kingston Chelsea & Westminster Health Authority*, Sainsbury Centre for Mental Health.

Sharma, T. and Carson, J. (1996) The idea of partnership is fine but what about perception, *Journal of Psychiatric and Mental Health Nursing*, 3: 133–5.

Town, N., Foster, R., Grant, S., Crosby, D., Emmerson, P., Williams, M., Edington, C., and Mountain, L. (1997) The County Durham Service Users and Carers Forum, *Journal Of Interprofessional Care*, 11, 2: 139–47.

Trivedi, P. (1996) Partners not adversaries, *Nursing Times*, 92, 21: 59–60.

Trivedi, P. (2001) Never again, *Openmind*, 110, July/Aug.: 19.

Truman, C. and Slade, M. (1999) Beyond tokenism: employing mental health service users as interviewers, *Clinical Psychology Forum*, 129: 39–41.

Wolf, R. (2001) Power of veto, *Openmind*, 108, Mar./Apr.: 13.

Wolfe, J., Gournay, K., Norman, S. and Ramnoruth, D. (1997) Care Programme Approach: evaluation of its implementation in an inner London service, *Clinical Effectiveness in Nursing*, 1: 85–91.

CHAPTER 2

A Carer's Perspective of Care Planning

Barbara Jones

Introduction

Nursing theories exist for the application of practical intervention for those suffering from severe mental illness. However, what of the carer, their role and expected involvement within the process of care for the person suffering? This chapter will explore Watson's Theory, its framework and concepts related to the patient and the family caregiver. First hand personal experience and opinions are provided for additional understanding of mental health nursing and its impact on the caregiver.

Decompensation, crisis or hospitalisation seldom occurs as an abrupt event. In the days, or even weeks prior to a person becoming mentally ill or relapsing, the family or caregivers are often privy to data that the person may likely not even be aware of. Tapping into this knowledge can afford the mental health professional with a valuable care-planning tool.

The family or caregiver can provide a timeline history of the illness and precipitants to the current event. These individuals, who collectively make up the nucleus of support for the person, are first hand observers of the behaviour, mannerisms and traits that make the patient unique. They see and live the cycles, phases and the crises along with the patient. They are the first responders in the tragedy of mental illness.

How Many People are Carers of People with Mental Health Problems?

According to the Carers National Association (CNA) (1998), the number of informal carers is steadily falling from 6.8 million in 1990 to 5.7 million in 1995, as a result of social and demographic trends. This figure is however, still very large, representing around 1 in 8 adults. Approximately eight of ten carers spend over 50 hours caring for a sick person, while 63 per cent of carers say that they cared for over 100 hours a week. The majority of carers (58 per cent) are women, and women are more likely to carry the main responsibility for caring, where there is more than one person with some responsibility (Department of Health (DoH), 1999a). Indeed, it is estimated that half of those with severe mental illness live with family or friends, and are likely to receive considerable support from them. According to one survey, carers receive little acknowledgement or support from doctors or other health professionals. Questionnaires were sent to 5000 members of the CNA and 3031 people replied. 70 per cent said that they spent at least seven hours each day caring for another person at home. Many respondents were elderly and more than half had substantial psychological or physical ill-health of their own (Wise, 1998).

Personal Account

I can relate first hand, the roller coaster existence that the individual with mental illness and the family experience. Day to day events can suddenly loom as crisis precipitants. There can be recurring episodes of discontinuing medications, because the individual felt 'normal', which the individual may not recognise as the result of therapeutic effect of the medications. Then, to the downward spiral effect of the individual's non-medicated status on their functioning abilities. The effect of that dysfunction on the family and relationship dynamics are all a part of what the caregiver experiences 24 hours, 7 days a week in their life. While medicated, the individual may be able to participate in the family unit. Examples that come to mind are cooking dinner, or helping with laundry. Then the cycle starts, the individual is less able to participate, less independent in their functioning. The care needs and responsibilities are transferred back to the caregiver. This sets up an imbalance in the caregiver's life.

The Sandwich Generation

Much has been noted regarding the 'sandwich generation'. This is the generation who while providing care for their own family and children, also care for their aged parents and hold down a fulltime job. There are those of us in this sandwich generation who must, in addition to the above commitments, take on a role with unknown care provision requirements. We must care for someone who cannot tell us what their needs always are. The amount of time required cannot be specified or planned. Often it is not possible to find a substitute to be a care provider.

Practicality of Care

Watson's theory of caring defines the human values that inspire strength a family finds to rally support for their loved ones. They do so in the face of

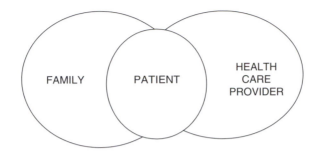

Figure 2.1   The mutual aspects of the relationships interactions

horrors that many cannot imagine. They can be victims of verbal, emotional and even physical abuse at the hands of a loved one who is not aware of what they are doing. Family members and caregivers have contained within their emotional being, a willingness to do what others do for money.

This theory in practice can assist the mental health professional with a guideline to identify the needs of the caregivers, and in so doing, the patient. The implied collaborative and mutual aspects of the relationships interactions, involved in the care of the patient, can be seen in Figure 2.1.

Akin to the foundation element of Watson's theory, the experience for my family member and our family has been one in which there were interrelations of those involved in providing care. From the very beginning the care provider (Mental Health Services) enlisted the participation of the family. We were drawn in to appointments, asked to offer input, identify concerns and strengths for our family member. The willingness of the professionals to listen to, and give validation to the concerns and needs of us as family members had significant and positive bearing on the readiness of the family (non-professional) caregivers to remain 'on the job'. I believe that the willingness of the professionals to value the family caregiver's observations assisted our family member in the tremendous effort required for him to trust someone who was outside of the family circle.

Watson's Theoretical Framework of Carative Factors

Watson notes that a transpersonal caring relationship is the foundation to her work in nursing theory. She states that transpersonal caring seeks to connect with the spirit or soul of the other through the processes of caring and healing and being in authentic relation, in the moment (Watson, 1996).

This is also recognisable as empathy (the placing of ones self in the situation of another). Identification with, and understanding of the impact of the illness, the planned intervention and the future, is a task that family caregivers and professional healthcare personnel alike can participate in. This participation can afford the patient with acceptance and promotes the positive support that will be required in the face of chronic mental illness. The development of a trusting authentic human caring relationship is noted as one of Watson's carative factors.

Her original work includes the following factors:

1. Formation of a Humanistic-altruistic system of values.
2. Instillation of faith-hope.
3. Cultivation of sensitivity to one's self and to others.
4. Development of a helping-trusting, human caring relationship.
5. Promotion and acceptance of the expression of positive and negative feelings.
6. Systematic use of a creative problem-solving caring process.
7. Promotion of transpersonal teaching/learning.
8. Provision for a supportive, protective, and/or corrective mental, physical, societal, and spiritual environment.
9. Assistance with gratification of human needs.
10. Allowance for existential-phenomenological-spiritual forces.

(Watson, 1979)

The following case example summarises Watson's theory.

(The scenario is true. Events and participant information has been changed to protect identities.)

Case Example

Jon is a middle-aged male service user (who is known to the services and has a ten-year history of schizophrenia) is brought voluntarily to the acute mental health unit for assessment. He has been reported in the community to be making declarative threats of violence toward a water department employee.

A Community Mental Health Nurse from the Crisis Team offers assessment of the person and is left with the impression that there is a case for safety concern. The person has a known diagnosis of mental illness, was initially agitated when he arrived at the unit, but has calmed down after being placed in a safe and non-stimulating environment. He is unwilling to contract for safety or adhere to risk management with the mental health nurse.

A family member (father) is notified of the plan to admit the person for a secure assessment under a section of the Mental Health Act (1983). When this family member arrives, Jon becomes agitated, demanding that the family member, 'Take him home, now'. He tells his father that 'the reason he was brought here has to do with a plan by the authorities to control him'.

The mental health nurse assesses Jon's perceptions and ability to reality test. The father is noted to be reorienting the son to the event and the actual tasks requested by the nurse involved. Jon again calms. With the father present in the room, the nurse again requests Jon to contract for safety by adhering to a risk management plan. At this point he agrees to contract, stating, 'I am angry, but I will not hurt anyone else, or myself'.

> ? *Point of Reflection*: Can you identify the three different assessments the nurse made in her interactions with the patient and his father?

The family caregiver in this scenario is experienced. The nurse is perceptive and experienced enough to the use of family as a collaborator in Jon's care. At many points in the scenario presented, varied actions and responses could have altered the outcome.

Consider the following possibilities:

The person could have refused to allow his family to be notified or the family could have refused to come to the hospital. The nurse could have jumped to the conclusion that the family member was causing Jon to become agitated and dismissed the opportunity to have him supported by a caring, trusted provider.

Ultimately the most important single factor in the plan is the person (Jon). In order for him to embrace the components of the plan, the interventions, in this case being admitted for assessment, he needs to have been part of the process. Knowing and feeling they have been involved and made choices (however limited they may be), allows them to come to terms with the arrangement. Watson offers the idea that promotion and acceptance of the expression of positive and negative feelings is a connection with the deeper spirit of self and the one being cared for (Watson, 1996).

The Care Plan for this patient included:

> I Discharge to his prior living situation. That is, home with family and community support.
> II An appointment with his Community Mental Health Nurse within 24 hours. This will include an assessment of his coping skills.
> III Review of his medication by the Psychiatrist.
> IV Recommendation for an occupational assessment (Given that the altercation, as perceived by the patient, was a result of his previous employment with the water department).

Establishing a care plan necessitates that the mental health nurse provide:

- Assessment of the situation, patient and *caregivers*. Measuring the physiological, psychological, psychosocial and spiritual needs of the *family* and the patient.
- The identification of needs.

- Plan of action to be carried out: With agreement, the various tasks will have identified within them, component roles for the participants in the plan. The patient will ..., the *caregiver* will ..., the healthcare professional will ... etc.
- Determine the necessary interventions. These may be pharmacological, emotional, social, educational, skills oriented tasks or a combination thereof.
- Evaluation of the intervention's outcome. The cycle of care will then be completed: a resolution of the event, or continuation with intermittent modifications as a chronic maintenance, or modified for enhancement of outcome, in which case the cycle will begin again.

The idea is to identify coping skills/mechanisms of both the individual and the family. Many detrimental coping skills and/or defence mechanisms lead to a break down of the function levels for one or both of the parties. Identification of those harmful skills, alongside the provision of education and positive reinforcement of beneficial coping skills can help to rest or alter the cycles.

As part of the nursing process (Assess Plan Implement Evaluate) the nurse should be able to identify the interventions needed, knowing who can participate in the provision of those interventions that is, the patient, the family, the healthcare professional, is expected to be part of nursing knowledge. The concept of team case management takes root here. A multidisciplinary team meeting for care planning is a valuable tool in returning the patients to their family in the community with the best possible opportunity for a positive outcome.

Establishing the care plan requires that the patient agree with the plan and the family caregiver is willing to take the responsibility delegated to him/her. The path to stabilisation is convoluted, 'Two steps forward, three steps back ...', is an apt description. Research evidence provides direct correlation of advantageous outcomes with supportive care relationships. Indeed, the carer's response to the ill family member is an important mediator of the illness outcome (Butzlaff and Hooley, 1998). This being said, the caregiver's perspective is worthy of review.

Caregiver's Perspective

The family caregiver plays a vital role in the treatment of anyone with a chronic mental illness. This care giving role is often thrust upon a family member who must provide not only supportive and appropriate care, but also become the case manager. The majority of family caregivers do not have clinical education in their backgrounds.

The caregiver has an ever-changing role with multiple responsibilities. They juggle work, home and care giving. They are often providers for other family members with a variety of needs. Seemingly minor distraction can turn into major disturbances in the tenuous day-to-day life of a family living with a member who suffers from mental illness. The nurse must be able to identify stressors and resources for caregivers.

These needs are beginning to be addressed with a focus on caregivers needs being identified (DoH, 1999a). It is up to the mental health nurse and multi-disciplinary team to ensure these needs are met (DoH, 1999b, 2002).

Research by Balachandran shows that not only is the health of the family member affected by the degree of social support received, the well-being of the caregivers is also affected by the level of social support they receive in helping the person cope with his/her mental health problem (Balachandran, 1985).

The World Health Report (2001) denotes principles of care should include partnerships with patients and families. It indicates that these groups have much to learn from each other. The sharing of information, exploration of reactions and previous effective (or ineffective) coping skills leads to the creation of a care plan that can be most effective in the management of the illness, and also improving the well-being of the individual suffering.

Retrospective evaluation of my own family's experience provides many examples where the care for the individual was directly impacted by the well-being of the family. The more stressed the primary caregiver or the family, then the more likely the individual sufferer was to react in an unpredictable attitude or behavior.

Knowing that there was someone else (the professional healthcare provider) that we as caregivers could turn to, meant that we were not alone in the experience.

Conclusion

The nurse as a health care professional has a duty to identify not only the needs of the patient, but the needs of the family or caregiver as well. Doing this will serve to enhance the quality of the therapeutic relationship for all three of the stakeholders offering care for the individual suffering mental illness. The nurse can influence the outcome of this therapeutic relationship by utilising the Carative Factors of Watson's theory. The strongest case is made for the use of self in the development of a trusting and caring triangular collaborative and therapeutic relationship.

The nurse is likely to be one of the first and closest healthcare providers involved with the family and the individual. The opportunity to make a difference comes early and at a time when the caregiver cannot recognise it. The responsibility of the nurse to open the door for discovery of the caregiver's inner strengths is an important one and should not be taken lightly. My own nursing knowledge was an inlet to teaching the rest of our family to embrace the willingness of the professional healthcare provider to assist us in caring for our family member. I certainly did not anticipate when I went to nursing school that it was to become a caregiver for my own family. However I am certainly glad I gained the skills to be an effective one.

In my own nursing practice, and in my own life I often utilise a variety of Watson's carative factors. Frequent use of these carative factors has made them become second nature. Many of my responses and reactions to what happens to my children, others or myself are directly related and impacted by those influences.

📖 Suggested Further Reading

Barrowclough, C., Lobban, F., Hatton, C. and Quinn, J. (2001) An investigation of models of illness in carers of schizophrenia patients using the illness perception questionnaire, *British Journal of Clinical Psychology*, 40: 371–85.

Boyle, E. and Chambers, M. (2000) Medication compliance in older individuals with depression: gaining the views of family carers, *Journal of Psychiatric and Mental Health Nursing*, 7: 515–22.

Chambers, M., Ryan, A.A. and Connor S.L. (2001) Exploring the emotional support needs and coping strategies of family carers, *Journal of Psychiatric and Mental Health Nursing*, Apr. 8, 2: 99–106.

Jubb, M. and Shanley, M. (2002) Family involvement: the key to opening locked wards and minds, *International Journal of Mental Health Nursing*, 11: 47–53.

Psychiatric News (1999) www.pscy.org/pnews/97-06-20/carter/html. *Carter Urges Psychiatrists to Support Family Caregivers*, 20 June.

References

Balachandran, R. (1985) The role of the family in the promotion of mental health of one of its members: a case study, *Indian Journal of Social Work*, 45: 403–13.

Butzlaff, R.L and Hooley, J.M. (1998) Expressed emotion and psychiatric relapse: A meta-analysis, *Archives of General Psychiatry*, 55: 547–52.

Carers National Association (1998) *Facts About Carers*, London: CNA.

Department of Health (1999a) *Caring about Carers: A National Strategy for Carers*, London: HMSO.

Department of Health (1999b) *National Service Framework for Mental Health*, London: HMSO.

Department of Health (2002) *Developing Services for Carers and Families of People with Mental Illness*, London: Department of Health Publications.

Watson, J. (1979) *Nursing: The Philosophy and Science of Caring*, Boston: Little, Brown and Company.

Watson, J. (1996) Watson's theory of transpersonal caring, in Walker, P.H. and Neuman, B. (eds.), *Blueprint for Use of Nursing Models: Education, Research, Practice, and Administration*, New York: NLN Press, pp. 141–184.

Wise, J. (1998) Carers are ignored by NHS, *British Medical Journal*, June: 1765.

World Health Organization Mental health Report: Internet site: http://www.who. int/whr2001/2001/main/Accessed: 24/04/2004.

Supportive Resources

Carers National Association
Ruth Pitter House
20/25 Glasshouse Yard
London EC1A 4JT
Tel: 020 7490 8818
Carersline: 0345 573 369
E-mail: info@ukcarers.org
Website: www.carersonline.org.uk

Crossroads – Caring for Carers
10 Regent Place
Rugby CV21 2PN
Tel: 01788 573653
E-mail: association.office@crossroads.org.uk
Website: www.crossroads.org.uk

PART II

Primary Care

CHAPTER 3

Primary Mental Health Care

Robert Tummey and Maureen Smojkis

Introduction

As a setting, primary care is generally preferred by mental health users and carers (Pilgrim and Rogers, 1993). It places the individual in the driving seat and adapts input to respond to ongoing needs. There are two features of provision that operate for the nurse in this area, these include a liaison aspect that focuses on:

(1) The interface between primary care services and mental health in isolation to secondary services and;
(2) The interface between primary and secondary mental health services.

For the purpose of this chapter, the main focus will be on the development of care planning within Primary Mental Health Care (PMHC). The intention is for an overview that illustrates the expanded role of the mental health nurse within this setting.

The main concepts will detail the planning of care for more common mental health problems as defined in the National Service Framework (NSF) (DoH, 1999). These will include issues such as depression, anxiety and grief reaction. Also exploring the alleviation of symptoms, stabilisation of functioning and working with the person to address their present ways of coping.

It has been a myth that Primary Care has confined itself to the 'worried well', when in fact they are the 'worried sick' (National Institute of Mental Health in England (NIMHE), 2003a). Indeed, issues described in mental health as 'common' or 'less severe' are now being acknowledged (Nolan and Badger, 2002) and recognised as being managed within the Primary Care setting for some time. Through a more functionalised team approach, integrative health and social service teams are working together to provide a coherent and a seamless service to individuals referred with mental health issues. Carer involvement is also a key element and helps inform a position of health that focuses on the normality of health input.

It is worthy of note that people who have a diagnosis of severe mental illness (SMI) can also suffer the same misfortunes in life as any other. Issues that may include:

- Bereavement,
- Separation/divorce,
- Traumatic events (including: road traffic accident etc),
- Anxiety and depression.

Diagnosis and previous presentation should not dismiss the claim for having real life experiences that cause distress. It does not mean that a previous dormant illness will return. It can mean that life experience influencing well-being at any given time should be treated accordingly, as with any other client in primary care. The person is more than a diagnosis. Primary care is the arena for normalising and is now recognised as a site of specialist mental health activity (NIMHE, 2003b). Interestingly, it provides the only point of contact for 30 per cent of people suffering SMI (SCMH, 2002).

Community mental health nurses (CMHN) in PMHC, usually work as part of a community mental health team (CMHT) covering a great deal of this work. These CMHNs will have established contact and work together with the person to optimise their potential to maintain a healthy well-being.

Partnership working with the client determines the potential for well-being and assists in the process of normality. Providing an input that draws on their strength and ability to navigate normal social goals. This provision is a recognisable one for the CMHN in PMHC for all referrals, be they from primary or secondary care.

Prevalence and Population

It is estimated that one in six people of working age will suffer some sort of mental health problem, requiring some form of intervention (DoH, 1999). These figures are alarmingly high and indicate the level of work still required for the achievement of an effective service. Primary care should be acknowledged for its provision as up to 50 per cent of all those with serious mental illness only use primary care services (DoH, 1999; Kendrick *et al.*, 2000). The prevalence is such:

- One in every 250 will be diagnosed with schizophrenia or bi-polar disorder.
- Bi-polar disorder affects 1 per cent of the population with a higher incidence in women,

Also, depression is one of the commonest mental illnesses encountered in primary care, with:

- 5 per cent of those attending their GP having a major depressive disorder;
- 5 per cent have dysthymia;

- 10 per cent have significant depressive symptoms which impair functioning (Lloyd and Jenkins, 1995);
- Lifetime prevalence of depression is 26 per cent for women and 12 per cent for men.

(Sobieraj *et al.*, 1998)

The Department of Health (1999) states that mental health is now receiving the attention and investment it deserves. The intention is to address the mental health needs of working age adults up to the age of 65, as it is estimated that one in six people in this age range experience a mental health problem. Referral on to specialist services for assessment and treatment occurs for 9 of every 100 consulting their GP with a mental health problem (DoH, 1999).

Findings of the first national survey of GPs and mental health in primary care (MACA, 1999) found that on average, GPs currently:

- Spend 30 per cent of their time on mental health problems,
- This is equivalent to one-and-a-half days of their working week,
- Spending 15 per cent on issues relating to anxiety and depression,
- 5 per cent on psychosomatic issues,
- 3 per cent on elderly mental health.

At the time of the survey over 50 per cent of those practices who responded had CMHNs and Counsellors attached, one in ten had access to a social worker, psychologist and psychiatrist. When asked to prioritise the support they wished to have attached to their practices, GPs listed CMHNs at the top.

Referrals

GPs and those who work within primary care can have their concerns raised when faced with a distressed person who requires assistance. Decision is then required for the appropriate avenue to take or which professional pathway needs to be engaged (Tummey, 2001). With the absence of crisis, a referral to PMHC will be warranted. This should be a direct point of access to the services, in line with the National Service Framework for Mental health (DoH, 1999). The referral process may include:

- The completion of a localised proforma by the GP and person to be referred.
- Telephone referral from the GP.
- Written referral in letter form.
- Referral by other Primary Care team members using the above system.
- Possible referral via other agencies, including voluntary sector, housing, accident and emergency departments or community midwife etc.

Box 3.1   Possible format for involvement

- Specific referral criteria and information
- Agreed time for appointment/lapse
- Time allotted for each patient
- Number of new assessments per week
- Administration: letters/notes/computer use

PMHC should be open to all referrals within primary and secondary care for suitable screening/assessment. However, the main referrer will be the GP or instigated through the GP via primary healthcare staff. An agreed format for involvement may differ across PMHC, dependent on home visit or GP surgery appointment. With a focus on 'screening', the PMHC services are offering the majority of assessments through a surgery appointment. For an example of the possible format for involvement please see Box 3.1.

Referrals from secondary care are usually following the reclassification of the Care Programme Approach (CPA) to standard or reduced need for secondary service involvement. Should the person have well-maintained mental health and engagement with the services then referral to PMHC care is acceptable. The GP or primary care team may also refer for the purpose of screening, assessment or monitoring.

Referral may also entail assessment of need or progression of established care interventions. For instance, the person may require or even prefer the administering of depot medication within primary care, to be seen at home or have a surgery appointment. Gender option may also become apparent, with requests for a specific gender in the delivery of care or administering of depot medication etc. The wishes of the client should be respected, although their agenda may be questioned.

Theoretical Framework

Focus should be on the effectiveness and ability to achieve a beneficial outcome within the agreed time. These should be based on the experience and expertise of the nurse and may be combined. However, use of any intervention should be evidence based and a therapeutic treatment of choice for specific presentation should be adhered to. Where the issue remains the mental illness, the theoretical approach will be similar to approaches purported in other chapters.

Cognitive Behavioural Therapy (CBT)   A directive approach that relies on contracted involvement. There is a requirement that the individual agrees with the treatment rationale and has the ability for self-help. The focus is on the behavioural, cognitive and physiological response to misinterpreted stimuli. CBT is indicated for anxiety and depression. However, it is required over a longer period for Serious Mental Illness, with a need to build rapport and ease in the involvement of its concepts. Nelson (1997) details this approach specifically with schizophrenia. [For further reference the reader is directed to Chapter 6 of this book].

Humanistic   The human needs of every individual should be the focus of attention for any nurse. The mental health nurse has a key involvement in identifying the needs of the person in relation to their current circumstances. Such human needs are described by Maslow (1954) and placed here with the importance they deserve:

> To be authentic, express our spiritual nature, affiliate and belong, be valued and value ourselves, love and be loved, express our sexuality, feel secure and attached, meet our physiological needs.

As an adjunct to humanistic philosophy, the person-centred approach developed by Carl Rogers integrates the concepts through an achievable counselling technique (Rogers, 1951). The focus is personal worth, self-esteem, potential for growth, listening/attending skills etc. Although there is a limited evidence base for the efficacy of this approach, the benefits for the ability to conduct effective interactions and therapeutic alliances are well documented. The approach regards the client as always knowing what hurts and in what direction they need to move for healing to take place (Rogers, 1967).

Medication   [For an explanation of medication management please see Chapters 5 and 6].

Solution-Focused Therapy (SFT)   PMHC teams are being trained in the use of SFT. O'Connell and Palmer (2003) state that people do better when it is noticed what they do well and how they cope. By identifying skills that the person has developed in other areas of their life those skills can be transferred to help solve current issues. SFT focuses on the future, identifying where the person wants to be and how the contact with the service can assist them in this move forward. By looking with the person, at times when the problem is less powerful and focusing on exceptions to the problem, the person begins to notice when they are finding their own solutions. This is ideal when interventions are limited by a fixed number of sessions.

Principles and Skills

A framework of capabilities in primary care has been outlined by Sainsbury Centre for Mental Health (SCMH, 2001). It broadly identifies the skills, knowledge and attitudes required of mental health practitioners to implement

---

Box 3.2   Skills for working in PMHC

- *Good listening/* attending skills.
- Working within *time-limited* ways.
- *Flexibility.* Flexible attitude will enhance the reciprocal nature of the partnership.
- *Self-Awareness.* Use of self as a therapeutic agent.
- *Observation.* Observing change.
- *Resourceful.* Knowledge and leaflets of the local services and self-help groups.
- *Realistic* goals and aspirations.
- *Cultural Awareness.* Inclusive of client diversity and inclusive practice.
- *Respect.* The person is not an illness, respect who they are.

---

the National Service Framework (DoH, 1999). These include the ability to:

- Assess the prevalence of mental health problems and needs amongst the population.
- Work in partnership with other agencies to secure wider public health of the local population and contribute to health improvement.
- Screen, diagnose and assess people experiencing mental health problems and those most at risk of mental illness.
- Assess health and social care needs and provide care and treatment to meet the needs of people with transient needs, including: support and counselling for anxiety, depression and grief reaction.
- Refer to and collaborate with specialist mental health services.
                        Adapted from 'The Capable Practitioner' (SCMH, 2001)

With specific regard to skills, the presence of a number of qualities identified in Box 3.2 will ensure effective liaison with primary care, secondary care and care of the client.

 Point of Reflection: Consider how many of the above attributes you have as a nurse?

Assessment

Approach

Within PMHC the approach at the assessment phase will be to determine the concerns presented by the person. This could be a screening process or more in-depth assessment, based on the effect of the difficulties on their mental health. There is still a need to obtain correct information of the mental health problem. Such an assessment will incorporate the assessing of need and explore the severity, duration and onset. The client will require the time and space to mention the difficulties they have encountered. The skilled practitioner may then interject with problem-free talk to determine the resources and strengths of the individual, eliciting times when these resources allow the problem to be reduced or be non-existent.

People who enter mental health services often have stories that are influenced by the values and prejudices they have encountered in the world. Nursing assessment should not be symptom focused or problem orientated (Watkins, 2001). It should be person focused and concerned with understanding the perception, experience and abilities of the client. That is not to say that the nurse ignore assessment criteria, but not conduct in a rigid, robotic and regimented way (Donald *et al.*, 2001).

It is also worth noting what is 'mental health'. Jenkins *et al.* (2001) believes this includes:

- A positive sense of well-being;
- Individual resources such as self-esteem, optimism, a sense of mastery and coherence;
- An ability to initiate, develop and sustain mutually satisfying personal relationships;
- Ability to cope with adversities.

Barker (1997) suggests that there are number of questions the practitioner should ask themselves, when engaged in assessment. Including:

1. Why am I doing this assessment?
2. What is the aim of the assessment – what do I want to find out about the referral?
3. When should I assess – is the referral urgent?
4. How will I get the information?
5. How will I judge what this information means (problem formulation)?
6. How might the client function differently if the problems are resolved?

Barker, P. (1997)

Process

The process for each clinical setting will be different according to need. Each setting will have its own local protocol for assessment and needs to be met. Some areas will require a more detailed approach, but this is dependent on the time allotted. Therefore, once you have allotted a time slot, keep to it. Introduce self and state your role and intention. Be aware that there may be issues surrounding your title (psychiatric) and so fears need to be allayed. Also, be open and honest, stating expectation for the time and request the client's expectations.

Barker (1997) reminds us that our reason for being there with the client is to respond to the person's experience of illness and engage in the experience of distress. Assessment is not merely a list of disparate areas of need to be met (Donald *et al.*, 2001) or the production of data, but a life story. It is not a collection of symptoms, but details of distress. We learn to gather the information and write the plan, but it is sensitive detail to the person that a foundation is made. Conversely, Newell and Gournay (2000) proclaim that there should be no innovation without evidence. Thus advocating a conviction that the task of nursing should be placed within the concept of evidence. The mental health nurse should be able to provide explanations for their involvement and interaction, based on the guidance of proof.

Methods of assessment and review, as described by Millar and Walsh (2000) are:

- Structured interview, using pre-determined questions in a set format.
- Unstructured interview, gleaning pertinent information from the general conversation.
- Psychometric tools, such as Beck's depression inventory.
- Observation of non-verbal information.

Whilst listening to the story of the person the nurse begins to move towards the person in a meaningful way, hearing things that will assist in the process of learning from each other. Hearing his or her own story unfold can enable the person to begin to move forward in an intentional way. The process of assessment is key to the development of a useful relationship between the person in care and the mental health service.

However, it is generally acknowledged that people who take up the offer of counselling or outpatient mental health appointments will attend between three and five sessions (MacDonald, 2001). One of the significant factors in the provision of community mental health care is the Did Not Attend (DNA) phenomenon. When meeting a person entering the service it is useful to be aware that this may be the only dialogue you may have together.

The protocol for the assessment should be comprehensive. Barker (2003) suggests that when we talk about assessment we should think about a tool kit, emphasising that each tool has a different function but that these tools are intended to illuminate our shared understanding of the person. Within the PMHC arena assessment can be multi-faceted and without co-ordination and understanding of commonalities and differences, disciplines can over indulge and create a repetitive experience for the person who is being assessed.

Information Gathering

Interaction initiated by the nurse will usually have an underlying intent most often of information gathering. In the first meeting some key thoughts that may be underpinning the questions may be:

- What brought this person here? How has the level of distress or symptoms altered?
- Why now? Is there any specific reason for the client to present now?
- What reason does the referring person give for this person being here? Scrutinise the referral.
- Is the reason the same as the persons? Does the person agree with the referral information?
- If they are different then how? What are the differences?

It is useful to gain this information from the written material provided by the referrer. This may be a letter or local proforma. However, discussion with the person is indicated in the spirit of partnership and collaboration. In order to elicit information from the persons wider support networks, it is necessary to reach agreement in discussing the issues with relatives, carers, friends or partner. One of the final sources for scrutiny will be the past case notes held at the GP surgery or CMHT. This allows a view of previous involvement and intervention. However, it needs to be reiterated that the client is the primary source of information and that secondary sources can offer further clarity if needed.

The nurse seeks to discover those things necessary and sufficient to define the person's problem. The use of a standardised assessment format may help this process. These are usually localised documents for each NHS Trust with criteria I have termed the six Ps of assessment (see Box 3.3).

An area that often receives little attention is physical health. It is worth taking time to explore the influence of any physical conditions through discussion with the client and any necessary health checks.

Box 3.3   Assessment format criteria

- PERSONAL DETAILS:
- PRESENTING ISSUES:
- PAST EXPERIENCES:
- PERIPHERAL/INFLUENCING FACTORS:
- POTENTIAL RISK:
- PLAN:

Tools Used

Various assessment tools may be used within PMHC. However, their use is not exclusive and should only be an additional indicator to a thorough assessment. Some used are:

Beck's Depression Inventory (Beck *et al.*, 1961).
Hospital Anxiety and Depression Scale (HADS) (Zigmond and Snaith, 1983).
Threshold Assessment Grid (TAG) (Slade *et al.*, 2003). Used to determine the
    severity of mental illness, particularly in PMHC (Mountfield, 2004).
Localised risk assessment tools.

[For details of assessment tools used for psychosis please refer to Chapters 5 and 6].

Risk Priorities

Issues of risk are necessary for exploration in all mental health settings. If an individual is at risk to themselves and/or others, then there is a recognised obligation to act (NMC, 2002a). PMHC is no different, with concern for risk in the following areas:

Suicide prevention: This is a major concern in mental health, as identified in the National Service Framework (DoH, 1999). [For further details, see Chapter 7: Crisis.]

Self-harm: This may be viewed along a continuum of self-harm behaviour. These range from 'good enough self-care through compromised self-care', mild self-harm (overworking, heavy smoking, nail-biting) through to moderate and severe self-harm (Turp, 2003).

Isolation: This can be apparent with any person referred, but especially vulnerable adults or those in 'at risk' groups (also, as a result of illness, stigma, fear or a combination).

Domestic abuse: This is a major cause of difficulty for women's health and quality of life. Therefore it needs to be the business of all health professionals (Tummey, 2003).

Children of parents with mental illness: They are at greater risk of neglect, abuse or physical injury than those families without mental illness.

Child Carers: Should be identified in families seen by PMHC. The child may take the role of carer in the form of 'parentification' for general functioning and crisis (DoH, 2003).

Risk is successfully assessed and managed every day in the UK. This is enhanced by good therapeutic relationships, thorough knowledge of the client's history, effective multidisciplinary team (MDT) working and clinical judgement that develops with experience (Turner, 2002). For an aid to assessing risk the reader is referred to Maphosa *et al.* (2000), who have developed a checklist of factors to consider. Management of risk is then about preventing future harm where time is available to plan interventions and management strategies (Ryan, 1999).

> **?** *Point of Reflection*: Consider how risk is managed in your service?

Care Planning

How Plan is Determined

People can and need to be active forces in their own recovery (Watkins, 2001). Based on the information gained, there is a need to determine the first course of action with the client. Where there is a clear issue, this needs to be incorporated into the plan through discussion. Indeed, maintaining the partnership requires the nurse to establish the expectations of the client. What is it they wish to gain from your involvement etc?

The structure of the care plan should be clear and understandable. Any tasks or goals identified are required to be achievable, acceptable and agreed. It is important not to work in isolation through the process of compiling the care plan. This is a document with shared information to be retained by the client and those involved in their care. People with mental health problems and their carers should be involved in the planning and delivery of care. Options and care pathways will be explored as a consideration of possible routes open to the person. However, a focus on strengths and ability to cope is also warranted, expanding on areas the person is doing well etc. The missing ingredient in so many care and treatment programmes is hope and belief in the potential for people to change and grow (Watkins, 2001). It is when people become self-determining and take responsibility for themselves and their lives that change begins (Watkins, 2001).

The issue of work will have to be discussed. It may have a major influence on an individual's identity and self-worth. This focus on inclusion also extends to people suffering SMI. Interesting statistics show that 15 per cent of people with SMI are employed (Evans and Repper, 2000) and 30–40 per cent are capable of working (Ekdawi and Conning, 1994). However, a normalising stance can be difficult to hold onto, particularly in a climate of biomedico, pseudoscientifico reductionism. Distress as illness in Western culture has become somewhat of an accepted truth (Watkins, 2001). This is both limiting and disabling.

Examples of Focus

The introduction of psycho-education may be necessary in dispelling the myths of mental illness. Help the person control symptoms and regain control of self. Information should be given regarding illness, drugs, relaxation and anxiety management.

Health promotion is another important area for PMHC. Establish physical well-being, explore the provision of a daily routine and ensure the person is taking time for self. Whilst health is the concern of the practitioner, it is also the responsibility of the client. Assistance and encouragement promotes partnership, but should never be dominated by the professional.

The use of an advanced directive (as an addition to the care plan) embraces the concept of collaboration and fosters a trusting relationship. Advanced directives are becoming more common and a step in the direction of empowerment (see Chapter 1). It needs to have meaning and credibility when defining the needs of the person during a period of acute illness. Agreement should be sought from the client, nurse and MDT (also involvement of the carer where appropriate and applicable).

Practical Application

For many years, there has been a novel outlook to planning care, by the mere token of completing a 'care plan'. Often this entailed the writing of stock answers that ensure adherence to professional obligation. Compiling a list of intentions created the framework. Establishing a therapeutic relationship requires trust and a certain degree of social skill that has been honed. Many people may find this difficult, including student nurses (MacInnes *et al.*, 2001). Therefore practising this skilful craft is a requisite requirement and not a potential objective for the client. The aim of psychiatric nursing is to make oneself available and to assist the patient (Altschul, 1997, p. 8).

Even professional help can reduce self-esteem by not involving people in their own care and focusing on disabilities, rather than strengths (Chadwick, 1997). The significance of collaboration cannot be over emphasised. The care plan should be a written record of agreed information on interventions and responsibilities. Practical application entails meeting the needs of the individual by providing the platform and resources necessary. Knowledge of local services and leaflets are essential and can help to introduce inclusion. Explicit detail of meetings or sessions is important. Ensure agreement for the time, duration and venue. Offer explanation of intended intervention:

- Counselling skills to assist the dealing and discussing of issues.
- Telephoning and writing of supportive letters (cross-referral, Housing, Finance etc).

Also, any identified requirements of the individual are to be explored and agreed. These may incorporate homework following each session, the focus of input and attendance to other services etc.

Have you a sufficient remit to assist the person? If the skills or resources of the nurse are inappropriate or inadequate, it may hinder progress or be harmful to be involved. Ensure delivery of any intervention is conducted with enough time and skill. As with treatment, care comes in many guises. It can be from what is perceived as the slightest word to the controlled intention of being with another. With one nurse it may be their manner or attitude that extends warmth and genuineness to those who have not had such. Another may possess the command of specific skills for the delivery of intervention. Greater skill is the combination.

Additional Care Planning

There may be a need for additions to the care plan as more information comes to light or as trust is gained. Indeed there may be several areas that require a focus, including co-morbidity, self-harm or physical issues. Some aspects of the care plan may overlap. Therefore try to remain clear and specific.

The example used is not based on real events, but an amalgamation of experience. Any resemblance to specific information or events is coincidental.

Case Example

Debbie is a thirty-five-year old woman. Her parents came to the UK from Jamaica seeking work in the 1960s. They met, married and had three children. Her experience of childhood was to be left to her own devices; if she chose not to go to school she didn't go. During her early life both parents drank heavily, she felt neglected. When she was sixteen Debbie met Alan, his parents had both arrived in England from Ireland also in the 1960s and also seeking work. Following Debbie's pregnancy at seventeen, Alan and Debbie married. Early in the marriage Debbie's husband began to emotionally, physically and sexually abuse her. This relationship is now over.

Referral

Debbie was referred by her GP because of a history of depression and suicide attempts; she has been known to the psychiatric services for some time. Debbie had an early life experience in which she felt she was not listened to. The importance of making a link with the person, exploring cultural commonalities and difference are key within the mental health and specifically PMHC. Within the first session at the surgery, a mental health assessment is necessary, identifying strengths for utilisation at a later stage of the interaction. What did Debbie want to work on? This looks at what the person wants – their preferred future.

Within the first sessions it is important that Debbie has an opportunity to tell her story. That she feels validated and heard. In terms of intervention, a combination of cognitive behavioural work and solution-focused is indicated.

An example of a second session:

How have things been since we last met?
What would it be useful for us to talk about today?

A situation may have occurred that would take precedence in the session, for example reoccurring thoughts of past events preventing Debbie from sleeping. Strategies need to be explored. This will entail identifying successful strategies from the past, providing education of the physiological experience occurring and developing an agreed programme to address sleep hygiene. Assisting Debbie to regain control of her sleep is the most important issue to her at present.

Following two further sessions, Debbie began to improve and made the decision to seek further assistance through a local self-help group.

Documentation

When writing any form of documentation within nursing there is a need for sensitivity and also a degree of recognition for the language used. Completing the assessment format, filling in the assessment tool, writing out the care plan, all require judgement and professional awareness. These documents are there for scrutiny and can be explored for their meaning, recalled in the context of any incident and accountable in the face of complaint. It is therefore necessary to take time to understand the meaning of what is written and communicated. Care plans are now written as contracts, with copies maintained by the client, carer and nurse, as per CPA (DoH, 1991).

For nurses, recording information about clients in their care is very important. Making records and interpreting them involves considerably more than dealing with facts. They are public documents in which the actions of the professional are stored for inspection or auditing (Crawford *et al.*, 1998). Any notes taken will need to be recorded and kept in line with NMC (2002b) guidelines.

Time Frame

A number of issues need to be addressed when determining the time frame. These will include:

- The number of sessions available (can be up to six or longer in some areas),
- A need to stay within boundaries set,
- Frequency and duration of sessions,
- Complete goals/objectives set or explore alternatives with flexibility.

There is also a need to be aware of other agencies involved. This will avoid duplication and if not adhered to, could even jeopardise the work in other areas. Also, be sensitive to the clients needs, as well as the surgery and your own.

Evidence Base

Crawford *et al.* (2001) highlights the benefit of CMHNs in primary care for the improved communication, closer working relationships with GPs and primary care teams, and ability to ensure standards one and two of NSF (DoH, 1999) become a reality. Other evidence has been provided throughout the chapter to form the effectiveness of PMHC.

Dissemination of Information

Concern for dissemination should be considered. The need to elicit information is important, but boundaries are required when sharing this. The competent practitioner should make the client aware of the professional requirements of role. There may be occasion when confidentiality is compromised and others are privy to disclosure. Honesty at the point of involvement is essential throughout any interaction. Be clear with the client if written notes are being taken and who has access. When writing letters to any member of the wider team, the client should be informed and aware. Be sure to identify where the information gained will be stored.

Clarity of your position as a health care professional who may need to divulge information to a third party is necessary. However, you should not attempt this in normal circumstances, without discussion with the client.

Reflective Practice

The introduction of reflective practice and availability of support can lead to the true integration of theory and practice. The reflective process can lead to skills being developed that are transferable across the range of mental health problems and adaptable to all practice settings. Effective helping is enhanced if there is a willingness to explore your own motivation (Hawkins and Shoet, 1989). Reflective practice provides a medium for nurses to share their experience with one another, and if facilitated well, can be a vehicle for health care improvement and development (Graham, 2000).

All nurses should engage in clinical supervision regardless of grade. Sufficient provision may include:

- Offering an opportunity to access individual clinical and educational supervision;
- Explore opportunities for determining your personal and professional needs.

Clinical supervision primarily ensures the maintenance of quality of work and protection of the client. The nurse is helped to develop knowledge, skills and attitudes in the context of a trusting and supportive relationship, also, offering support to the nurse working in difficult and demanding situations, often in a climate of change (MacDonald, 2001).

Practice Development

Due to the setting of PMHC there is a requirement to be proficient in computer skills. The recording of information is often computerised. In-house training should be sought. With regards to higher education there are currently no specific academic pathways for PMHC. However, a number of Higher Education Institutes offer undergraduate and postgraduate degree programmes for CMHNs.

Some exciting new developments are occurring across the UK to assist in the provision of services for people suffering from mental health problems. Recent introductions to PMHC include graduate workers to support delivery of brief interventions and gateway workers to improve the gateway to specialist services (Ekers *et al.*, 2004).

Projects involving client held case records are becoming more common across mental health settings. McGreevey (2003) found that most clients are satisfied with retention of their records and this appears to be tangible proof of the partnership we strive for with clients. They demonstrate nurse–client negotiations and sometimes the differing perspectives recorded for both to share (McGreevy, 2003).

Conclusion

The field of mental health is diverse and interesting, with a number of areas to work. Within PMHC there is an opportunity to be at the point of access for provision. Specific skills are necessary, with assessment and intervention a standard practice for the skilled practitioner in this area. Indeed, many CMHNs regard primary care work with enthusiasm, for the opportunity to advise GPs, provide care in a less stigmatising environment and be involved in mental health promotion (Badger and Nolan, 2000). This chapter has identified the purpose and process of primary care and navigated a course that is client-led, hopefully, through enthusiasm, offering advise and promoting mental health.

📖 Suggested Further Reading

Barker, P. (1997) *Assessment in Psychiatric and Mental Health Nursing: In Search of the Whole Person*, London: Stanley Thornes.

Forster, S. (ed.) (2001) *The Role of the Mental Health Nurse*, Cheltenham: Nelson Thornes.
Newell, R. and Gournay, K. (eds) (2000) *Mental Health Nursing: An Evidence-based Approach*, London: Churchill Livingstone.
Watkins, P. (2001) *Mental Health Nursing: The Art of Compassionate Care*, Oxford: Butterworth-Heinemann.

References

Altschul, A. (1997) A personal view of psychiatric nursing, in Tilley, S. (ed.), *The Mental Health Nurse: Views of Practice and Education*, Oxford: Blackwell Science.
Badger, F. and Nolan, P. (2000) Primary mental health care: whose role is it anyway? *Nursing Standard*, 15, 9: 43–5.
Barker, P. (1997) *Assessment in Psychiatric and Mental Health Nursing: In Search of the Whole Person*, London: Stanley Thornes.
Barker, P. (ed.) (2003) *Psychiatric and Mental Health Nursing: The Craft of Caring*, London: Arnold.
Beck, A.T., Ward, C.H., Mendelson, M., Mock, J.E. and Erbaugh, J.K. (1961) An inventory to measure depression, *Archives of General Psychiatry*, 4: 561–71.
Chadwick, P.K. (1997) Recovery from psychosis: learning more from patients, Journal *of Mental Health*, 6, 6: 577–88.
Crawford, P., Brown, B. and Nolan, P. (1998) *Communicating Care: the Language of Nursing*, Cheltenham: Stanley Thornes Ltd.
Crawford, P., Carr, J., Knight, A., Chambers, K. and Nolan, P. (2001) The value of community mental health nurses based in primary care teams: 'switching the light on in the cellar', *Journal of Psychiatric and Mental Health Nursing*. 8: 213–20.
Department of Health (1991) *The Care Programme Approach*, London: HMSO.
Department of Health (1999) *National Service Framework for Mental Health: Modern Standards and Service Models*, London: DoH.
Department of Health (2003) *Caring About Carers*, London: HMSO.
Donald, S., Lancaster, R. and Forster, S. (2001) The nurse as assessor, in Forster, S. (ed.) *The Role of the Mental Health Nurse*, Cheltenham: Nelson Thornes.
Ekdawi, M. and Conning, A. (1994) *Psychiatric Rehabilitation: A Practical Guide*, London: Chapman and Hall.
Ekers, D., Lovell, K. and Richards, D. (2004) Primary care challenge in the 21st century, *Mental Health Nursing*, 24, 2: 6–7.
Evans, J and Repper, J. (2000) Employment, social inclusion and mental health, *Journal of Psychiatric and Mental Health Nursing*, 7: 15–24.
Graham, I.W. (2000) Reflective practice and its role in mental health nurses' practice development: a year-long study, *Journal of Psychiatric and Mental Health Nursing*, 7, 109–17.
Hawkins, P. and Shoet, R. (1989) *Supervision in the Helping Relationship*, Buckingham: Open University Press.
Jenkins, R., McCulloch, A., Freidli, L. and Parker, C. (2001) *Developing a National Mental Health Policy, Maudsley Monographs 434*, London: Psychology Press.
Kendrick, T., Burns, T., Garland, C., Greenwood, N. and Smith, P. (2000) Are specialist mental health services being targeted on the most needy patients? – the effects of setting up a special services in general practice, *British Journal of General Practice*, 50: 121–6.

Lloyd, K. and Jenkins, R. (1995) The economics of depression in primary care, Department of Health Initiatives, *British Journal of Psychiatry*, 166, suppl. 27: 60–2.

MACA (1999) *First National GP Survey of Mental Health in Primary Care*, MJM Healthcare Solutions.

MacDonald, N. (2001) The nurse as supervisor, in Forster, S. (ed.), *The Role of the Mental Health Nurse*, Cheltenham: Nelson Thornes.

MacInnes, D., MacDonald, N. and Morrissey, M. (2001) The nurse as therapist and counsellor, in Forster, S. (Ed.) *The Role of the Mental Health Nurse*, Cheltenham: Nelson Thornes.

Maphosa, W., Slade, M. and Thornicroft, G. (2000) Principles of assessment, in Newell, R. and Gournay, K. (eds), *Mental Health Nursing: an Evidence-based Approach*, London: Churchill Livingstone.

Maslow, A. (1954) *Motivation and Personality*, New York: Harper and Row. Cited in Watkins, P. (2001) *Mental Health Nursing: The Art of Compassionate Care*, Oxford: Butterworth-Heinemann.

McGreevy, P. (2003) Proof of partnership, *Mental Health Nursing*, 23, 1: 24.

Millar, E. and Walsh, M. (2000) *Mental Health Matters in Primary Care*, Cheltenham: Stanley Thornes.

Mountfield, L. (2004) Using an assessment tool for mental health referrals, *Nursing Times*, 100, 22: 38–40.

Nelson, H. (1997) *Cognitive Behavioural Therapy with Schizophrenia: A Practice Manual*, Cheltenham: Stanley Thornes.

Newell, R. and Gournay, K. (eds) (2000) *Mental Health Nursing: An Evidence-based Approach*, London: Churchill Livingstone.

NIMHE (2003a) *Primary Care Programme for Consultation*, London: National Institute of Mental Health in England.

NIMHE (2003b) *Cases for Change: Primary Care*, Leeds: National Institute of Mental Health in England.

Nolan, P. and Badger, F. (eds) (2002) *Promoting Collaboration in Primary Mental Health Care*, Cheltenham: Nelson Thornes.

Nursing and Midwifery Council (2002a) *Code of Professional Conduct*, London: NMC.

Nursing and Midwifery Council (2002b) *Guidelines for Records and Record Keeping*, London: NMC.

O'Connell, B. and Palmer, S. (2003) *Handbook of Solution Focused Therapy*, London: Sage.

Pilgrim, D. and Rogers, A. (1993) Mental health service users' views of medical practitioners, *Journal of Interprofessional Care*, 7: 167–76. Cited in NIMHE (2003) *Cases for Change: Primary Care*, Leeds: National Institute of Mental Health in England.

Rogers, C. (1951) *Client-Centred Therapy*, London: Constable.

Rogers, C. (1967) *On Becoming a Person*, London: Constable.

Ryan, T. (1999) *Managing Risk and Crisis in Mental Health Nursing*, Cheltenham: Nelson Thornes.

Sainsbury Centre for Mental Health (2001) *The Capable Practitioner*, London: SCMH Publications.

Sainsbury Centre for Mental Health (2002) *An Executive Briefing on Primary Care Mental Health Services*, London: SCMH Publications.

Slade, M. *et al.* (2003) Threshold Assessment Grid (TAG): the development of a valid and brief scale to assess the severity of mental illness, *Social Psychiatry and Psychiatric Epidemiology*, 35: 78–85.

Sobieraj, M. *et al.* (1998) The impact of depression on the physical health of family members, *British Journal of General Practice*, 48: 1653–5. Also in Plummer, S. and Gray, R. (eds) (2000) Community mental health nurses, primary care and the national service framework for mental health, *Nursing Standard*. 15, 7: 47–52.

Tummey, R. (2001) A collaborative approach to urgent referrals, *Nursing Standard*, 15, 52: 39–42.

Tummey, F. (2003) Domestic abuse: the hidden factor, *Mental Health Nursing*, 23, 2: 4–6.

Turner, T. (2002) Risky Business, *Nursing Times*, 98, 8: 24–5.

Turp, M. (2003) *Hidden Self-Harm*, London: Jessica Kingsley.

United Kingdom Central Council (1999) *Fitness for Practice*, London: UKCC.

Watkins, P. (2001) *Mental Health Nursing: The Art of Compassionate Care*, Oxford: Butterworth-Heinemann.

Zigmond, A.S. and Snaith, R.P. (1983) The hospital anxiety and depression scale, *Acta Psychiatrica Scandinavica*, 67: 361–70.

CHAPTER 4

Mental Health Liaison

Dave Roberts and Linda Whitehead

Introduction

Mental health work in the general hospital setting is traditionally referred to as 'consultation liaison', 'liaison psychiatry' or more simply, 'liaison'. However, mental health liaison is emerging in the UK as the most common title for this work. It is not exclusive to the general hospital, but describes the interface between mental health services and non-mental health colleagues. It is also frequently used to describe liaison between mental health services and primary care services in the community (Tunmore, 2002). However, for the purpose of this chapter, mental health liaison in the general hospital will be the focus and the care of the adult with physical health problems.

Nurses practising within this speciality are generally known as 'liaison mental health nurses' (LMHNs). We will also use the term 'patient' in preference to 'client' or 'service user', remaining consistent with the usual terminology within the general hospital setting.

It is useful to briefly review the distinctions between consultation, liaison and collaboration:

Consultation: Mental health consultation is essentially a process of advising and supporting the non-mental health worker on mental health issues. As a style of working it assumes the mental health consultant is outside of, and separate from, the team directly caring for the patient. It does not assume a long-term or regular working relationship.

Liaison: Liaison is a process involving a number of activities, including consultation, support, supervision, education and research. It can be conceptualised as an integration of mental health knowledge and skills with other specialities (e.g. medical, nursing) or as the interpretation or translation of mental health concepts into a form that is understandable and useable by non-mental health workers (Roberts, 2002a).

Collaboration: Increasingly, the process of liaison is viewed as one of collaboration. The mental health worker is seen as a member of the team, with a different professional perspective, different skills to offer, but sharing common aims. Each party takes responsibility for the aspect of work that falls within their expertise.

The General Hospital Setting

The general hospital is an unfamiliar environment for many mental health nurses. It is divided into a number of medical specialist units, often with different modes of working. The liaison mental health nurse may work within specific units (Accident & Emergency, oncology), or have a hospital-wide remit. Either way, the LMHN will need to adjust to the working practices prevalent within the setting.

Priorities may differ. Many hospital units have acutely ill people and physical health priorities predominate. Interpersonal aspects of care may not be seen as essential. On the other hand, units caring for chronic conditions, where recurrent admissions are common and relationships are built up over time, may place a higher priority on communication and psychosocial aspects of care.

Adjusting to the pace of care is necessary. Acute units in particular may be driven by a fast pace and high patient turnover. The LMHN may be expected to provide fast results to complex problems.

Hierarchies are apparent and may influence involvement. There is less of a tradition of flattened hierarchies within the general hospital. The medical profession is very powerful and the role of the ward sister or manager is often central. The LMHN will need to understand how these affect the referral process and lines of communication. This will improve their integration.

The LMHN may have a role in educating staff about the particular needs of vulnerable and marginalised groups. There are numerous examples of patients being marginalised within general hospital settings because of personal characteristics, or because they do not fit with expectations of how patients should behave. This can include people with substance abuse and mental health problems.

Prevalence and Population

A number of mental health problems and psychiatric disorders are commonly encountered in the general hospital setting. These are highlighted in the Boxes 4.1 and 4.2.

Problem behaviours are also encountered and explored below:

Suicide   About 5000 people die as a result of suicide each year and suicide reduction has been a key Government health target (DOH, 1999, 2002). Risk factors associated with suicide have been described elsewhere (Whitehead and

Royles, 2002). The risk of suicide associated with certain medical conditions is not well recognised (see Box 4.3).

Box 4.1   Mental illness in the general hospital setting

- *Depression* occurs commonly in chronic physical illness, with prevalence between 10 per cent and 50 per cent. It is particularly common in neurological conditions.
- *Anxiety* is frequently encountered in response to the uncertainty of illness, or associated with specific hospital situations, e.g. investigations, waiting for test results.
- *Adjustment reactions and disorder* are commonly found in people going through periods of change as result of physical illness, e.g. adjusting to a diagnosis of cancer. This can include the consequences of illness and treatment, e.g. role change, body image change.
- *Stress and trauma reactions* may be encountered particularly in Accident and Emergency Departments (A&E).
- *Post Traumatic Stress Disorder* is now being recognised increasingly in association with hospital circumstances. This can include after childbirth, or periods in Intensive Care Units.
- *Perinatal disorders*, e.g. postnatal depression, puerperal psychosis.
- *Psychotic episodes*. These are unusual but may occur in any part of the general hospital including the A&E department.

Box 4.2   Substance abuse in the general hospital setting

- *Alcohol intoxication*, especially in A&E.
- *Alcohol dependency*. Health problems associated with alcohol dependence are common in the general hospital, e.g. gastrointestinal disease. Medical assessments do not always include an alcohol history, so withdrawal syndrome is sometimes an unexpected complication of inpatient treatment.
- *Opiate overdose* and other problems associated with drug dependency.

Box 4.3   Increased risk of suicide

Medical conditions with an increased risk of suicide:
HIV/AIDS, Malignant neoplasm, Esp. head and neck cancers, Huntingdon disease, Multiple sclerosis, Peptic ulcer, Renal disease, Spinal chord injury, Systemic lupus erythematosus.

(Harris and Barraclough, 1994)

Self harm Rates of self-harm appear to be increased in those with painful, debilitating or, on occasions, life threatening conditions. The numbers of presentations following deliberate self-harm (DSH) to A&Es in the UK each year have been estimated as being between 150,000 and 170,000 (Kapur *et al.*, 1999). The rate of specialist assessment is increased when patients are admitted to hospital following DSH and specialist assessment is thought to reduce the risk of subsequent repetition (Kapur *et al.*, 2002).

Somatoform disorders	Organic states
<ul><li>Somatisation disorder</li><li>Hypochondriasis and conversion disorder</li><li>Pain disorder</li><li>Body dysmorphic disorder</li></ul>	<ul><li>Toxic confusion states/delirium</li><li>Neurological disorders</li></ul>

Referrals

The number of referrals to liaison services in the UK, vary considerably. A prevailing view is that referral rates are rising as services prove their worth and develop and expand. The nature and rates of presentation vary also according to specific specialities and localities within different general hospitals. Unfortunately the numbers referred to services often relate to the knowledge, awareness and interests of the individual clinicians involved rather than the specific needs of patients.

In many services patients referred following DSH constitute the highest single patient group. Criteria for the referral of such patients to mental health services vary considerably. The Royal College of Psychiatrists (1996) recommends that all hospitals have formal systems in place for the suicide risk and psychosocial needs of all such patients to be assessed; underlined by the National Suicide Prevention Strategy (DoH, 2002). Further guidance is to be provided by the National Institute for Clinical Effectiveness (NICE).

Referral mechanisms in mental health liaison differ. Some groups of patients may be referred for mental health assessment routinely, for example, according to local protocols or clinical care pathways. Others may be referred only after individual consultations between referrer and service provider. In all cases it is preferable that the patient is involved in the decision making process.

Only in cases when the patient is considered legally incompetent would it be appropriate to refer patients against their will. This said, misconceptions about mental health in general are still common and sensitivity, patience and common sense may be necessary to obtain agreement for referral for mental health assessment. Cross referral between consultant teams remains the norm in many hospitals. However, direct referrals between general nurses and mental health nurses is increasing. This referral mechanism is more common where specialist LMHNs form direct relationships with particular specialist teams or departments, for example, in oncology or haematology (Roberts, 2002b).

Though this chapter focuses primarily on the needs of adult patients (18–65 years), because of their physical proximity and specialist skills of many liaison services, some individuals outside this age group may be referred, assessed and treated as a matter of both good practice and local convenience. In these cases good working relationships and clear care transfer protocols are needed between liaison services and both community child and adolescent services and elderly care services. In other areas direct links between these community based services and the general hospital are well established and liaison services may have little role other than co-ordination and occasionally, emergency assessment of younger or older patients in the general hospital.

Theoretical Framework

Much of the health care system is based on medical or nursing specialisation. The most obvious example is the division between mental health and physical health services. This is, philosophically, a product of the Cartesian division between mind and body. It also fits within the '*medical model*' of health, which emphasises processes of diagnosis and treatment based in traditional reductionist models of science. Implicit within mental health liaison is the *biopsychosocial* or *integrationist* model. That is, mental health liaison is based on an integration of physical, mental and social elements in the assessment and management of presenting problems. This is largely synonymous with the philosophical term *holism*. The aim is to integrate the efforts of the whole health care team, crossing traditional philosophical and professional boundaries and promoting a collaborative approach to assessment and care.

The Collaborative Model of Liaison is the defining model of mental health liaison. It comprises the following elements: consultation, supervision and support, education and research.

Consultation is responding to a request for help or advice. It may have a *clinical* or *organisational* focus.

Clinical consultation involves either:

* *mental health* assessment and/or treatment of a referred patient;
* or advice on *nursing care* of a patient without necessarily seeing the patient directly.

Organisational consultation can have a focus on either:

* *professional* issues such as stress management among the referring team;
* or *systemic* issues involving the health care environment or system within care is delivered.

Supervision and support will help the referring team to develop their own skills in the management of basic mental health problems, and build confidence in the provision of psychosocial aspects of care.

Education in mental health matters and psychosocial aspects of care will complement supervision and support in the development of skills and confidence.

Research undertaken collaboratively consolidates working relationships and helps to cross inter-professional boundaries of knowledge.

Regular consultation, education, supervision and support are the basis of the collaborative model. Regular feedback to the referrer informs a *referral loop*, as greater knowledge among the referring team informs the referral process.

Principles and Skills

In a recent survey of UK LMHNs, the theoretical models of Crisis Intervention, Cognitive Behaviour Therapy (CBT) and Counselling were cited as the most commonly used (Roberts and Whitehead, 2002).

Crisis Intervention   Given the fact that many patients presenting to liaison mental health services are experiencing some form of social or psychological crisis it is unsurprising that crisis intervention was the model most widely used. Although there is relatively little UK literature on the subject, the crisis intervention model (Hobbs, 1984) has been particularly useful in the management of DSH.

Problem solving   This is a practical short-term focused therapy (Hawton and Kirk, 1989) commonly used in conjunction with crisis intervention. As a psycho-educational approach, problem solving has been shown to be one of the only effective interventions for use following DSH (Hawton *et al.*, 1998).

Cognitive Behaviour Therapy (CBT)   CBT is a very commonly used therapy in the treatment of depression, and of a number of somatoform disorders. It has been described in the work of LMHNs with chronic fatigue syndrome (Deale and Chalder, 2002), pain disorders and DSH (Atha *et al.*, 1989).

Counselling   This may be regarded as the basic model that underpins many other approaches. LMHNs working with cancer patients have described an integration of CBT and Rogerian counselling (Gardner, 1992; Tunmore, 1989).

In addition to the above models, knowledge of *Systems Theory* is necessary to understand the context of health care. In particular, to undertake systemic consultation within the complex system that is the general hospital (Roberts, 1997).

Assessment

Approach

Psychosocial assessments of individual patients in liaison settings, is similar to that associated with other community and hospital contexts. It should be timely, comprehensive and problem based. There are however frequent differences in the focus of the psychosocial assessment arising out of particular types of referral or presentation.

In consultation work, the focus of assessment is on the patient, though the ward environment may be a relevant factor, which in itself requires assessment. For example, confused behaviour shown by an elderly patient, may be aggravated, by being nursed in a central position of a very busy and noisy acute ward. A calmer environment may have a positive effect in such a situation.

At other times, although it is the patient that is referred, the 'problem' may be systemic in origin. For example, a patient in A&E, distressed following a road traffic accident, might be referred when staff tolerance and skill at dealing with distress is reduced in the absence of senior staff.

Once referred, developing a collaborative relationship with the patient is essential. In an environment where patients are faced with a large range of different health professionals, formal introduction of the LMHN, their role and mental health background is essential.

Issues of consent apply in the general hospital as elsewhere. Establishing appropriate consent for interview is vital especially if the patient appears cognitively impaired or is otherwise unwell. All patients should be informed routinely of their referral to any mental health service by the referrer and appropriate consent obtained.

Privacy, safety and the physical circumstances of the patient warrant attention. For example, patients who are mobile may be assessed in dedicated or improvised interview rooms. Others, who are being nursed in bed or who are less mobile may require alternative arrangements. Creativity and flexibility from all parties (the patient, general hospital staff and mental health staff) will allow some degree of privacy and appropriate levels of safety to be achieved. Similarly the *timing and duration* of any interviews may need to take into account the patient's physical capacity as well as hospital resources, routines and priorities.

Process

Understanding the reason for the interview   An explanation of the assessor's understanding of the reason for the referral and the nature and process of the assessment should also be given. The patient's understanding of the reason for the referral should also be established to avoid misunderstandings, which may later adversely affect the therapeutic relationship or the care given.

Relative/carer involvement   Many patients are either accompanied by or visited regularly by relatives or carers during their general hospital care. Their presence provides the opportunity, not only to obtain corroborative information for assessment purposes (with permission), but also allows for their involvement in the care giving process. Information giving and education approaches may be used and this contact may also provide the opportunity for the needs of carers to be identified.

The therapeutic use of the assessment interview   This is often desirable given the brevity of many liaison contacts. Benefits may accrue from, immediately challenging hopelessness and suicidal thoughts and the initiation of problem solving in those with depressed mood. Similarly, the opportunities offered by the frequent presence of relatives and other carers can allow the possibility of marital or family work during admission.

Information Gathering

Multiples sources of information are necessary in addition to that from the patient interview itself. Information may be obtained from written medical notes, discussions with hospital medical and nursing staff, relatives and carers and telephone contacts with GPs and other community based agencies. History taking in liaison settings has many similarities with other mental health assessments in other contexts. Topics of specific relevance are summarised in Box 4.4.

Determination of a problem list and needs should be considered. As far as possible, agreement with the patient should be reached on the nature and priority of problems to be addressed. Risk factors, medical or psychiatric diagnoses may also form part of the problem list.

Tools Used

The following assessment tools are used:

- Hospital Anxiety and Depression (HAD) Scale (Zigmond and Snaith, 1983). This questionnaire is designed for identifying clinically significant levels of anxiety and depression in the physically ill.
- Beck Intent Scale (Beck *et al.*, 1974a). This is useful for establishing the suicidal motivation of a specific incident of self-harm.
- Hopelessness scale (Beck *et al.*, 1974b). Hopeless is a factor in predicting suicide risk.
- Locally agreed tools and guidelines for risk assessment.

Risk Priorities

This is an essential feature of mental health assessments in the liaison setting. Inquiries about suicidal thoughts are important in all liaison assessments given the raised risk of suicide associated with many physical illnesses (see Box 4.3).

Box 4.4   Mental health assessment

Areas of the mental health assessment interview of particular relevance in liaison settings

- Chronological account of events leading to admission to hospital following treatment subsequent to DSH particular attention should be given to the events, planning, thoughts, feelings and expectations associated with the self-harm (Whitehead and Royles 2002).
- Detailed medical history especially current illness and medications including the implications of both the illness and its treatment.
- Psychiatric history especially current diagnoses and treatments including medication.
- History of self-harm and suicide attempts whether or not these have come to the medical attention previously (especially presentations following DSH).
- Current and past use of alcohol and any prescribed, non-prescribed or street drug.
- Risk of harm to self from suicide, repeated self-harm, self-neglect, non-compliance with treatment, and to others by violence, exploitation and so on.
- Usual coping strategies/resources including, for example, problems solving, supports available both in hospital and at home.
- Home situation including homelessness, finances.
- Current mental state especially:
  - cognitive functioning (level of consciousness, attention, orientation and memory)
  - mood including depression, hopelessness and suicidal ideas, anxiety,
  - hallucinatory or illusory experiences in any sensory mode.

Similarly, the risk of aggressive or violent behaviour to hospital staff is raised in many medical conditions characterised by disturbances in cognitive function, for example, toxic confusional states, acute intoxication with alcohol or other-drugs. The risk of repeated self-harm, may be noted separately. The assessment of risk is most effective when carried out within a multidisciplinary team, in order to reduce overly defensive practice or inappropriate clinical risk taking.

Care Planning

How Plan is Determined

Care planning in mental health liaison, is determined by the assessment process. There are two key elements in care planning:

1. *Direct* care involves seeing the patient face-to-face and intervening directly. The main form of direct care is mental health consultation. Systemic consultation may involve some direct elements.

2. *Indirect* care, where the LMHN gives advice on nursing care or treatment. This includes nursing care, professional and systemic consultation.

An initial assessment of care needs will include an assessment of the likely period of stay in the general hospital. The majority of patients admitted for treatment of overdose stay less than 24 hours. Therefore, planning will involve subsequent care on an outpatient or domiciliary basis. However, some patients will require an extended period of assessment and care in the hospital (e.g. patients experiencing acute liver failure following paracetamol overdose). Care for patients with chronic physical illness, such as cancer, will be complicated by fluctuations in health status, the side effects of treatment, and re-admissions for treatment of infections. In this case, it is imperative that the patient and their family understand how to maintain contact with the LMHN.

Not all liaison services, particularly emergency services for DSH, will provide follow-up after the initial assessment, so consideration will need to be given for referral to other agencies. In many cases this will be the patient's local mental health service. However, many patients' problems will not fall within the remit of the average mental health team. This may be because they have special needs, because of their age (under 18 or over 65), or their problems (e.g. substance misuse). It may be because they fall below the threshold of severe mental illness. Only a minority of people who take overdoses are mentally ill; most are in crisis, and for this client group, there may be limited community resources. The LMHN will need to develop knowledge of local services providing counselling for individuals and couples, specialist counselling and support for young people, advice on debt management and so on.

Practical Application

Some mental health liaison services will provide specialist follow-up for certain categories of patient. This may include:

- DSH services for people in continuing crisis after the overdose. As many people do not reach the threshold for referral to a community mental health team, support may be offered to people after DSH during the period of crisis.
- Psycho-oncology services are located in a number of major cancer centres in the UK. They are geared to the particular needs of cancer patients, many of whom are going through periods of adjustment rather than mental illness.
- Services for somatoform disorders or conditions that commonly present in physical health settings, for example, somatisation disorder, chronic fatigue syndrome. These will often be based on CBT and offer a series of outpatient treatments.

Future contact options may be offered on discharge. For example, within DSH services, a point of contact may be offered via the Green Card or Open Access system. The evidence for the effectiveness of this in preventing further DSH is equivocal. However, many patients find having the choice an aid to emotional containment and personal coping.

Case Example

Tina was admitted unconscious to an A&E ward following an overdose of 25 tablets of amitriptyline (50mg) and referred next day to the DSH team.

Assessment: Initial assessment identified abnormal cognitive state with altered conscious level, disorientation, visual hallucinations and poor short-term memory suggesting a diagnosis of a confusional state relating to the ingestion of the tricyclic antidepressants.

The initial plan was to delay the assessment process until Tina had recovered from the toxic effects of the overdose.

A secondary assessment was completed 24 hours later when Tina's cognitive state had returned to within the normal range.

Patient defined problems:

- Extreme distress associated with loss of relationship with long-term partner three weeks ago.
- Fears she will be unable to cope with her children without the support of parents who are on holiday for a further seven days.
- Six-month history of depression associated with poor sleep and appetite, difficulty concentrating and loss of energy and enjoyment.

Clinician defined problems:

- Episodic heavy drinking over the last six months coinciding with deterioration in relationship with partner.
- Poor coping when emotionally overwhelmed leading to increased risk of further overdoses especially if she continues to drink.
- Problematic use of low-dose amitriptyline as a hypnotic.

Care plan:
In hospital:

- Monitor mental state whilst in hospital.
- Contact relatives and GP to gain further details.
- Involve Health Visitor to discuss support for the children.

On discharge:

- Arrange three subsequent weekly outpatient appointments to review mental state.
- Advise on reducing alcohol intake.
- Advise on sleep hygiene.
- Advise on ways of coping when emotional under stress.
- Review and agree alternative ways of coping when suicidal, offer contact numbers.
- Discuss use of amitriptylline as hypnotic with GP, and discuss introduction of alternative antidepressant.
- Review again at the end of three meetings and consider further support.

Documentation

Active communication and liaison with all appropriate agencies is essential in the general hospital setting. This includes liaison with general hospital-based services, other mental health services, and with primary care. Direct verbal communication, often by phone, is desirable, especially if there are risk factors that need to be highlighted. However, this should always be followed up with written communication. In situations of risk or crisis, effective communication is paramount.

Documentation should always include an assessment of ongoing risk if DSH has been involved, if suicidal ideas are present or if there are other worrying features, such as depression in the chronically ill. This should be accompanied by a detailed care plan, which identifies which agencies are providing follow-up. Professionals involved should be mentioned by name so that there is no confusion of responsibilities.

LMHNs may be employed by a mental health trust or by the general hospital. They may share common case notes or hold them separately. It is important that any contact with the patient, whilst in hospital, is documented in the general hospital medical or nursing notes.

Time Frame

Some care episodes may involve assessment and intervention on only one occasion. In this case, the assessment itself may be seen as having a therapeutic effect, by focusing on current and past problems, highlighting both previous effective and ineffective coping. If follow-up is planned, an estimate of the frequency and duration of contact should be made, and agreed with the patient. This may be based on the expected duration of a specific therapy, for example, 12–16 sessions of CBT. Or it may be based on an expectation of the duration of the current crisis, to be reviewed at a later date. This could include an initial series of four meetings at weekly intervals.

Frequency and duration will depend on the priorities established at the time of assessment and/or discharge, and on the focus of the intervention.

Evidence Base

Evidence for the effectiveness of Mental Health Liaison is integrated throughout the chapter.

Dissemination of Information

Special attention should be given to *issues of confidentiality* in the very public environment that is the general hospital. Documentation should be appropriate to purpose (medical notes often have a wider readership than the equivalent psychiatric notes) and care should be taken that discussions with other hospital staff take place out of earshot of the patient and others.

Documentation should be disseminated to key parties, always involving primary care, usually the GP, on discharge. It may help to have standard documentation in the form of a summary so that key information is readily accessible and easy to read.

Reflective Practice

Many LMHNs work in relative isolation, and so need to think carefully about how to monitor their practice and ensure that it is safe and consistent.

Clinical Supervision is the main means for achieving this. Thought needs to be given to the source of the supervision, and the LMHN should ensure they have a choice over who it is. Managerial supervision alone will not be enough. The supervisor should be someone the LMHN respects, and who has relevant experience. If it is not possible to find someone with specific experience in the field of mental health liaison, then another experienced mental health practitioner may be able to offer generic mental health supervision.

Personal reflection may be used as a supplement to supervision, and is another way of developing skills and monitoring practice. This may involve the use of a reflective diary, or adopting a critical incident approach to reflective practice. Reflection within multidisciplinary teams, involving non-mental health colleagues, can be used, based on debriefing or defusion following specific clinical incidents.

There is a lack of published accounts of reflective practice in mental health liaison, one exception being an account of a challenging scenario in outpatient liaison work (Roberts, 1999).

Practice Development

There are currently limited opportunities for specialist education in mental health liaison in the UK. In spite of this, many LMHNs manage to further develop their work through education programmes. In a recent national survey, half the sample had undertaken English National Board qualifications after qualifying in mental health nursing. Of 78 respondents, 11 had a Community Psychiatric Nursing Certificate, 12 had a qualification in teaching, 6 in CBT and 5 in counselling (Roberts and Whitehead, 2002). Many mental health nursing skills are transferable. In addition, education skills are readily transferable and useable in the general hospital setting.

Conclusion

Mental health liaison is a complex activity. It involves not only intervening at times of crisis in people's lives, but doing this in an environment that is not always conducive or sympathetic to the goals of mental health liaison. There is not only a need to effectively engage the patient and their carers, but also to translate action plans and care packages into terms that will be understood by the referring agents. Mental health nurses can build on their sound relationship-building and interpersonal skills to develop collaborative working relationships with colleagues in the general hospital.

Suggested Further Reading

Gunnell, D. (1994) *The Potential for Preventing Suicide*, Bristol: University of Bristol.
Hawton, K. and Catalan, J. (1987) *Attempted Suicide, A Practical Guide to its Nature and Management*, Oxford: Oxford University Press.
Regel, S. and Roberts, D. (eds) (2002) *Mental Health Liaison – A Handbook for Nurses and Health Professionals.*, London: Bailliere Tindall.

References

Atha, C., Salkovskis, P. *et al.* (1989) Accident and emergency: Problem-solving treatment, *Nursing Times*, 85, 17: 45–7.
Beck, A., Schuyler, D. and Herman, I. (1974a) Development of suicidal intent scales, in Beck, A., Resnik, H. and Lettieri, D. (eds), *The Prediction of Suicide*, Philadelphia: Charles Press.
Beck, A.T., Weissman, A. *et al.* (1974b) The measurement of pessimism: the hopelessness scale, *Journal of Consulting and Clinical Psychology*, 42, 6: 861–5.
Deale, A. and Chalder, T. (2002) Chronic fatigue syndrome: a cognitive behavioural approach, in Regel, S. and Roberts, D. (eds), *Mental Health Liaison – A Handbook for Nurses and Health Professionals*, London: Bailliere Tindall.

DoH (1999) *Saving Lives: Our Healthier Nation*, London: Stationary Office.

DoH (2002) *National Suicide Prevention Strategy*, London: HMSO.

Gardner, R. (1992) Psychological care of neuro-oncology patients and their families, *British Journal of Nursing*, 1, 11: 553–6.

Harris, E.C. and Barraclough, B.M. (1994) Suicide as an outcome for medical disorders, *Medicine*, 73, 6: 281–96.

Hawton, K. and Kirk, J. (1989) Problem-solving, in Hawton, K., Salkovskis, P., Kirk, J. and Clark, D. (eds), *Cognitive Behaviour Therapy for Psychiatric Problems – A Practical Guide*, Oxford, OUP.

Hawton, K., Arensman, E. *et al.* (1998) Deliberate self harm: systematic review of efficacy of psychosocial and pharmacological treatments in preventing repetition, *British Medical Journal*, 317, 7156: 441–7.

Hobbs, M. (1984) Crisis intervention in theory and practice: a selective review, *British Journal of Medical Psychology*, 57, Pt 1: 23–34.

Kapur, N., House, A. *et al.* (1999) General hospital services for deliberate self-poisoning: an expensive road to nowhere?, *Post Graduate Medical Journal*, 75, 888: 599–602.

Kapur, N., House, A. *et al.* (2002) Effect of general hospital management on repeat episodes of deliberate self poisoning: cohort study, *British Medical Journal*, 325: 866–7.

The Royal College of Psychiatrists (1996) *The General Hospital Management of Adult Deliberate Self Harm*, Royal College Of Psychiatrists.

Roberts, D. (1997) Liaison mental health nursing: origins, definition and prospects, *Journal of Advanced Nursing*, 25: 101–8.

Roberts, D. (1999) Using the internal supervisor, in Spouse, J. and Redfern, L. (eds), *Successful Supervision in Health Care Practice: Promoting Professional Development*, Oxford: Blackwell Science, pp. 43–9.

Roberts, D. (2002a) Working models for practice, in Regel, S. and Roberts, D. (eds), *Mental Health Liaison – A Handbook for Nurses and Health Professionals*, London: Bailliere Tindall.

Roberts, D. (2002b) Mental health liaison in cancer care, in Regel, S. and Roberts, D. (eds), *Mental Health Liaison – A Handbook for Nurses and Health Professionals*, London: Bailliere Tindall.

Roberts, D. and Whitehead, L. (2002) Liaison mental health nursing: an overview of its development and current practice, Regel, S. and Roberts, D. (eds), *Mental Health Liaison – A Handbook for Nurses and Health Professionals*, London: Bailliere Tindall.

Tunmore, R. (1989) Liaison psychiatric nursing in oncology, *Nursing Times*, 85, 33: 54–6.

Tunmore, R. (2002) Liaison mental health nursing in community and primary care, Regel, S. and Roberts, D. (eds), *Mental Health Liaison – A Handbook for Nurses and Health Professionals*, London: Bailliere Tindall.

Whitehead, L. and Royles, M. (2002) Deliberate self harm – assessment and treatment interventions, Regel, S. and Roberts, D. (eds), *Mental Health Liaison – A Handbook for Nurses and Health Professionals*, London: Bailliere Tindall.

Zigmond, A.S. and Snaith, R.P. (1983) The hospital anxiety and depression scale, *Acta Psychiatiea Scandinaviea*, 67, 6: 361–70.

PART III

Severe and Enduring Mental Illness

CHAPTER 5

Early Intervention in Psychosis

Mark Rayne

A civilisation is measured by its treatment of its most vulnerable groups. We must remember that citizens in care are no less citizens and their voices should be heard, their views respected and their interests defended. (Edna Conlan, United Kingdom Advocacy Network)

Introduction

Delayed presentation of any health condition, can have major consequences for treatment and prognosis. This has rightly led to increased emphasis upon early detection and National health promotion, as referenced in the NHS Plan (Department of Health (DoH), 2000). Psychosis is no different. It presents in early adulthood, with a peak age of presentation or onset around 19 years.

The time frame from emergence of initial symptoms of psychotic illness to receiving specialist psychiatric treatment is an average of 12 months. However, generally the amount of time young people have to wait for help is one–two years and even longer in inner city areas (Birchwood *et al.*, 2001). This treatment lag is linked to great distress and increased probability of early relapse in the future.

However, there are a number of difficulties for early detection of psychosis that include:

- Placing a diagnosis on a young person.
- Issues of knowledge and confidence in the management of symptoms.
- Accessibility of secondary care services.
- The stigma of seeking help and having contact with Mental Health Services.

Together with a general lack of knowledge of mental health there can be a lack of confidence in engaging young people and the special needs and agendas that young people have. Parents do not know what to do, or who to contact when a mental health crisis occurs and it is not a topic discussed openly in families. Indeed, young people do not feel empowered to seek help.

The general public image of psychosis is negative, probably exaggerated by the media. Therefore, individuals may have a real fear of what may happen to them if they seek help. However, schizophrenia does not have to be a chronic disabling condition. Young people generally recover from the first episode of illness and over eighty per cent of individuals achieve remission of symptoms from their first episode of psychosis within six months. For the purpose of this chapter, the positive and beneficial input of a specific early intervention service will be explored.

Prevalence and Population

On average, 20 people per 100,000 will develop psychosis per year, rates ranging between 10–15 per 100,000 in less deprived areas compared with 55–60 per 100,000 in areas of high deprivation Department of Health (DoH, 2001). 80 per cent of first episode psychosis presentations are young people aged between 16–30 at onset with a median age of 19 years in males and 22 years in females.

The prevalence of Schizophrenia is important for this chapter, but the reader is directed to Chapter 6 for a detailed and comprehensive account.

Referrals

One of the most important ways to improve outcome in psychosis is to initiate treatment early. This means that individuals presenting with signs of psychosis need to be identified early and referred for assessment and treatment promptly. Results from the Early Psychosis Prevention and Intervention Centre (EPPIC) program in Melbourne, Australia, suggest that individuals receiving optimum treatment within six months following onset of psychosis have better recovery than those receiving treatment after a delay of greater than six months. For further information, please see: http://home.vicnet.net.au/eppic (2004).

Young people with first episode psychosis usually access mental health services in the UK as a result of crisis intervention or formal hospital admission; in the absence of an early intervention service. Routine referral to the mental health service often results in a poor uptake from young people. This may be due to issues of fear, stigma and unsuitable location of the service (usually in non-youth friendly locations). They are then discharged back to referrers for non- attendance ('two strikes you are out, attitude').

Non-attendance can be viewed as the young person making an informed choice not to attend their appointment and not requiring it. However, non-attendance can indicate withdrawal from contact and the start of the early signs of psychosis.

Referral pathways are complex and can vary. They may be dependant upon:

• Availably of mental health literacy,
• Access to non-stigmatising signposting and assessment,

- Initial psychosis detection skills of staff at primary level and,
- Ability of community and health services to communicate together.

Referral Process

The referral process for young people with psychosis into mental health services is usually through the Primary Care route via their GP. This relies heavily upon the young person initiating help, whereas the more usual path is that of concerned relatives informing the GP of apparent deterioration in the young person's behaviour from normal self. Young people doubt the usefulness of professional help and their negative stereotypes of mental illness and fear of mental health services form barriers to self-referral (Lincoln and McGorry, 1995).

The Early Intervention approach attempts to stream the referral process for young people into youth friendly services. This will mean:

- Links with youth and community agencies for training.
- To develop joint locations to see young people.
- Increasing the skills of workers in psychosocial interventions to engage and help the young person manage their symptoms.
- Engaging the wider family and young persons support network, as psychosis and its effects will touch all.

Theoretical Framework

Medication

The use of medication to treat the symptoms of psychosis has been a mainstay of treatment for many years since the discovery of Chlorpromazine, in the 1950s. The medications used are known collectively as antipsychotics, and are split into the older treatments (Typical) and the newer treatments (Atypicals). Both typical antipsychotics and atypical antipsychotic treatments are effective against positive symptoms of the illness. There is no clear evidence that atypical antipsychotics are more effective or more tolerated than typical antipsychotics. However, Geddes *et al.* (2000) state that conventional antipsychotics (the older typical) should be used in the initial treatment of an episode of schizophrenia unless the person has not previously responded to these drugs or has unacceptable extra pyramidal side effects. Whereas, Emsley (1999) suggests that atypical antipsychotics have fewer side effects and as a result can help with compliance to treatment. This is important with young people and their first illness and may help prevent crisis or relapse.

Psychosocial Interventions

Cognitive Behavioural Therapy (CBT) and Behavioural Family Therapy (BFT) to treat psychotic symptoms has been increasingly used with individuals with schizophrenia and medication resistant symptoms:

- CBT hastened the time to recovery by between 25 and 50 per cent and halved the time spent in hospital compared with controls (Drury *et al.*, 1996).
- Cognitive therapy shows a greater level of 'perceived control' of symptoms than other groups (Drury *et al.*, 1996).
- Relapse outcomes are statistically superior for family treated patients at six-month follow-up (Barraclough *et al.*, 1999).
- Individuals with families assigned to any form of social intervention had a two-year relapse rate of 40 per cent, whereas the relapse rate for individuals whose families were offered no help was 75 per cent (Leff *et al.*, 1990).

However, the use of CBT and BFT has not been extensively researched in acute first episode psychosis. This is a consideration that needs to be taken into account.

Hearing Voices

Research in Holland showed that two-thirds of the people interviewed, who were hearing voices, were living their lives without using mental health services (Romme and Escher, 1993). However, in a further study, 77 per cent of the people interviewed with schizophrenia and 100 per cent with dissociative experiences, had suffered major life changes or traumatic life events prior to the onset of hearing voices (Romme, 1996).

Romme *et al.* (1992) identified individuals' personal coping styles for voice hearing. Four coping styles were highlighted: *distraction, ignoring the voices, select-ive listening, setting limits on their influence.* The management of voices techniques by Romme *et al.* (1992), are shown to help individuals cope with issues of power against the voices, compelling them to act or to harm themselves and also to reduce the feeling that voice hearers are ostracised and not part of society. One of the most powerful ways of doing this is by introducing them to other voice hearers and other styles of coping to improve self-esteem and confidence.

Relapse Prevention Strategies

One of the most important determinants of relapse is duration of illness prior to starting antipsychotic medication. Despite high remission rates after a first episode psychosis, the risk of relapse is also high (Wiersma, 1998), reaching 81.9 per cent in one recent study at five years follow-up (Robinson *et al.*, 1999). Prevention of relapse is therefore important in first episode psychosis as most individuals are young (Lieberman *et al.*, 1993), and are likely to be pursuing important social and occupational goals. These will be disrupted by the symptoms and treatment associated with psychotic relapse.

It is suggested that each relapse may result in the growth of residual symptoms (Wiersma, 1998) such as hearing voices, paranoia and periods of depression.

These residual symptoms may also accelerate social disablement (Hogarty, 1991). The early warning signs approach to relapse prevention seeks to identify the earliest signs of impending relapse and to offer timely and effective intervention to arrest their progression towards frank psychosis (Spencer, 2001).

Employment/Vocation

Unemployment rates and loss of educational chances are common in those with severe mental illness. In schizophrenia the return to vocation is known to be a protective factor against relapse. There are two main themes of employment help that can be offered to individuals recovering from mental health episodes. Namely:

- Prevocational Training. A period of preparation before an individual is deemed capable of entering competitive employment.
- Supported Employment. Placing people in competitive employment without any preparation but with support whilst in the employment (Crowther *et al.*, 2001).

With prevocational training and supported employment, individuals can have a chance of achieving the 'reason to get up in the morning'. But there is still a lot of education to be done with employers and the community before there is any form of equality at the job interview stage.

Principles and Skills

Knowledge of how to help others is a component of 'mental health literacy'. The public have difficulty in dealing with mental disorders. Knowledge may be insufficient, as they may not know how to behave or be afraid of making mistakes (Brandli, 1999). These difficulties can also apply to Primary Care and Specialist Mental Health Staff if they have not had appropriate training and supervision.

There can be a considerable gap between the skills of staff trained in psychosocial interventions and those that have not. This can affect the quality and consistency of interventions offered to individuals and their families, at a time when there is a great need for information, education and debriefing. The IRIS group (1999) and DoH (2001) set out key principles for the assessment and care planning for individuals with a first episode psychosis. These are:

- Increase stability in the lives of service users, facilitate development and provide opportunities for personal fulfilment.
- Provide a user centred service available for age 14 to 35 that effectively integrates child, adolescent and adult mental health services and works in partnership with primary care, education, social services, youth and other services.
- At the end of the treatment period, ensure that the care is transferred thoughtfully and effectively.

Box 5.1   Principles of care

- Culture, age and gender sensitive.
- Family orientated.
- Meaningful and sustained engagement based on assertive outreach principles.
- Treatment provided in the least restrictive and stigmatising setting.
- Separate, age appropriate facilities for young people.
- Emphasis on normal social roles and service user 's development needs, particularly education and achieving employment.
- Emphasis on managing symptoms rather than diagnosis.

    (IRIS Guidelines, 1999; Policy Implementation Guide (DoH, 2001))

For service provision, evidence indicates that the principles of care in Box 5.1 are important.

Assessment

Approach

Assessment should be service user centred, with a multidisciplinary assessment, co-ordinated by the care co-ordinator. There should be sufficient time to build a therapeutic rapport with the individual and family, allowing an opportunity to discuss the impact of the psychosis.

In the majority of cases, symptoms and behaviours are preceded by less specific and severe symptoms, termed 'prodromal symptoms'. These are rarely viewed with concern, as they are very similar to adolescent behaviours common everywhere. They include social isolation; changes in sleep patterns and changes in diet. It is only when the symptoms of more clear psychosis appear such as voices or bizarre behaviour that frighten families, that help is sought and usually as a crisis.

The initial assessment meeting should be relaxed and non-clinical in nature. It should include time to build a trusting relationship. The location of the initial and following contacts are important. They should be somewhere that is youth friendly and where there is no perceived power imbalance as in a clinical environment. The initial contact should be a social interaction, getting to know the young person and their issues. The issues of formal mental health assessments and rating scales can only be introduced once a rapport has been built and some degree of trust established, as disengagement from a clinical approach is all too common.

The needs of young people are complex and good links into other services and networking skills are an important attribute of the nurse. Needs may include, housing, employment, money, vocation, relationships etc.

Process

The assessment should be comprehensive, using a minimum of jargon and a clear explanation of the assessment processes.

The assessment should include:

- Psychiatric history – from the young person and family to include, onset of symptoms, any family history, the presentation of the symptoms and duration of untreated illness.
- Mental status examination – to include the young persons perceptions of the symptoms, onset and including information from the family.
- Risk assessment – to include risk history, coping strategies, support networks and include the family in the assessment.
- Social functioning assessment – friendships, interests, hobbies, isolation and socialisation.
- Psychological assessment – any unresolved issues, psychological counselling history.
- Occupational assessment – employment/vocation/interests.
- Family/support assessment – any needs for carer assessment, support, information, education, needs of other family members with mental health issues.
- Service users aspirations and level of understanding – what are their hopes and feelings for the future and what do they understand/attribute to their current situation.
- Contribution from others who are important to the service user – asking the individual if they wish anyone to contribute to the assessment process.

 Point of Reflection: Are choices of engagement offered, and are they youth sensitive?

Information Gathering

Information is gained from a variety of sources at different times during the assessment process. It is important to collate the information received and ensure the sources are clearly documented. Information will vary in accuracy so it is important to cross reference against information already held.

Tools Used

A selection of assessment tools that can inform the assessment process are listed in Box 5.2.

Box 5.2   Useful assessment tools

- Early Signs Scale (ESS) (Birchwood *et al.*, 1989).
- Health Of the Nation Outcome Scale (HONOS) (Wing *et al.*, 1996).
- Liverpool University Neuroleptic Side Effect Rating Scale (LUNSERS) (Day *et al.*, 1995).
- Lancashire Quality of Life Assessment (Oliver, and Mohamad, 1992).
- Positive and Negative Syndrome Scale (PANSS). (Kay *et al.*, 1987).
- Calgary depression scale (Addington *et al.*, 1993).

Risk Priorities

The long period of untreated psychosis before first treatment has been shown to involve distress for individuals and their relatives. This includes ineffective and demoralising attempts to get help and the experience of traumatic events. Approximately 20–30 per cent of young people experiencing their first onset of psychosis have been a danger to themselves or others before receiving effective treatment, including suicide attempts (Lincoln and McGorry, 1999).

Around 10–15 per cent of people with psychosis commit suicide and the risk of this is greatest early in the illness (two-thirds of suicides occur within five years). Suicide is preceded by factors such as depression and particularly hopelessness, which are potential targets for psychosocial interventions (IRIS Guidelines, 1999).

Care Planning

How Plan is Determined

> A practical and pragmatic approach should acknowledge the strengths and potential abilities of people who use services to decide for themselves what they want to do and what they need some help with. (Edna Conlan, 1990)

In the early detection of psychosis, individuals and family members should have information made available to them on treatments and help available. With such information, they will be able to make choices of treatment they wish to accept, which are evidence based and deemed to help in the management of the psychosis. 'Health literacy' is the term applied, for the ability to gain access to, understand and use information in ways which promote and maintain good health (Nutbeam *et al.*, 1993). In mental health, literacy has been 'comparatively neglected' (Jorm, 2000).

Diagnosis can be difficult in the early phase of psychotic illness and so care planning needs to focus on the management of symptoms together with time to allow any symptoms to stabilise before a clear diagnosis is made. An initial care plan should be produced within a week of assessment and be regularly reviewed. It should be flexible enough to adapt to the changing needs of the individual.

Psychosocial therapies should be offered together with medication, psycho-education and the location of support groups to help the recovery process. Family therapy and the promotion of carer support groups should also be offered to all families. There is also a need to look at addressing the basics of everyday living including housing, benefits and vocational and social aspirations. This information can be attained by use of the Lancashire Quality of Life scale and by introducing others to co-work, including youth and community agencies. A relapse prevention and crisis plan should be developed with the Individual and family/involved others and families should know when and how to access help. This can be achieved by incorporating the identification of personal coping strategies, collaborating with the individual and family to identify early warning signs, agreeing on a contacts list and rehearsing a contingency plan.

Hospitalisation should be avoided if at all possible, but if it is required then separate age, gender and culture appropriate accommodation should be provided. The team should review the effectiveness of interventions offered and involve the service user and family/involved others in each of the review stages.

Prescribed medication should be checked to ensure that it is in line with National Institute for Clinical Excellence (NICE, 2002). Prescribing should be of low dose atypical antipsychotic medication, with information on side effects, issues of compliance and contact numbers; if there are any issues that the individual or family wish to discuss.

The option of referral to hearing voices groups, family therapy and cognitive behavioural therapy should also be explained and offered.

 Point of Reflection: What is the level of mental health literacy in your area and do people positively engage services?

Practical Application

In early psychosis, there is a need to offer early and sustained interventions. The interventions should be undertaken by a dedicated, community based co-ordinator utilising an assertive approach. Two key principles to aid engagement are that the individual is:

- seen at a low-stigma setting of their choice as opposed to an outpatient environment.
- failure to initially engage should not lead to closure of the case (creative engagement options should be explored).

It is important to involve the whole family and care team in the relapse plan. Not only does it improve and clarify the roles and responsibilities when relapse is impending, it reduces the stress on families making them feel empowered and more confident to cope. It also prevents the trauma of crisis for the individual and improves their trust and relations with the helping services (Programme In Community Mental Health Value Base, 1997; IRIS Guidelines, 1999).

There has been little research undertaken on how to positively engage individuals with first episode psychosis. Birchwood *et al.* (2001) suggest that engagement should include finding a common ground with the individual, an avoidance of a premature confrontation of their explanation of their illness and treatment delivered in as flexible a manner as possible. It is only when professionals engage young people to form a therapeutic alliance, that young people remain in contact with services. This forming of a therapeutic alliance is very difficult for professionals to achieve. There are also real issues of young people not feeling part of society or what it has to offer them; social isolation is common in adolescents and more common in adolescents with psychosis.

The care plan is practically applied through collaboration with the individual and family to develop an ownership that makes the care plan a working and relative document to them. The care plan should be balanced with the needs of the individual and the needs of the service offering the support. It should be developed and managed by all, co-ordinated by the case worker, and reviewed as often as any of the contributors deem necessary to make it a live and fluid document reflecting the changing needs of the individual, family and care team.

> **?** *Point of Reflection:* Do individuals receive evidence-based interventions? Are staff competent to deliver them?

Additional Care Planning

A lot of young people who experience mental health issues will self-treat with illicit drugs and alcohol. They are easy to obtain and most times reduce presenting psychotic symptoms. Regular assessments of any co-morbidity issues is important and help for substance misuse should be available by liaison and joint working with relevant agencies (see Chapter 13). Treatment for psychosis should be concurrent with treatment for substance issues. It is important that agencies communicate due to issues of prescription of antipsychotic medication alongside treatments for detoxification/substance management together with issues of duplication or omission of treatments etc. Another reason is the issue of compliance and disengagement due to side effects of treatments.

Forty-five per cent of people with first-episode psychosis have symptoms similar to post traumatic stress disorder (PTSD) linked to their illness and its treatment. Early use of the Mental Health Act and high doses of antipsychotics with side effects contribute to this. These factors also increase the risk of long-term treatment reluctance and service disengagement (IRIS Guidelines, 1999).

The example used is based on real events, but an amalgamation of experience. Any resemblance to specific information or events is coincidental.

Case Example

Personal History

Jane is a female of 19 years of age and the youngest of three siblings. She lives at home with both parents. Jane completed her first year at college and achieved a good grade. She did not enrol for the second year. Jane's cannabis use began at the age of 14 years (in excess of two roll ups' per day). She is not currently using cannabis. The family and Jane herself report changes in coping around two years ago (This coincided with the first year of her 'A' levels). There was a rapid decline in social functioning noted during the period of independent living, with emerging paranoid beliefs.

A referral was made to early intervention services following refusal to see her GP.

Jane was not engaged with the service at this point so the parents were offered home support by the early intervention service. Jane later agreed to an initial meeting with the early intervention service.

Initial Assessment

Upon initial assessment and observation Jane showed evidence of self-neglect and poor personal care. There was very poor eye contact and Jane's posture was guarded and she appeared very agitated. There was some evidence provisionally of thought disorder and she expressed suspicious beliefs. Her affect was flat and she complained of altered sleep patterns. Her general engagement initially was very poor.

Flash cards were used that helped to identify some initial symptoms, which helped with communication and engagement. The team then tried to promote insight into possible psychosis in a very non-threatening manner.

Care Plan

Attempts were made to engage Jane by following her agenda and ensuring her control of the process. All of the interventions were on a social level thus enabling Jane to identify her needs and identify possible solutions.

Through discussion and collaboration, a number of interventions were undertaken with Jane and her family. These included:

- Behavioural Family Therapy with Jane and her family to discuss Jane's psychosis and the impact upon them all, which includes an element of problem solving.
- Education and benefit's advice.
- To slowly introduce the idea of 'medication' to Jane discussing how it may help overcome symptoms of her psychosis, side effects and compliance. Atypical anti-psychotic medication was eventually prescribed through agreement.
- To offer family support and jointly develop a crisis and contingency plan with Jane and her family.
- With agreement commence CBT to help Jane to recognise symptoms of her psychosis and to offer management techniques.
- All interventions were within an assertive outreach model and included facilitating re-socialisation for Jane.

Documentation

The individual should be registered on enhanced Care Programme Approach (CPA). They will have complex and ongoing needs and receive a multidisciplinary service approach throughout the three-year critical period of engagement within early intervention.

Joint documentation should be used (medical together with nursing, social work and O.T), with all disciplines having access and input to joint assessments and ongoing care plans and reviews. This aids consistent approach and better communication between disciplines involved in the care.

Time Frame

Where disabilities develop, they usually do so during the first three years (the so-called 'critical period'). Unemployment, impoverished social network, loss of self-esteem can develop aggressively during the critical period; the longer these needs are not dealt with, the more entrenched they become (Birchwood *et al.*, 1998). Also, where a pattern of repeated relapse develops, it begins during the critical period (Wiersma *et al.*, 1998).

The team should stay involved with the individual for the duration of the critical period. The approach is similar to assertive outreach (see Chapter 8) with frequent contacts, outreaching to the individual, their family and involved others and complementing their existing support networks. The approach will hope to achieve:

- an improvement in ability to manage symptoms of psychosis,
- an increased quality of life,
- improved socialisation and re-establishment of social networks and,
- gaining of goals and aspirations around vocation and employment.

Evidence Base

Early intervention in psychosis is an exciting and positive proposition. Young people have a better chance of recovery if they get help earlier and if the help offered is youth friendly and the interventions are evidence based and do not lead to disengagement from services (Birchwood, 2001).

This chapter has pulled together some evidence for early intervention but the most compelling argument is the ethical one; as long duration of untreated psychosis causes extreme suffering and burden to the individual and all who care for them. Early intervention goes some way to reduce this suffering, which should be enough evidence.

Dissemination of Information

Any work and information recorded should be as open, collaborative and accessible as possible by all who are involved in the care process. It is really important that no one is excluded from the information sharing loop as there is a need to share information on:

- care planning,
- medication,
- reporting and reviewing adverse side effects,
- early warning signs of relapse and risk behaviours,
- feelings expressed by the individual.

Families are valuable allies in the process and need to be able to communicate with all of the care team. To exclude them from the information sharing process is to leave them to manage in isolation.

Confidentiality can be a difficult issue. There is a need to promote trust with the individual and allow them to talk about their feelings. An open and honest approach from the onset of engagement is vital, with agreement of what is confidential and what is shared.

Reflective Practice

Individuals with first-episode psychosis may present with very complex issues both psychologically and socially. There are case management issues around disengagement, self-harm and risk taking behaviours within early intervention teams. Therefore, team, peer and individual supervision should be accessed on a regular basis (both a structured and ad hoc). Joint supervision with other young peoples agencies and Child and Adolescent Mental Health Services (CAMHS) is a valuable experience for EI case managers to gain knowledge and help confidence. This ensures collaborative working and especially helps the transition process between agencies.

It is important that case discussion and sharing information takes place within the team. This helps the supervision and case management process and when covering sickness and absence. It is also a valuable way to share any successes in engagement approaches, positive outcomes and collaborations made with other agencies.

The formation of any new team should encourage collaborative processes and relationships within the team and celebrate new ways of working with young people with psychosis.

Practice Development

Training and the sharing of skills between youth, mental health and other agencies is necessary. Some workforce initiatives are underway, including graduate and assistant case managers being recruited into early intervention teams. Teams are also developing strong links with Connexions, youth organisations and learning mentors in schools. Service users are employed in teams as 'Service User Trainers'. This helps to improve the power imbalance and reduce anxiety, especially at first contact with mental health services. Also, carers are being employed to look at the needs of carers through Carer Education and Support Programmes.

This re-engineering of the workforce is essential to help deliver the early intervention approach, to engage individuals and families and to maintain engagement with mental health services.

Conclusion

There is a need to continue the engagement process once the young person is in services by the use of the best treatment options possible with information, treatments with minimal side effects and the choice of other treatment options to help the adjustment to the illness. There is also a need to assess the individual 'holistically' including needs for appropriate housing, employment, educational and finances.

Within this chapter, the rationale and evidence for an early intervention approach with young people with first-episode psychosis has been discussed. Early Intervention teams are developing at different rates and around different service delivery models. The one thing they all have in common is the passion of clinicians who want to do things differently. Realising that historical approaches to mental health service delivery with this client group is fraught with disengagement, long durations of untreated illness, formal admissions to stigmatising services and the development of new long-term no-hopers.

However, for me early intervention is about changing the prognosis for young people with psychosis, from professional pessimism to one of professional optimism.

Acknowledgements

The author would like to acknowledge the contribution made by Victoria Ellen Swain, Team Leader, South Staffs Early Intervention Service to this chapter.

Suggested Further Reading

Birchwood, M. (2001) *Early Intervention in Psychosis*, London: Wiley Press.
Haddock, G. and Slade, P. (1997) *Cognitive-Behavioural Interventions with Psychotic Disorders*, London: Routledge.
Nelson, H. (1997) *Cognitive Behavioural Therapy with Schizophrenia: a practice manual*, Cheltenham: Stanley Thornes.
Read, J. and Reynolds, J. (1996) *Speaking Our Minds: An Anthology*. Houndmills: MacMillan Press.

References

Addington, D. *et al.* (1993) Rating depression in schizophrenia: a comparison of a self report and observer report scale, *Journal of Nervous and Mental Disease*, 181: 561–5.
Barraclough, C., Tarrier, N., Lewis, S., Sellwood, W., Mainwaring, J., Quinn J. and Hamlin, C. (1999) Randomised controlled effectiveness trial of a needs based psychosocial intervention service for carers of people with schizophrenia, *British Journal of Psychiatry*, 174: 505–11.
Birchwood, M., Fowler, D. and Jackson, C. (2001) *Early Intervention in Psychosis*, London: Wiley Press.
Birchwood, M., Todd, P. and Jackson, C. (1998) Early intervention in psychosis. The critical period hypothesis, *British Journal of Psychiatry*, 172, suppl.33: 53–9.
Birchwood, M. *et al.* (1989) Predicting relapse in schizophrenia, *Psychological Medicine*, 19: 649–56.
Brändli, H. (1999) The image of mental illness in Switzerland, in Suimon, J., Fischer, W. and Sartorius, N. (eds): The Image of Madness. The Public Facing Mental Illness and Psychiatric Treatment, Basel: Karger, pp. 29–37.
Crowther, R., Marshall, M., Bond, G. and Huxley, P. (2001) Helping people with severe mental illness to obtain work: systemic review, *British Medical Journal*, 322: 204–8.
Day, J., Wood, G., Dewey, M. and Bentall, R.P. (1995) A self-rating scale for measuring neuroleptic side effects. Validation in a group of schizophrenic patients, *British Journal of Psychiatry*, 166: 650–3.

Department of Health (2000) *NHS National Plan*, London: Stationery Office.

Department of Health (2001) *The Mental Health Policy Implementation Guide*, London: HMSO.

Drury, V., Birchwood, M.Cochrane, M. and Macmillan, F. (1996) Cognitive Therapy and recovery from acute psychosis: a controlled trial, *British Journal of Psychiatry*, 177: 8–14.

Early Psychosis Prevention and Intervention Centre (EPPIC):http://home.vicnet. net.au/eppic/

Emsley, R.A. (1999) Risperidone in the treatment of first episode patients, *Schizophrenia Bulletin*, 25: 721–9.

Geddes, J., Freemantle, N., Harrison, P., Bebbington, P. (2000) Atypical Antipsychotics in the treatment of Schizophrenia: systematic overview and meta regression analysis, *British Medical Journal*, 321: 1371–6.

Hogarty, G.E. (1991) Family psycho education, social skills training and maintenance chemotherapy in the aftercare treatment of schizophrenia, *Archives of General Psychiatry*, 48: 340–1.

IRIS Group (1999) Initiative to reduce the Impact of Schizophrenia (I.R.I.S) Guidelines.

Jorm, A.F. (2000) Public knowledge and beliefs about mental disorders, *British Journal of Psychiatry*, 177: 396–401.

Kay, S.R., Fiszbein, A. and Opler, L.A. (1987) The positive and negative syndrome scale (PANSS) for schizophrenia, *Schizophrenia Bulletin*, 13, 2: 261–76.

Leff, J., Berkowitz, R. and Shavit, N. (1990) A trial of family therapy versus a relatives group for schizophrenia: Two year follow up, *British Journal of Psychiatry*, 157: 571–7.

Lieberman, J., Jody, D., Geisler, S., Loebel, A., Szymanski, S., Woerner, M. and Borstein, M. (1993) Time course and biological correlates of treatment response in first episode schizophrenia, *Archives of General Psychiatry*, 50: 369–76.

Lincoln, C.V. and McGorry, P. (1995) Who cares? Pathways to psychiatric care for young people experiencing a first episode of psychosis, *Psychiatric Services*, 46: 1166–71.

Lincoln C and McGorry, P.D (1999) Pathways To care in garry pychosis: Clinical and Consumer Perpectives, In *The Recognition and Management of Barly Psychosis*, MaGorry, P.D, and Jackson, H.J (eds), Cambridge: Cambridge University Press, pp. 51–79

McGorry, P. (1995) Psycho education in first episode psychosis: a therapeutic process, *Psychiatry*, 58: 313–28.

National Institute for Clinical Excellence. (2002) *Guidance on the Use of Newer (Atypical) Antipsychotic Drugs for the Treatment of Schizophrenia*, London: NICE.

Nutbeam, D., Wise, M. and Bauman, A. (1993) *Goals and Targets for Australia's Health in the Year 2000 and Beyond*, Canberra: Australian Government Publishing Service.

Oliver, J. and Mohamad, H. (1992) The quality of life of the chronic mentally ill, *British Journal of Social Work*, 22: 391–404.

Robinson, D., Woerner, M.G. and Alvir, J.M. (1999) Predictors of relapse following response from a first episode of schizophrenia, *Archives of General Psychiatry*, 56: 241–6.

Romme, M. and Escher, S. (eds) (1993) *Accepting Voices*. London. MIND Publications.

Romme, M. (1996) Patients and non-patients experiencing auditory hallucinations, *Yijdschrift voor Psychiatrie*, 38: 648–59.

Romme, M.A., Honig, E.O., Noorthoorn, E.O. and Escher, A.D. (1992) Coping with hearing voices: an emancipatory approach, *British Journal of Psychiatry*, 161: 99–103.

Spencer, E. (2001) Management of first episode psychosis, *Advances in Psychiatric Treatment*, 7: 133–42.

Wiersma, D. (1998) Natural course of schizophrenic disorders, *Schizophrenia Bulletin*, 24: 75–85.

Wing, J.K., Curtis, R.H. and Beevor, A.S. (1996) Health of the Nation Outcome Scales (HoNOS), *British Journal of Psychiatry*, 174: 432–4.

CHAPTER 6

Rehabilitation and Recovery: Evidence-based Care Planning for Enduring Mental Disorder

William Spence

Introduction

The development of the evidence base for psychosocial interventions (PSI) together with improved antipsychotic medication has underpinned an increasingly upbeat approach to working with people with enduring mental disorder (EMD). For the purpose of this chapter, the term 'enduring mental disorder' is preferred to 'serious mental illness', in line with the World Health Organization. Recovery from EMD is acknowledged by the government, who suggest services:

> create an optimistic, positive approach to all people who use mental health services. The vast majority have real prospects of recovery – if they are supported by appropriate services, driven by the right values and attitudes. (DoH, 2001, p. 24)

Evidence-based interventions in schizophrenia have been driven in the UK by the government's prioritisation of this group (DoH, 1999) and the burgeoning research evidence relating to it. In particular several areas can be identified where the evidence base for practice has increased over recent years. These include:

- The role of medication and its management.
- Expressed emotion and family intervention studies.
- Recognition of stress and vulnerability in relapse.
- Early detection and intervention in psychosis.
- Information processing in symptom management.
- Psychological interventions including Cognitive Behavioural Therapy (CBT).

Research on a variety of models of evidence-based practice (EBP) with people experiencing EMD indicates reduced relapse, improved social functioning, relapse prevention, effect of medication and family intervention (Leff and Vaughn, 1976).

Prevalence and Population

Mental disorder has been found to be the leading cause of disability in the world (Murray and Lopez, 1996) and psychotic disorders are associated with increased mortality (Allbeck and Wistedt, 1986).

Prevalence

1. Community sample studies suggest that the lifetime prevalence rate of schizophrenia is 0.7 per cent (Levav *et al.*, 1993).
2. The WHO calculates the range of annual incidence to be from 0.12 to 0.69 per cent (Hafner, 1995) using data from eight national studies, while median annual incidence across participating WHO sites was 0.22/100 (Bromet *et al.*, 1996).
3. Variation on prevalence has been more extensively studied and adult point prevalence ranges between 1 and 7.5 per 1000 and lifetime prevalence between 1 and 18 per 100 (Warner and Girolamo, 1995).
4. Around 250,000 people in the UK endure schizophrenia or schizophrenia like disorder (OPCS, 1995).
5. It can be seen that around 29 million people worldwide suffer from schizophrenia of which 20 million live in developing or least developed countries (Barbato, 1998).

Recovery   Around 20 per cent of individuals with schizophrenia make a recovery, around 70 per cent have relapsing disorder and about 10 per cent are seriously disabled by it (NICE, 2002b).

Positive symptoms   Schizophrenia sufferers frequently describe hallucinations and delusions. Johnstone *et al.* (1991) found more than 30 per cent of this group to experience moderate to severe levels of hallucinations and around 50 per cent to experience moderate to severe levels of delusions.

Onset   There are many risk factors associated with schizophrenia (Jablensky and Eaton, 1995). Family history and social class have been found to be strongly associated with the onset of schizophrenia (Bromet and Fennig, 1999). The familial recurrence of schizophrenia has been well established and originates in Koller's 1895 (cited in Jablensky, 1997) case control study of mental disorders where the inheritable risk of the psychoses was highlighted.

Genetics   Combined studies have estimated the proportion of affected offspring where the relative is similarly affected (Gottesman and Shields, 1982), see Box 6.1.

Box 6.1   Affected offspring

Parent – 5.6 per cent.
Sibling – 10.1 per cent.
Sibling (one parent also affected) – 16.7 per cent.
Children – 12.8 per cent.
Children (both parents affected) – 46.3 per cent.
Grandchildren – 3.7 per cent.
Unrelated – 0.86 per cent.

These studies often did not use; standardised diagnostic criteria, controls, blinding or age correction, and these are significant methodological weaknesses (Read *et al.*, 1992). Further strong evidence comes from monozygotic and dizygotic twin studies. Jones and Cannon (1998) estimate that the morbid risk in affected monozygotic twins will be over 50 per cent, whether reared apart or not, and they estimate that the overall heritability for liability to schizophrenia is between 60 and 70 per cent. However the discordance rate for monozygotic twins has been reported to be as high as over 50 per cent (Gottesman and Shields, 1976) and this supports the centrality of environmental factors in schizophrenia's aetiology.

Social Class   Social class influence on schizophrenia prevalence has long been acknowledged and it has been estimated that three times as many people from the lowest social class will suffer in comparison to those in the highest social class (Eaton, 1988). Whether the environmental stressors of lower socio-economic strata are implicated or whether affected individuals simply drift socio-economically downwards is not clear although most practitioners will be familiar with this phenomenon.

Gender   An over representation of males in schizophrenia first episode studies has been noted (Murray and van Os, 1998) although the lifetime risk seems to be equal for both groups using cumulative incidence in the 12–60 years range (Hafner, 1995). Over a six-year period some 65.2 per cent of first admission schizophrenia sufferers in one American county were male (Bromet and Fennig, 1999). In this study the mean age of first admission males across schizophrenia and schizoaffective disorder was three years less than that of females and those groups diagnosed with psychotic bipolar disorder and psychotic depression were both younger than that of females by a mean six years. It may be that females are more susceptible to the later onset and better prognosis type of schizophrenia although the reasons for this are not clear (Piccinelli and Gomez Homen, 1997).

Culture   There seem to be elevated levels of schizophrenia and other forms of psychosis in African Caribbean people, and seemingly low rates among South

Asian people (Cochrane and Bal, 1989). These observations are however based on rates of contact with services and represent a weak and unreliable estimate of prevalence among these groups (King *et al.*, 1994; Harrison *et al.*, 1988). Claims that the incidence of schizophrenia is declining (Der *et al.*, 1990) have caused some controversy although when rigorous assessment criteria (Hafner, 1995) are applied, no clear increase or decrease is evident (Helgason, 1990).

> **?** *Point of reflection:* Does your team have a clear idea of the prevalence and incidence of EMD in the locality served? How is this used to plan and evaluate services?

Referrals

Most referrals will be made to the community mental health team (CMHT) or assertive outreach team. CMHTs seem to be prioritising work with those experiencing EMD. However many CMHTs are less than clear about their goals and operational ambitions, despite being considered the 'mainstay' of the system (DoH, 2000). Ovretveit *et al.* (1988) and Onyett (2003) offer direction and advice regarding case allocation and management. An anticipated benefit of multidisciplinary team (MDT) working is the allocation of care to the most appropriately skilled staff, although in many instances this does not happen (Searle, 1991). To ensure that the referral process improves the care offered, it is essential that the care of those with EMD is prioritised. A shared philosophy of care and a shared understanding of the roles of contributing professionals, will contribute to improved teamwork.

> **?** *Point of reflection:* How are decisions made in your MDT team, for example, ward team or CMHT?
> How clearly does your team prioritise the needs of those with EMD?
> Does your team have a shared philosophy and an agreed operational policy relevant to those with EMD?

Theoretical Framework

Biopsychosocial Approach

The biopsychosocial approach (Engel, 1980), fits well with the stress vulnerability model (SVM) (Zubin and Spring, 1977; Nuechterlein and Dawson, 1984) advocated as the basis for working with people experiencing EMD. Here the biological aspect of schizophrenia's aetiology may be acknowledged and flexibly integrated with psychological and social factors to inform care planning. The utility of the SVM (Zubin and Spring, 1977) in schizophrenia work has become well established and is supported by the range of evidence-based interventions that have emerged since the late 1980s. The understanding of vulnerability should however be expanded to include the psychological processes associated with learning and responses to the environment in addition to the biological vulnerability, which is most readily acknowledged by the medical model.

Medication Management

Antipsychotic drug treatment remains the 'mainstay' of effective treatment of schizophrenia to be used alongside a range of psychosocial interventions (University of York, 1999, p. 1). Benefits of antipsychotic medication have been clearly identified (Kane, 1996), reducing relapse by 39 per cent in service users with a schizophrenia diagnosis who live in high stress families, although this advantage drops to 3 per cent where the family demonstrates low stress (Leff and Vaughn, 1976). Medication is not curative, but may have beneficial effects in 70–80 per cent of individuals (Pratt, 1998) although non-concordance has been estimated to be as high as 80 per cent (Corrigan, 1990). The promotion of concordance is a significant role for mental health nurses. Four aspects of medication management have been identified as important in promoting concordance:

- A client-centred approach.
- The development of a therapeutic relationship with the person.
- Knowledge about antipsychotic medication.
- Assessment skills (Harris *et al.*, 2002).

The older antipsychotics are equipotent in comparison to the newer atypical drugs with the exclusion of Clozapine, which has been shown to be markedly superior in its amelioration of negative symptoms, reduced severity and reduced frequency of extrapyramidal effects (Mortimer, 1994). The consideration of the use of the newer drugs has been sanctioned in England and Wales by the national institute for clinical excellence as a first choice option for people with newly diagnosed schizophrenia (NICE, 2002a). Limited concordance has been linked to a number of factors that practitioners should explore with the service user, with a view to negotiating progress (Hughes *et al.*, 1997).

Cognitive Behavioural Therapy

Cognitive behavioural therapy (CBT) seeks to explore the links between the individual's feelings and thinking patterns that relate to his/her distress. Individuals are encouraged to:

- Explore the evidence for distressing beliefs.
- Challenge the assumptions and other cognitions that they hold in relation to the belief.
- Develop rational alternatives to these (Beck *et al.*, 1985).

Many excellent texts exist that will assist both the neophyte and experienced practitioner in the application of CBT to those experiencing EMD (Birchwood and Tarrier, 1994; Kingdon and Turkington, 1994; Fowler *et al.*, 1995; Chadwick *et al.*, 1996; Haddock and Slade, 1996; Barrowclough and Tarrier, 1997 and Nelson, 1997). However, several problems in applying CBT to EMD have been noted by Fowler *et al.* (1995):

- Many people experiencing psychosis have difficulty in describing automatic thoughts and dysphoric feelings.
- Some also find direct enquiry about feelings to be threatening or even confusing.
- Some may reject the cognitive model altogether preferring to accept negative self-appraisals and reject the notion that these beliefs may be subject to change through reinterpretation.

> **?** *Point of reflection:* To what extent does your team acknowledge the factors that contribute to breakdown as highlighted by the SVM (Zubin and Spring, 1977)?

Principles and Skills

The therapeutic relationship is central to the delivery of all evidence-based interventions if it is one that attracts less research attention and this may be due to the difficulties in quantifying its elements and their effects. Interpersonal skills such as listening, eye contact, the expression of empathy and belief in medication have been shown to promote adherence (Meichenbaum and Turk, 1987).

The motivational interviewing approach to health behaviour change offers much promise. It is characterised by a non-directive, client-centred counselling style (Rollnick and Morgan, 1985). This approach is highly collaborative in nature and relies on the practitioner advising on medication management and providing feedback to the service user (Miller and Rollnick, 1991). The practitioner adopts an empathic approach, providing a range of change options and promotes personal responsibility and self-efficacy (Miller and Rollnick, 1991). The provision of written information should be tailored to service users understanding and circumstances (Ley, 1982). Psychoeducation more generally has been found to have a positive effect on well-being (Pekkala and Merinder, 2003).

The skills required for the delivery of CBT for EMD are many. Blackburn and Davidson (1995) list six characteristics that may be seen as the main features of the cognitive therapy style. A collaborative approach is essential, particularly where the person may be reluctant to engage. With questioning an essential part of the approach, it must be undertaken using a gentle, warm and empathic manner to avoid confrontation. The use of good listening skills is necessary for attending to the overt and implied meanings of the person's communication. Initially, nursing interventions may be 'low key'. However, appropriate professional boundaries must be maintained and integrated with a flexible approach to working with EMD where techniques are chosen and sequencing planned in an individualised manner.

Blackburn and Davidson (1995) advocate the 'judicious' use of humour and this may be seen as a very complex skill. The nurse must balance the assessment of many variables that impact on the perception of humour with the spontaneity that will enable humour to strengthen the therapeutic relationship. This is not a straightforward task. Nurses, of course, must have an understanding of the cognitive behavioural model that may be more straightforwardly gained from work with depression and anxiety in addition to broad clinical experience (Kingdon and Turkington, 1994).

Nurses must be persistent and creative in their approach to this group and be committed to teamwork. Service users will almost certainly appreciate a problem-solving approach and open mindedness. Perhaps, more fundamentally, nurses must be sensitive to the protection of the dignity and personal autonomy of the person with EMD, particularly where the individual's attention to this is temporarily reduced as a result of reduced mental health.

> **?** *Point of reflection:* Consider the source of support for practitioners in your team who work with those experiencing EMD?

Assessment

Approach

Barker (1997) offers a detailed discussion of the person-centred assessment process, advocating the use of formal and informal methods. The goal is to: quantitatively determine the scale of the problem, clarify the context or condition under which psychotic phenomena occur, appreciate the purpose of the person's behaviour and the variation in the problem which helps the practitioner understand the seriousness of the difficulty. Formal methods, or those involving assessment instruments/rating scales derived through research, have grown in popularity.

However, before selecting a rating scale, practitioners must be confident in their ability to understand the significance of the scale's reported psychometric properties and the way in which it might best be used to inform practice decisions. Barnes and Nelson (1994) caution that scales' comprehensiveness, sensitivity to change, and specificity should be considered prior to selection.

Process

Systematic assessment should begin with global assessment, followed by more specific assessment informed by the data collected. The care plan may be directed by the Care Programme Approach (CPA) documentation (DoH, 1990). Care should be taken with regard to the validity and reliability of this where local adaptations have been incorporated, especially with regard to assessment prompts, including risk assessment. The desire to reach agreement with service users and informal carers on the content of the care plan may result in delays in updating this document in the light of specific assessments. Local administration systems should aim to support the dynamic nature of assessment and care planning as far as possible. Ideally service users should be assessed over a period where they are free from the effects of antipsychotic medication. Although, the anticipated benefit of these drugs to a psychotically disturbed person often outweighs the benefits of drug free assessment at a crisis point. Antipsychotic polypharmacy should normally be avoided.

The drug attitude inventory (Hogan *et al.*, 1983) may be helpful in the detailed assessment of service users' views of their prescription and may assist the practitioner in tailoring interventions to improve concordance. The assessment of the unwanted effects of psychotropics has not always been afforded the salience by practitioners that these potentially disabling effects warrant. Bennett *et al.* (1995a) found that Community Mental Health Nurses (CMHNs) on average assessed only a few of the 13 commonest groups of unwanted effects – (1) hypotension (2) behavioural problems (3) dystonia (4) akathisia (5) parkinsonism (6) tardive dyskinesia (7) malignant syndrome (8) weight gain (9) sexual difficulties (10) gastric difficulties (11) blurred vision (12) urinary and (13) skin complications.

Information Gathering

Assessment information gathering is an ongoing process. Whilst care planning and delivery can never be informed by complete information, practitioners must use judgement in reaching a practicable and safe balance of information and action. Assessment will begin at the first contact and terminate at the close of the last contact of the care episode. Information gathering will be governed by an ethical code (NMC, 2002) and will seek to answer the question, 'what does it mean to be this person?' (Barker, 1997). This poses a particular challenge in psychosis where its medicalisation may have contributed to the invalidation of the sufferer's experiences as symptoms of illness. Nurses must approach these phenomena as people's responses to life and relationships and gather information accordingly.

The adoption of a holistic approach will ensure that relevant information that is easy to overlook is incorporated in assessment. Conceptual and theoretical models of nursing may guide information gathering, however effective practice in this area will be highly dependent on well developed interpersonal skills conducive to the development of trust in the working alliance. Here, counselling's core conditions (Rogers, 1951) of empathy, unconditional positive regard or warmth and authenticity/genuineness will assist in the development of a trusting relationship. Informal or unpaid carers can wherever possible be part of this working alliance. Informal carers are often second only to the service user in their ability to reliably provide valid information and their salience to the care process is only in recent times coming to be recognised.

Tools Used

Many global and specific assessment instruments exist and Gamble (2000) and Barnes and Nelson (1994) offer a very useful overview of these.

The Manchester scale (KGV) (Krawiecka *et al.*, 1977) has become widely used in assessment. Its simplicity, brevity of administration, high inter rater reliability, sensitivity to change (Owens and Johnstone, 1980) and its suitability for use by inexperienced practitioners (Manchanda *et al.*, 1989) make it a most practical global assessment instrument.

The Brief Psychiatric Rating Scale (Overall and Gorham, 1962) is a general scale designed for general use and not specifically schizophrenia. Although its use is frequently reported (Manchanda *et al.*, 1989), its utility in schizophrenia work is less helpful (Barnes and Nelson, 1994). The instrument may best be considered an effective measure of change in general psychopathology.

The Knowledge About Schizophrenia Interview (KASI) (Barrowclough and Tarrier, 1997) has become an established instrument in the assessment of the psychoeducation need of the sufferer's significant others. Barrowclough and Tarrier (1997) also provide useful information designed to address the common queries and knowledge gaps of significant others.

The Camberwell Assessment of Need (Phelan *et al.*, 1995, Slade *et al.*, 1999) is a standardised assessment of service user need, which may be incorporated into routine care (Gilbody *et al.*, 2001) to determine both met and unmet service needs.

The development of unwanted drug effect rating scales enables practitioners to build a detailed picture of the person's experience while promoting collaboration and involvement in care. The use of these has been recommended by the Department of Health (DoH and RCN, 1994). Several such scales are available:

- The Liverpool University Neuroleptic Side Effect Rating Scale (LUNSERS) (Day *et al.*, 1995) is widely used by practitioners.
- Abnormal Involuntary Movement Scale (AIMS) (Munetz and Benjamin, 1988 and National Institute of Mental Health, 1977).
- The UKU side effect rating scale (Lingjaerde *et al.*, 1987) for use by CMHNs (Bennett *et al.*, 1995b).
- The Simpson Angus scale (Simpson and Angus, 1970).

Barnes and Nelson (1994) have described several of the above tools in a practical review of assessment tools relevant to psychoses.

- The cognitive assessment of voices interview schedule (Chadwick *et al.*, 1996) provides practitioners with a systematic framework for discussing and assessing the experience of hearing voices.

Scales are best employed in the spirit of openness, involvement and participation, which is conducive to service user empowerment (White and Hellerich, 1992) and nurses must be cautious of adopting the erroneous and frequently found assumption that psychometrically established knowledge is not contaminated by subjectivity (Spence, 2000).

Risk Priorities

The assessment and management of risk is a critical element in caring for those with EMD. A systematic approach to this has become critical to meaningful care planning for this group, as recent tragedies (Ritchie *et al.*, 1994; Greenwell *et al.*, 1997) have evidenced failures in risk management. The increased severity of mental health problems to be found in community patients and supervised discharge have served to emphasise the importance of rigorous risk management procedures. This group may be vulnerable to various types of risk including the risk they present to self, for example, self-harm including suicide, financial, exploitation, unwanted drug effects, and to others like verbal and non-verbal violence including damage to property, offending and sexual activity.

Risk is the likelihood of an event occurring and its assessment should consider the individual, his or her circumstances and the individual's response to these. This highlights the dynamic nature of risk assessment where all these variables are subject to fairly rapid change and the importance of the regular and frequent appraisal and recording of this. Risk assessment instruments must not form the sole source of information used when risk is assessed. The individual's history of risk, particularly to self and others, should be used to inform the assessment of risk but not dictate it. The potential for the person's history of risk to stigmatise should be carefully balanced with the value of this information in informing care planning.

In assessing risk for suicide, violence and aggression the scales advocated by Hawton (1994) and Wykes *et al.* (1994) will be of use in planning care. It is important that risk assessment covers the dimensions of frequency and severity. It should be seen as an approach rather than a skill (Snowden, 1997), which is integrated with everyday practice.

> **?** *Point of Reflection:* To what extent would you say that risk assessment has become an integral way of working for your team?

Care Planning

How Plan is Determined

The Tidal Model, developed by Barker (2001a), assumes nursing to be an interactive developmental human activity concerned with the person's further development. It assumes that the experience of mental distress is evidenced by observable behavioural disturbance or private events known only to the individual. This is then translated into a disturbance of every day living.

The nurse – patient relationship for Barker (2001b) is one of mutual influence where the narrative is used to guide the practitioner in care planning (Barker, 2002). Within this model, the water of an ocean represents the 'dynamic effect of experience'. The horizon represents the illusory boundaries of the self and the limitless nature of personal experience and shipping represents the journey of life. The model is relevant to the care of people experiencing EMD and sees the focus of mental health care as empowerment and community delivery of care. Nursing care involves a temporary unity of service user and nurse and an acknowledgement that people are constantly changing.

This model directs that care planning includes the person's own words to communicate the lived appreciation of these problems. Empowering interventions seek to help people gain control over their lives by the strengthening of individual competencies and capacities (WHO, 1986, 1997). Care planning should seek to enable the service user's understanding of what is happening to him/her and devise steps to assist the individual realise her/his aspirations for what should happen next. This model may be used to frame CBT and family work. It requires the practitioner's acceptance of the SVM emphases on environmental factors in relapse and the importance of the service users' life history in explaining supportive and stressful experiences in addition to interpersonal, spiritual and physical strengths and weaknesses.

Care planning for people experiencing EMD has been greatly influenced by the CPA (DoH, 1990) and its recommendation that service users and carers are involved in this process. Patient involvement in decision-making is driven by the desire to provide a service that is responsive to patient's needs, the right of users to be involved in decisions relating to them and the therapeutic value of involvement (Hickey and Kipping, 1998). The Nursing and Midwifery Council (NMC) (2002) requires nurses to involve patients in care planning wherever 'practicable'. Involving patients in the care planning process may increase concordance with the care plan (Favod, 1993), maximise the effectiveness of the care delivered (Valimaki and Leino-Kilpi, 1998) and is entirely consistent with the collaborative approach of CBT.

Planning however is often dominated by a biomedical preoccupation with problems, which may undermine patients' personal aspirations, hopes, goals and intentions. Anthony and Crawford (2000) found mental health nurses to support consumer involvement in care planning and its basis in the service users' expressed needs. However they also found that staff attitudes and conflicting staff roles, among other things, militated against this.

Practical Application

Seeking the agreement of all involved in care planning represents one practical challenge and the care programme approach is designed to enable this under the auspices of the care co-ordinator. Nurses should be careful to ensure that goals reflect the patient's perspective and wishes as far as practicable and that they are attainable. Realisable goals may be set and progress towards them assessed. Workers in this area must adapt to a scale of ambition for recovery that is usually less rapid but, perhaps more incremental, than in acute work. Support through supervision in adopting this facet of work in EMD is indicated.

The active involvement of patients, their informal carers and other professional carers supports the need for high levels of nursing accountability in care planning. The conceptual underpinnings of care planning will be readily apparent in the documentation, and nurses must ensure that this is consistent with the team's approach where this has been clarified. The implementation of planned care must be a collaborative effort and the genuineness of this collaboration may be tested where practitioners are asked to support informed and competent non-concordance with it. Informal carers are very important collaborators and their support in realising agreed objectives will be paramount.

Such tripartite negotiations demand high levels of interpersonal skills and supervisory support of practitioners, particularly where conflict arises. Ultimately the nurse must balance the demands of individualised care with those of her/his employer, professional body and societal expectations. As an employee the nurse must remember that he/she cannot fulfil the role of independent advocate for the service user or informal carer where the need for this arises.

Additional Care Planning

The need to maintain a dynamic record of care that reflects the virtually contractual nature of the involvement of all parties is essential. Ongoing and specific assessment results will influence the plan and mechanisms must be in place to support this. The plan is a dynamic documentation of aspirations and interventions and this must be supported by the practitioner's conceptual model where the environment and people are assumed to be continually changing.

Case Example

Background

John is in his mid-fifties and lives with his partner. Both have a diagnosis of schizophrenia and are regularly admitted to hospital on several occasions each year.

Problem

John believes that his neighbour in the flat upstairs moves around his home in a similar pattern to himself as part of his close observation of John's movements.

Plan

With few other unsubstantiated beliefs and a high level of community functioning at the time of intervention, it was agreed with John that the temperate challenge to this idea was likely to reduce the strength of his belief in it. John's perception, of supporting evidence for this belief, was sought and subject to non-threatening exploration and limited challenge. Noises emanating from the flat upstairs acted as activating events for John. The noises led John to make inferences about this neighbour's intentions, 'this guy is watching my every move … I think that he must be up to no good … watching me and recording my movements' Although this inference may be seen as quite arbitrary in nature, John felt that he had selectively chosen a situation and took this out of context (the high likelihood that both men would be in similar flat areas at many times) and had continued to consider most noise from the flat above in this context. He acknowledged that he had ignored many important features in his formulation, for example, that neighbour noise was inevitable in a flat and probably independent of his own movements, that he had not met his neighbour and had no reason to believe that he was collecting information about him, that the quietness of the neighbourhood tended to make noises above very noticeable. He also saw that he had magnified the significance of the noises and that the application of the erroneous algorithm represented an overgeneralisation. The consequences of these interpretations caused John anxiety consistent with their significance and intervention focused on weakening these inferences. These interventions were founded on a developing nurse–patient relationship that had developed over several months through rehabilitation work associated with discharge from a long stay hospital ward to community living once more. The CBT approach here was well accepted by John who was well educated and saw himself as an accomplished if unpublished author.

Time frame: Three–Four months

Short term

Acknowledgement of the cognitive approach and acceptance of its potential to help. Reduction in the strength of beliefs.

Long term

The patient's goal, following education of the approach, was to reduce belief strength to the point where this no longer caused significant concern. John's understanding of the information processing basis of CBT is evident in his statement of goals: 'I want to get to the bottom of these noises and reach a point where they do not worry me any more.'

Documentation

Mental health nurses are obliged to incorporate the patient and carers' views in the care plan. This is stipulated in the CPA, a framework for the continuity of documentation and care provided (DoH, 1990). However, in a study by Rose (2001) the majority of patients did not know what CPA was for. The nurse's responsibilities with respect to record keeping are clear. The NMC believes that, 'good record keeping is a mark of the skilled and safe practitioner, whilst careless or incomplete record keeping often highlights wider problems with the individual's practice' (NMC, 2002, p. 7). The care plan should be accessible to the service user and this may be achieved by providing a copy for her/him. With the service user's permission the informal carers may be provided with a copy and their contribution to care recorded in this document.

Time Frame

The care plan should be reviewed on an ongoing basis and a meeting formally convened by the care co-ordinator as necessary. This can be at various intervals dependent on the need of the service user and those involved in their care. The time frame for care plan review will depend on many factors including the changing health of the patient, the complexity of needs, agencies and professional involved and the level of CPA applicable. Service users should be involved with every change of the plan. Professional input will ideally be made available until no longer necessary and this will be determined by a combination of service user need and operational policy direction on inclusion and exclusion criteria. In practice this may reflect service rationing at the expense of individualised and evidence-based care and the criteria for this should be made explicit.

Dissemination of Information

Challenges to the service user's confidentiality may arise where care plan disclosure may be indicated and where permission to share this with others is absent. There is no formulaic solution that can be offered here. Practitioners will be required to balance trust in the therapeutic relationship, with public and service user protection and the value of informal carer involvement with their professional responsibilities. It is important that practitioners are able to discuss these complex issues with colleagues in reaching decisions that are balanced and informed by the reflective process.

? *Point of reflection:* How might service users and their informal carers become optimally involved in the planning of care? Are the needs of informal carers systematically assessed and addressed?

Reflective Practice

Schön (1983) highlighted the importance of reflection, in enhancing professional practice. He drew attention to the weakness in professionals' faith in the application of theory to practice. The value of intuitive knowledge in guiding professional practice has been incorporated in the Johns (1995) model of reflective practice, which has developed Carper's (1978) patterns of knowing.

Reflection in practice involves a form of action research where the professional considers practice as it is delivered. This is associated with skilled practice (Conway, 1994) and may differentiate between differing levels of professional competence. Reflection on action occurs after the event, or may involve pausing in the midst of intervention to consider options (Conway, 1994). However reflection on practice may lead the evidence-based practitioner to challenge the status quo and to subsequent conflict (Hargreaves, 1997). This highlights the need for strategic consideration of the practice context where practice development is planned.

Reflective practice skills are important in working with people with EMD and their carers, given the complexity of the skills required. Reflective skills are essential and development of these in any staff group must be considered a priority.

Practice Development

In 1997, almost half of CMHNs reported specialisation with those experiencing EMD and this was a growth of almost 43 per cent over the 1985–96 period (Brooker and White, 1997). Also, almost 16 per cent reported approach specialisation in psychosocial intervention at this point (Brooker and White, 1997).

The national service framework's (DoH, 1999) aspirations for mental health promotion (especially with regard to those with EMD) have been met by what can only be described as, a lacklustre response from over stretched NHS trusts. The evolving evidence for early interventions, covered in Chapter 5 of this book, supports ill health prevention methods in this at-risk group. However, everyday practice has yet to fully embrace this evidence in the UK although the political imperative to do so already exists (DoH, 2000, 2003; NICE, 2002b). Group and community level targeting of ill health preventative interventions will require significant practice development in mental health nursing and a significant change in professional preparation for this role. Nurses seem well positioned to embrace the growing demand for power sharing with patients and their informal carers.

Conclusion

Nursing practice faces many challenges in the good ship NHS. One such challenge is the prioritisation of those with EMD and the delivery of evidence-based care to this group. Nurses are rising to the challenge and, with some artistry, are assimilating the evidence base in their every day practice. The CBT approach and associated skills sit harmoniously with a nursing quest to assist individuals in making sense of their experience of disorder. The integration of emerging research with traditional values of compassion and client-centredness within nursing will continue to challenge mental health nurses for the foreseeable future.

📖 Suggested Further Reading

Kavanagh, D.J. (1992) *Schizophrenia: An overview and practical handbook*, London: Chapman and Hall. (Although a little dated, this text is a well-referenced resource book).

Harris, N., Williams, S. and Bradshaw, T. (2002) *Psychosocial interventions for people with schizophrenia: A practical guide for mental health workers*, New York: Palgrave Macmillan. (This text provides a 'practical guide' to evidence based practice in this area).

References

Allbeck, P. and Wistedt, B. (1986) Mortality in schizophrenia, *Archives of General Psychiatry*, 43: 650–3.

Anthony, P. and Crawford, P. (2000) Service user involvement in care planning: The mental health nurse's perspective, *Journal of Psychiatric and Mental Health Nursing*, 7: 425–34.

Barbato, A. (1998) *Schizophrenia and Public Health*, Geneva: World Health Organization.

Barker, P. (1997) *Assessment in Psychiatric and Mental Health Nursing: In Search of the Whole Person*, Cheltenham: Nelson Thornes.

Barker, P. (2001a) The Tidal Model: Developing an empowering, person-centred approach to recovery within psychiatric and mental health nursing, *Journal of Psychiatric and Mental Health Nursing*, 8, 3: 233–40.

Barker, P. (2001b) The Tidal Model: A radical approach to person-centred care, *Perspectives in Psychiatric Care*, 37: 2.

Barker, P. (2002) The Tidal Model: The healing potential of metaphor within the patient's narrative, *Journal of Psychosocial Nursing*, 40: 43–50.

Barnes, T.R.E. and Nelson, H.E. (1994) *The Assessment of Psychoses: A Practical Handbook*, London: Chapman Hall.

Barrowclough, C. and Tarrier, N. (1997) *Families of Schizophrenic Patients: Cognitive Behavioural Intervention*, Cheltenham: Stanley Thornes.

Beck, A.T., Hollon, S.D., Young, J.E., Bedrosian, R.C. and Budenz, D. (1985) Treatment of depression with cognitive therapy and amitryptiline, *Archives of General Psychiatry*, 42: 142–8.

Bennett, J., Done, J. and Hunt, B. (1995a) Assessing the side effects of antipsychotic drugs: A survey of CPN practice, *Journal of Psychiatric and Mental Health Nursing*, 2: 177–82.

Bennett, J., Done, J., Harrison-Read, P. and Hunt, B. (1995b) Development of a rating scale/checklist to assess the side effects of antipsychotics by community psychiatric nurses, in Brooker, C. and White, E. (eds), *Community Psychiatric Nursing: A Research Perspective, Vol. 3*, London: Chapman and Hall.

Birchwood, M. and Tarrier, N. (1994) *Psychological Management of Schizophrenia*, Chichester: Wiley.

Blackburn, I. and Davidson, K. (1995) *Cognitive Therapy for Depression and Anxiety*, Oxford: Blackwell Science.

Bromet, E.J., Jandorf, L., Fennig, S. *et al.* (1996) The Suffolk County Mental Health Project: demographic, pre-morbid and clinical correlates of 6-month outcome, *Psychological Medicine*, 26, 5: 953–62.

Bromet, E.J. and Fennig, S. (1999) Epidemiology and natural history of schizophrenia, *Biological Psychiatry*, 46, 871–81.

Brooker, C. and White, E. (1997) *The Fourth Quinquennial National Community Mhealth Nursing Census of England and Wales*, Manchester: University of Manchester.

Carper, B. (1978) Fundamental patterns of knowing in nursing, *Advances in Nursing Science*, 1, 1: 13–23.

Chadwick, P., Birchwood, M. and Tarrier, P. (1996) *Cognitive Therapy for Delusions, Voices and Paranoia*, Chichester: Wiley.

Cochrane, R. and Bal, S.S. (1989) Mental hospital admission rates of immigrants to England: a comparison of 1971 and 1981, *Social Psychiatry and Psychiatric Epidemiology*, 24: 2–11.

Conway, J. (1994) Reflection, the art and science of nursing and the theory–practice gap, *British Journal of Nursing*, 3, 3: 114–18.

Corrigan, P. (1990) From non-compliance to collaboration in the treatment of schizophrenia, *Hospital and Community Psychiatry*, 41, 11: 1203–11.

Day, J., Wood, G., Dewey, M. and Bentall, R.P. (1995) A self rating scale for measuring neuroleptic side effects: Validation in a group of schizophrenic patients, *British Journal of Psychiatry*, 166: 650–3.

Department of Health (1990) *The Care Programmed Approach for People with a Mental Illness Referred to the Specialist Psychiatric Services*, HC 23, London: Department of Health.

Department of Health (1999) *National Service Framework for Mental Health*, London: the Stationery Office.

Department of Health (2000) *Mental Health Policy Implementation Guide*, London: Department of Health.

Department of Health (2001) *The Journey to Recovery – The Government's Vision for Mental Health Care*, London: Stationery Office. Available at: http://www.doh.gov.uk/mentalhealth/journeytorecovery.pdf

Department of Health (2003) *Early Intervention for People with Psychosis*, London: Stationery Office. Available at: http://www.nimhe.org.uk/downloads/early.pdf

Department of Health and The Royal College of Nursing (1994) *Good Practice in the Administration of Depot Neuroleptics*, London: HMSO.

Der, G., Gupta, S. and Murray, M. (1990) Is schizophrenia disappearing, *Lancet*, 335: 513–16.

Eaton, W.W. (1988) The use of epidemiology for risk factor research in schizophrenia: An overview and methodologic critique, in Tsuang, M.T. and Simpson, J.C. (eds), *Handbook of Schizophrenia, Vol. 3: Nosology, Epidemiology and Genetics of Schizophrenia*, Amsterdam: Elsevier Science Publishers BV, pp. 169–204.

Engel, G.L. (1980) The clinical application of the biopsychosocial model, *American Journal of Psychiatry*, 137: 535–44.

Favod, J. (1993) Taking back control, *Nursing Times*, 89: 68–70.

Fowler, D., Garety, P. and Kuipers, E. (1995) *Cognitive Behaviour Therapy for Psychosis: Theory and Practice*, Chichester: Wiley.

Gamble, C. (2000) Assessments: a rationale and glossary of tools, in, Gamble, C. and Brennan, G. (eds), *Working with Serious Mental Illness: A Manual for Clinical Practice*, London: Balliere Tindall.

Gilbody, S.M., House, A.O. and Sheldon, T.A. (2001) Outcome measures and needs assessment tools for schizophrenia and related disorders (Cochrane Review), in *the Cochrane Library*, 2, Oxford: Update Software.

Gottesman, I. and Shields, J.A. (1976) Critical review of recent adoption, twin and family studies of schizophrenia: Behavioural genetics perspectives, *Schizophrenia Bulletin*, 2: 360–401.

Gottesman, I. and Shields, J. (1982) *Schizophrenia: The Epigenetic Puzzle*, Cambridge: Cambridge University Press.

Greenwall, J., Procter, A. and Jones, A. (1997) *Report of the Inquiry into the Treatment and Care of Gilbert Kopernik-Steckel*, Croyden: Croyden Health Authority.

Haddock, G. and Slade, P. (1996) *Cognitive Behavioural Interventions with Psychotic Disorder*, London: Routledge.

Hafner, H. (1995) Epidemiology of schizophrenia. The disease model of schizophrenia in the light of current epidemiological knowledge, *European Psychiatry*, 10: 217–27.

Hargreaves, J. (1997) Using patients: exploring the ethical dimension of reflective practice in nurse education, *Journal of Advanced Nursing*, 25: 223–8.

Harris, N. (2002) Neuroleptic drugs and their management, in Harris, N., Williams, S. and Bradshaw, T. (eds), *Psychosocial Interventions for People with Schizophrenia: A Practical Guide for Mental Health Workers*, New York: Palgrave Macmillan.

Harris, N., Williams, S. and Bradshaw, T. (2002) *Psychosocial Interventions for People with Schizophrenia: A Practical Guide for Mental Health Workers*, New York: Palgrave Macmillan.

Harrison, G., Owens, D., Holton, A., Neilson, D. and Boot, D. (1988) A prospective study of severe mental disorder in Afro-Caribbean patients, *Psychological Medicine*, 18: 643–57.

Hawton, K. (1994) The assessment of suicidal risk, in Barnes, T.R.E. and Nelson, H.E. (eds), *The Assessment of Psychoses: A Practical Handbook*, London: Chapman and Hall.

Helgason, L. (1990) Twenty years' follow-up of first psychiatric presentation for schizophrenia: what could have been prevented?, *Acta Psychiatrica Scandinavica*, 81: 231–5.

Hickey, G. and Kipping, C. (1998) Exploring the concept of user involvement in mental health through a participation continuum, *Journal of Clinical Nursing*, 7: 83–8.

Hogan, T.P., Awad, A.G. and Eastwood, R.A. (1983) A self-report scale predictive of drug compliance in schizophrenics: reliability and discriminative validity, *Psychological Medicine*, 13: 177–83.

Hughes, I., Hill, B. and Budd, R. (1997) Compliance with antipsychotic medication: From theory to practice, *Journal of Mental Health*, 6, 5: 473–89.

Jablensky, A. and Eaton, W.W. (1995) Schizophrenia, in Jablensky, A. (ed.), *Epidemiological Psychiatry*, London: Balliere Tindall, pp. 283–306.

Johns, C. (1995) Framing learning through reflection within Carper's fundamental ways of knowing in nursing, *Journal of Advanced Nursing*, 22: 2226–34.

Johnstone, E.C., Owens, D.G.C., Frith, C.D. and Leavy, J. (1991) Clinical findings: Abnormalities of mental states and their correlates. The Northwick Park follow up study, *British Journal of Psychiatry*, 159: 21–5.

Jones, P. and Cannon, M. (1998) The new epidemiology of schizophrenia, *Psychiatric Clinics of North America*, 21: 1–25.

Kane, J.M. (1996) Schizophrenia, *New England Journal of Medicine*, 334: 34–41.

King, M., Coker, E., Leavey, G., Hoare, A. and Johnson-Sabine, E. (1994) Incidence of psychotic illness in London: comparison of ethnic groups, *British Medical Journal*, 309: 1115–19.

Kingdon, D.G. and Turkington, D. (1994) *Cognitive Behavioral Therapy of Schizophrenia*, Hove: Psychology Press.

Koller, J. (1895) Beitrag zur Erblichkeitsstatistik der Geisteskranken im Canton Zurich; Vergleichung derselben mit der erblichen Belastung gesunder Menschen durch Geistesstorungen u. dergl. Arch. Psychiatr. 27: 269–94, cited by Jablensky, A. (1997) The 100-year epidemiology of schizophrenia, *Schizophrenia Research*, 28: 111–25.

Krawiecka, M., Goldberg, D. and Vaughan, M. (1977) A standardised psychiatric assessment scale for rating chronic psychotic patients, *Acta Psychiatrica Scandinavica*, 55: 299–308.

Leff, J.P. and Vaughn, C.E. (1976) The influence of family and social factors on the course of psychiatric illness: A comparison of schizophrenic and depressed neurotic patients, *British Journal of Psychiatry*, 129: 125–37.

Levav, L., Kohn, R., Dohrenwend, B.P., Shrout, P.E., Skodol, A.E., Schwartz, S., Link, B. and Naveh, G. (1993) An epidemiological study of mental disorders in a 10 year cohort of young adults in Israel, *Psychological Medicine*, 23: 691–707.

Ley, P. (1982) Giving information to patients, in Eiser J.R. (ed.), *Social Psychology and Behavioural Medicine*, New York: Wiley.

Lingjaerde, O., Ahlfors, U.G., Bech, P., Dencker, S.J. and Elgen, K. (1987) The UKU side effects rating scale: A new comprehensive rating scale for psychotropic drugs and a cross sectional study of side effects in neuroleptic-treated patients, *Acta Psychiatrica Scandinavica*, 334, 76: 6–100.

Manchanda, R., Hirsch, S.R. and Barnes, I.R.E. (1989) A review of rating scales for measuring symptom changes in schizophrenia research, in Thompson, C. (ed.), *The Instruments of Psychiatric Research*, London: John Wiley and Sons, pp. 59–86.

Meichenbaum, D. and Turk, D.C. (1987) *Facilitating Treatment Adherence: A Practitioner's Guidebook*, New York: Plenum Press.

Miller, W.R., and Rollnick, S. (1991) *Motivational Interviewing: Preparing People for Change*, New York: Guilford Press.

Mortimer, A.M. (1994) Newer and older antipsychotics: A comparative review of appropriate use, *CNS Drugs*, 2, 5: 381–96.

Munetz, M.R. and Benjamin, S. (1988) How to examine patients using the Abnormal Involuntary Movement Scale, *Hospital and Community Psychiatry*, 39, 11: 1172–7.

Murray, R.M. and van Os, J. (1998) Predictors of outcome in schizophrenia, *Journal of Clinical Psychopharmacology*, 18, 2: S2–S4.

Murray, C.J.L. and Lopez, A.D. (1996) Evidence based health policy: Lessons from the Global Burden of Disease Study, *Science*, 27: 740–3.

National Institute for Clinical Excellence (2002a) *Guidance on the Use of Newer (Atypical) Antipsychotic Drugs for the Treatment of Schizophrenia*, London: NICE.

National Institute for Clinical Excellence (2002b) *Schizophrenia: Core Interventions in the Treatment and Management of Schizophrenia in Primary and Secondary Care, Clinical Guideline 1*, London: NICE.

National Institute of Mental Health (1977) *ECDU Awareness Manual: Abnormal Involuntary Movement Scale*, Washington: Department of Health and Welfare.

Nelson, H. (1997) *Cognitive Behavioural Therapy with Schizophrenia: A Practice Manual*, Cheltenham: Stanley Thornes.

Nuechterlein, K. and Dawson, M.E. (1984) A heuristic vulnerability-stress model of Schizophrenia, *Schizophrenia Bulletin*, 10: 300–12.

Nursing and Midwifery Council (2002) *Guidelines for Records and Record Keeping*, London: NMC. URL: http://www.nmc-uk.org/nmc/main/publications/guidelinesForRecordkeep.pdf Retrieved, 15 December 2003.

Onyett, S. (2003) *Team Working in Mental Health*, Basingstoke: Palgrave/Macmillan

OPCS (1995) *OPCS Survey of Psychiatric Morbidity in Great Britain*, London: HMSO.

Overall, J. and Gorham, D. (1962) The brief psychiatric rating scale, *Psychological Reports*, 10: 799–812.

Ovretveit, J., Temple, H., and Coleman, R. (1988) The organisation and management of community mental health teams, in Echlin, R. (ed.), *Community Mental Health Centres/Teams Information Pack*, Surrey: Good Practices in Mental Health Interdisciplinary Association of Mental Health Workers.

Owens, D.C.G. and Johnstone, E.C. (1980) The disability of chronic schizophrenia–their nature and factors contributing to their development, *British Journal of Psychiatry*, 36, 384–95.

Pekkala, E. and Merinder, L. (2003) Psychoeducation for schizophrenia (Cochrane Review), in *The Cochrane Library*, Issue 1, Chichester, UK: John Wiley and sons, Ltd.

Phelan, M., Slade, M., Thornicroft, G., Dunn, D., Holloway, F., Wykes, T., Strathdee, G., Loftus, L., McCrone, P. and Hayward, P. (1995) The Camberwell Assessment of Need (CAN): The validity and reliability of an instrument to assess the needs of people with sever mental illness, *British Journal of Psychiatry*, 167: 589–95.

Piccinelli, M. and Gomez Homen, F. (1997) *Gender Differences in the Epidemiology of Affective Disorders and Schizophrenia*, Geneva: World Health Organization.

Pratt, P. (1998) The administration and monitoring of neuroleptic medication, in Brooker, C. and Repper, J. (eds), *Serious Mental Health Problems in the Community: Policy, Practice and Research*, London: Balliere Tindall.

Read, T., Potter, M. and Gurling, H.M.D. (1992) The genetics of schizophrenia, in Kavanagh, D.J. (ed.), *Schizophrenia: An Overview and Practical Handbook*, London: Chapman and Hall.

Ritchie, J.H., Dick, D. and Lingham, R. (1994) *The Report of the Inquiry into the Care and Treatment of Christopher Clunis*, London: HMSO.

Rogers, C.R. (1951) *Client-centred Therapy*, London, Constable.

Rollnick, S. and Morgan, M. (1985) Motivational Interviewing: Increasing readiness for change, in Washton, A. (ed.), *Psychotherapy and Substance Abuse: A Practitioner's Handbook*, New York: Guilford.

Rose, D. (2001) *Users' Voices: The Perspectives of Mental Health Service Users on Community and Hospital Care*, London: Sainsbury Centre.

Schön, D. (1983) *The Reflective Practitioner. How Professionals Think in Action*, London: Temple Smith.

Searle, R.T. (1991) Community Mental Health Teams: Fact or Fiction? *Clinical Psychology Forum*, 31: 15–17.

Simpson, G.M. and Angus, J.W.S. (1970) A rating scale for extra pyramidal side effects, *Acta Psychiatrica Scandinavica*, suppl., 212, 46: 11–19.

Slade, M., Thornicroft, G., Loftus, L., Phelan, M. and Wykes, T. (1999) *CAN: Camberwell Assessment of Need*, London: Gaskell.

Snowden, P. (1997) Practical aspects of clinical risk assessment and management, *British Journal of Psychiatry*, 170, suppl., 32: 32–4.

Spence, W. (2000) Serious mental illness – The language of moral panic, in Cotterill, L. and Barr, W. (eds), *Targeting in Mental Health Services: A Multidisciplinary Challenge*, Aldershot: Ashgate.

University of York (1999) Drug treatments for schizophrenia, *Effective Health Care*, 5: 6.

Valimaki, M. and Leino-Kilpi, H. (1998) Preconditions for and consequences of self determination: The psychiatric patient's point of view, *Journal of Advanced Nursing*, 27: 204–12.

Warner, R. and Girolamo, G. (1995) *Schizophrenia*, Geneva: World Health Organization.

White, D.R. and Hellerich, G. (1992) Postmodernism reflections on modern psychiatry: The diagnostic and statistical manual of mental disorders, *The Humanistic Psychologist*, 20, 1: 75–91.

World Health Organization (1986) *Ottawa Charter for Health Promotion: An International Conference on Health Promotion*, 17–21 November, Copenhagen: WHO.

World Health Organization (1997) *The Jakarta Declaration on Leading Health Into the 21st Century*, Geneva: WHO.

Wykes, T., Whittington, R. and Sharrock, R. (1994) The assessment of aggression and potential for violence, in Barnes, T.R.E. and Nelson, H.E. (eds), *The Assessment of Psychoses: A Practical Handbook*, London: Chapman and Hall.

Zubin, J. and Spring, B. (1977) Vulnerability: a new view of schizophrenia, *Journal of Abnormal Psychology*, 86: 260–6.

CHAPTER 7

Crisis Resolution/Home Treatment

Clare Hopkins and Stephen Niemiec

Introduction

Mental health crisis assessment and resolution are not new concepts in mental health nursing (Stein and Test, 1980; Hoult and Reynolds, 1984). However, the Department of Health (DoH) has highlighted the need for dedicated crisis services especially in urban areas (DoH, 1998), emphasising the need to offer care in the least restrictive environment and provision of alternatives to hospital (DoH, 1999; Mental Health Act, 1983). The NHS Plan (DoH, 2000) goes further with a commitment to establish 335 crisis teams by 2004. All people in contact with specialist mental health services will be able to access crisis resolution services at any time.

This political impetus for the development of crisis resolution and home treatment services (CRHTs) reflects the significance international impacts of such services have on both people's lives and on mental health services (MHS) themselves (Hoult and Reynolds, 1984; Marks *et al.*, 1994). Importantly they also reflect the increasing power of the user and carer voices in the design of MHS to provide a greater range of options for treatment and care which are more responsive around the clock (Faulkner, 1997; Cohen, 1998; Mental Health Foundation, 2002).

However, the development of crisis services in the UK has been slow and erratic. Allen (1999) and Orme (2001) both suggest that this is because of a lack of consensus on what is actually meant by the term 'crisis', how crises might best be resolved and the most suitable model for setting up such services. It is also true that the absence of sufficient numbers of clinicians used to the CRHT models in the UK led to a dearth of models which reflect fidelity to model principles (Niemiec and Tacchi, 2003). Services existing before the National Service Framework Policy Implementation Guide (DoH, 2001) were set up with little consideration of differences between crisis intervention and crisis resolution (the latter specifically offering assessment and treatment following referral).

Box 7.1   CRHT model

- Service availability 24 hours a day, 365 days a year.
- Multidisciplinary team – medicine, nursing, social work, occupational therapy and possibly psychology.
- Practitioner's mobile telephone.
- Provide care to the person in crisis in their homes.
- Provide intensive support. Visits may occur two or three times each day in the acute phase of the crisis and stay involved until crisis resolved.
- Help the person to learn from the crisis.
- Offer support to family/carers intensively from the point of assessment.
- Act as gatekeepers for inpatient beds.
- Work collaboratively with inpatient services to reduce the length of admissions when this has been necessary.

Some services have evolved out of existing local services. Others have been developed in response to local needs (Harrison *et al.*, 1999). Typically those providing crisis resolution rather than crisis intervention, have made the greatest impact upon whole systems within mental health services (Niemiec and Tacchi, 2003). The CRHTs which made significant impact upon bed occupancy, average length of patient stay and which received positive feedback from users and carers held fidelity to the model (see Box 7.1). The plan of care for the person in crisis requires ease of access and rapidity of response, plus the ability to adapt quickly to an ever-changing clinical and domestic environment. Throughout the chapter the term *crisis resolution* will be used to describe the short-term intervention to support people experiencing a mental health crisis in their homes.

Prevalence and Population

Anyone can experience a mental health crisis. However, people who have previously experienced mental illness may be especially vulnerable at times of stress (Coffey, 1998). Therefore, crises can precipitate or be a consequence of mental illness (Rosen, 1998).

In a survey of psychiatric morbidity in the UK, the prevalence rate for probable psychotic disorder was 5 per 1000 of the population and 164 per 1000 adults experienced a neurotic disorder, most commonly a mixed anxiety and depressive disorder (Meltzer, 2001).

It is estimated that Crisis Resolution Teams will treat 100,000 people a year who would otherwise need to be admitted to hospital (DoH, 2000). Each team is likely to serve a population of approximately 150,000 and to be involved with between 20 and 30 service users at any one time. Services should be designed to be responsive to local need. It is expected that provision of crisis resolution services will lead to a 30 per cent reduction in the need for psychiatric inpatient beds (DoH, 2001). Greater reductions may also be achieved (Niemiec and Tacchi, 2003).

Referrals

Referral criteria for crisis teams are diverse. Some services accept only referrals for people already known to mental health services, others from a variety of primary and secondary services (GP, Social Worker, psychologist, mental health workers and others). A few services take referrals from service users themselves (Orme, 2001).

Despite this diversity, the core referral criteria (secondary to living in the team's catchment area) are that the person is:

- experiencing a crisis as a result of serious mental illness and;
- vulnerable and disabled to the extent that they need intensive or extended hours treatment and support and;
- would otherwise be likely to require inpatient treatment and,
- over the age of 16 and below the age of 65.

(Sainsbury Centre for Mental Health (SCMH), 2001b)

There is also general agreement that crisis care is ineffective and therefore not offered for some presentations (see Box 7.2).

A triage system carried out by an experienced clinician is often used as a means of filtering and prioritising the work of the team, ensuring that resources are allocated according to apparent need and level of risk. This triage function is vital to the smooth running and effectiveness of any crisis team. It provides a sense of security and flow to what is often a very busy clinical service and will ensure that referrals are only accepted if they meet the inclusion criteria for the team (Brimblecombe, 2001b).

Box 7.2   Presentations not for crisis care

- Mild anxiety disorders.
- Organic illnesses including dementia.
- Primary problem of drug or alcohol abuse.
- Learning disabilities.
- Exclusive diagnosis of personality disorder.
- Recent history of self-harm but not suffering from a psychotic illness or severe depressive illness.
- Crisis related solely to relationship issues.
- Experiencing a *psychiatric emergency* rather than a *mental health crisis*.

(DoH, 2001; SCMH, 2001b)

Theoretical Framework

Gerald Caplan first formulated crisis theory in the early 1960s. According to Caplan and Felix (1964) the experience of crisis is universal. People face crisis when they encounter an obstacle to important life goals; one that is not amenable to the person's usual coping strategies. A period of disorganisation ensues, when the person is upset and attempts to remedy the situation. Three phases of crisis were identified:

1. The 'onset' phase when there is an increase in tension as the person becomes aware that the problem cannot be quickly and easily solved.
2. The 'breakdown/disorganisation' phase. Tension and anxiety may rise to intolerable levels and coping strategies may rapidly become exhausted. At this point the person in crisis may turn to others for help. They may cease to be able to meet their own needs and responsibilities at this point.
3. The 'resolution' phase. Because crises are often passing events, a resolution of some kind may occur. However, this resolution may be either positive or negative. If it is positive, the person will have learned new ways to help themselves in future. If negative, potentially damaging ways of dealing with the situation may be learned and become established.

(Caplan and Felix, 1964)

Crisis theory suggests that intervening at the point where mental health crisis has brought breakdown and disorganisation provides optimum opportunity to help the person to find positive solutions and coping strategies instead of negative, short-term ones.

Schnyder (1997) adapted Caplan's theories into a 7-stage model of crisis intervention which incorporates a systemic perspective. It builds upon the person's existing positive coping strategies during the course of a short-term intervention. The seven stages of the model are: (1) establishing contact, (2) analysing the problem, (3) defining the problem, (4) setting the goal(s), (5) working on the problem, (6) termination and (7) follow-up.

> **?** *Pause for thought*: Cast your mind back to the last time you felt yourself to be in a crisis. What strategies did you use? Did they work? If they did not work what did you do next?

Principles and Skills

Assessment and planning care for the person in mental health crisis is a complex and subtle craft. It involves having the personal and interpersonal skills to bring *calm* to a potentially fraught situation and to build a rapid rapport with both the person in crisis and those around them (both family and professional carers). This requires the clinician to *contain their own anxiety* and be able to find ways of containing the anxiety of others (McGlynn and Smyth, 1998). Those who work with people in crisis must carry a (metaphorical) *toolkit of therapeutic skills* and be able to judge accurately which therapeutic approach is demanded by each situation. This will require a considerable ability to be *flexible and creative* in the response to each situation (SCMH, 2001a).

The clinician will need to use well-honed skills of *observation, listening and questioning* which are guided by the situation rather than a formulaic approach. They must be able to 'hear the unsaid' and to 'notice the previously unnoticed' and be able to make sense of situations rapidly in order to *assess risk accurately*. A *thorough and contemporary knowledge* of all aspects of mental illness and possible interventions, combined with the skill to integrate the information gained from all sources into a coherent *formulation* (SCMH, 2001a). *Communication skills* – sharing information with both the main players in the crisis as well as other professionals is also essential.

Negotiation will play a very important part in both the assessment process and also during discussions about what is to happen subsequently. *Assessing the risks* and possibilities to all concerned rapidly and *negotiating creative solutions* based on this risk assessment is a key crisis skill. At times the correct response to a crisis will be to take no action at all (Kolberg, 1999). In this situation the clinician will need to be confident in their decision, where necessary taking time away from the situation in order to reflect and consult other members of the interdisciplinary team about the approach to adopt. *Being a team worker* is fundamental to crisis care and a major support to the individual clinician.

Assessment

Approach

Crisis situations provide a special opportunity for assessment. The fact that assessment will take place *rapidly* acknowledges the need for immediate response in the crisis. Crisis theory suggests that this immediacy allows the clinician to start the process of positive *resolution* of the crisis, at the time when the person and those around her/him are most amenable to finding solutions and making changes.

In many situations crisis assessment offers therapeutic opportunities for the person to articulate not only the details of their experience but also to begin to formulate, perhaps for the first time, what it means to them. Important people in the person's life may be present by agreement. The clinician, through sensitive questioning and listening, may act as a catalyst to the forging of new joint understandings and empathy (Rosen, 1998).

Although it is important to ascertain the antecedents and contributory factors resulting in crisis, the crisis plan is not established to address these issues in the short term. Plans to refer the person for longer-term intervention may be necessary once the immediate crisis has been resolved (Aguilera, 1994).

Gaining an understanding of how the crisis is being defined by the person, those around them and wider society, will help the clinician to facilitate this understanding (Kolberg, 1999). The words used to talk about what is happening are extremely important. Is the crisis (and therefore the person at the centre of it) being described in terms of helplessness in the face of overwhelming events? For example, has John become 'mad' because of the desertion of his wife? Are words of responsibility and blame being used to describe the crisis? For example, talking of John's failure to take the medicine prescribed for him and blame for causing disruption to the entire family. McNamee (1992) suggests that using this relational and linguistic approach to crisis is important as it shows how crisis is constructed collectively. By being prepared to listen rather than attempting to 'fix' the problem they will open up, rather than restrict the options for reconstruction available to the person in crisis (Kolberg, 1999).

Process

Once it is established that the person in crisis meets the inclusion criteria for the team and potential issues of risk to the clinician have been explored, crisis teams aim to assess the person as rapidly as possible, often within two hours (Brimblecombe, 2001b).

However, if any information exists which suggests that the clinicians would be at risk from the person themselves, their family, neighbours or animals, then assessment in a neutral, safe environment should be arranged (Sutherby and Szmukler, 1995).

An essential skill of rapid assessment is the development of engagement. In particular, observation of the social conventions necessary to facilitate acceptability is fundamental. Greetings, introductions, explanations and observation of social boundaries whilst displaying an accepting and non-judgemental approach – 'being ordinary' (Taylor, 1994; Hill and Michael, 1996) will help to develop this early rapport. Having prior knowledge of, or seeking advice regarding cultural issues and norms is also essential.

An explicit explanation about the role of the team and the reason for the visit will help to allay anxieties and misperceptions which could hinder the assessment and subsequent planning of care (Kolberg, 1999). Those people who have previous experience of admission to hospital compulsorily or voluntarily may assume that the reason for the visit is to arrange admission. This may excite expectations or fears that jeopardise the therapeutic relationship (Brimblecombe *et al.*, 2003).

Negotiating who will be present at the assessment is another important precursor to beginning the assessment interview. Ensuring the person in crisis is able to give informed consent to the inclusion of others may represent a delicate ethical balance because of their level of agitation or confusion. Including and co-ordinating the multiple perspectives of all participants is also a key skill in obtaining a thorough assessment of the situation (Sutherby and Szmukler, 1995).

Information Gathering

The key source of information, prior to meeting the person is the referrer. Information should be gathered about the person, their situation and crisis and any history of previous crises, mental illness and potential risks. Although a rapid and timely response is necessary this should not be at the expense of inadequate preparation and information gathering (SCMH, 2001b). Being in crisis may mean that the person does not present an orderly or coherent verbal account of their history. Risk factors identified through previous behaviour can be used to ensure the safety of the person, family and clinician. Integrating all perspectives of the crisis is a vital part of the information gathering process.

Tools Used

There are no standardised and validated assessment tools for use in crisis assessment. However any of the assessment tools used in mental health care may also be used effectively as part of a comprehensive assessment of crisis.

Use of a standardised assessment tool could offer an effective means of ensuring that, where a series of clinicians is visiting the person in crisis, a baseline has been established and changes can be swiftly identified. However, in the initial stages of crisis the person may not have sufficient concentration to complete written assessment tools.

All members of the multidisciplinary team should use a standardised assessment format. It is important that each area of the personal dimension is included. CRHT works best when a full bio-psychosocial assessment has occurred. This would include:

- A reason for presentation
- Service users view of the situation
- Their desires and expectations
- A mental status examination
- Personal and social history
- A genogram
- Psychiatric history
- Predisposing factors and maintaining factors of the crisis
- Risk assessment and risk management plan
- The formulation

The assessment represents a vast domain of personal and family information. It is important that this information be summarised in such a way as to communicate the essential features of the person's situation in as short a time as possible to the team. A model for formulation preparation is provided below.

	Precipitating	Predisposing	Maintaining
Biological			
Psychological			
Social			

In addition to providing concentrated information, the formulation will point to the care and treatment required from the team, enabling multidisciplinary working. The development of the formulation sets the scene for the care plan.

Risk Priorities

Being in crisis brings special risks. Self-control and the control each individual has over their life or behaviour may be temporarily lost or abandoned. Specifically, the risk of self-harm, with or without suicidal intent, needs to be considered and a management plan negotiated. Any risk of harm to others must be systematically considered and assertively questioned. Questioning and observation must be used to detect possible risk through neglect and chaos to both the person and others who might depend upon them, especially children. Assessment of risk will be both formal and include intuitive 'gut feelings' of the clinician. This is an intangible process based upon experience and knowledge and must never be ignored (Raven, 1999; Morgan, 2000). Effective assessment of risk is, of necessity, a fluid and continuous process.

Constant reappraisal of risk is especially important when the treatment is in the person's own home. Commitment to the treatment plan may change unobserved and the means to harm may be more readily acquired. It is important that the risk management plan is negotiated with the person and family members. Direct contact to the crisis team should be offered whilst under their care.

Care Planning

How Plan is Determined

There are several important components to the planning of care with people who are experiencing a mental health crisis. The planned care must be *responsive* to the individual needs of the person and their carers during the current crisis. It should be *negotiated* with the person and those who will support her/him at home and be sufficiently *flexible* to accommodate changing need.

In order to plan care with the person in crisis, three ingredients must be available:

- A high degree of engagement between the person and the crisis resolution team.
- Adequate informal carer support.
- Issues of risk and safety must have been assessed and positively balanced through the negotiation of a plan.

The philosophy which underpins treatment at home recognises that admission to hospital at a time of crisis may lead to the phenomena which the psychiatrist R.D. Scott described as 'closure' (Reed, 2000). Removing a person from their family and social environment at the time of crisis risks a change in the perceptions of others about that person. Not only is there a risk that they will be seen as being 'the problem', but others may feel the need to withdraw emotionally as an act of self-protection and a process of dehumanisation takes place (Scott, 1980).

Planning, which facilitates recovery in the same environment in which the crisis occurred, offers both the person and their carers the opportunity to witness and take part in resolving and containing the crisis, thereby heightening the possibility that relationships will be maintained. Treatment at home should also guard against the development of dependence on mental health services.

Practical Application

Engagement

People in crisis may feel powerless, helpless and as a result, hopeless. They are vulnerable and open to suggestion – either positive or negative. Engaging them in a dialogue about the situation and negotiating a plan of care which is solution focused – rather than problem saturated – is vital. Ensuring that, as far as possible, the person's personal power does not become subordinate to the power of the clinician is also vital to the promotion of autonomy and hope (Leiba, 1995; Cutcliffe and Barker, 2002). Being explicit about the type of help the team can provide and the possible duration of their input is important in providing transparency and certainty (Whittle and Mitchell, 1997).

Safety

An important decision in planning care for the person in mental health crisis relates to whether care and treatment may be safely and appropriately offered by the team. Admission may be necessary or advisable. Two variables impact immediately on this decision and these are often interlinked:

(1) The level of perceived risk which exists, taking into consideration levels of intent, hopelessness, impulsivity and the availability of the means of harm and

(2) The quality of sources of informal support if they are to remain at home including the willingness of the person and their carers to negotiate a plan which will ensure the care and security of the person in crisis.

Research by Brimblecombe (2000) highlighted the fact that suicidal thoughts and impulses are no bar to treatment of the person in their home. Although high levels of expressed suicidal ideation are given as the main reason for admission to hospital (Brimblecombe *et al.*, 2003). However, the plan must be regularly reassessed for continuing safety and if this cannot be assured then admission to hospital may need to be arranged (Brimblecombe, 2001a).

Whether or not the person has a circle of supportive family and friends will be significant in their continuing safety in the community, as will the willingness of the person and carers to negotiate a plan of care with the team. Simply gaining an undertaking from the person that they will agree to maintain their own safety is insufficient and may in fact precipitate further risk (Farrow, 2003). Negotiating and planning individualised care which promotes hope is essential if risk is to be managed successfully (Barker and Cutcliffe, 2000).

Support

The possibility of planning care in 'the least restrictive environment' (DoH, 1998, 1999, 2001) may rely on the accessibility of non-professional care and support. Crisis resolution services have a significant role in supporting carers in *their* support of the person. Having support from family or friends may be what the person in crisis needs most. However, by the time the team becomes involved a great deal of stress may have occurred and strains and stresses in relationships may be evident (Sutherby and Szmukler, 1995). Being a 'carer' may be difficult, onerous and may pose a conflict to their wishes and aims. If the relationship with the person in crisis is already fragile and full of conflict, or if the carer is at the end of their tether and do not know how to cope, then the carers' role may seem like an unbearable burden (Simmons, 1990; Fulford and Farhall, 2001).

The clinician will need to maintain vigilance for those occasions when support at home cannot be fostered or when carers become exhausted by the emotional labour of caring. The family's personal circumstances may make care at home impossible. Indeed, the person's behaviour may have caused a serious rift in either close personal relationships or within the wider community (Sutherby and Szmukler, 1995; Östman and Kjellin, 2002).

Supporting carers is of key importance if they are to maintain this vital role. Many services provide telephone support 24 hours a day to offer advice or a listening ear. Additional creative care planning might include arranging periods of respite from the caring role. Role modelling coping strategies to manage difficult behaviours or situations may also provide support and reassurance (McGlynn and Smyth, 1998).

Case Example

Jane is a 25-year-old mother of two children, aged 7 and 5. She and her husband Andy have experienced a number of life stresses, which have affected them greatly. Andy lost his job 10 months ago and since then the family have been living on benefits. The struggle to make ends meet whilst caring for a young family has taken its toll on their relationship.

Two weeks ago Jane's mother died suddenly. Jane had experienced sleep difficulties over the past four months, had lost her appetite and had become somewhat emotionally withdrawn from Andy and the children. Since the news of her mother's death she has become almost mute and has seemed to be unaware of the children's needs.

This afternoon Andy found Jane preparing to take a large overdose of paracetamol. After a struggle he managed to take the tablets away from her. After a home visit by the GP Jane was prescribed anti-depressant medication (safe in overdose) and referred to the Crisis Team. Andy arranged for the children to stay with a neighbour and thereafter refused to leave Jane alone for a moment until the team arrived.

When the crisis resolution team arrive for assessment they find a very tense situation between Jane and Andy. She has now become extremely tearful and is highly resentful of Andy's constant vigilance.

The two clinicians manage to negotiate a compromise with the couple that they will speak with Jane alone initially whilst Andy goes to the neighbours to say goodnight to the children. When he returns they will all talk together.

Assessment of Jane reveals that she is experiencing a severe depression as a result of recent events. On reflection she is now horrified by the impulsive attempt to overdose and does not feel at risk of repeating these actions.

When Andy returns the two clinicians engage both Andy and Jane in a discussion about what care is necessary and agree where it will take place. During this time Jane remains tearful and distraught and Andy expresses his anxiety about his ability to maintain Jane's safety.

Six weeks passed and Jane's mood improved considerably. The anti-depressant medication was proving effective and she feels more able to care for her children. Andy is extremely pleased with her improvement in mood and ability to express her grief about the death of her mother.

At the final care planning session, the following plan is negotiated:

- If improvement in mood continues, Jane will be discharged back into the care of her general practitioner in seven days' time *(Providing the family with certainty about the ending of the relationship with the team and who will be providing follow-up support)*.
- If after that time, she or Andy note that she is becoming low in mood or withdrawn, or if she feels that she may act to harm herself in any way, she

will immediately contact her GP or tell Andy and ask him to make the contact for her *(Indicators of relapse are identified collaboratively and a plan agreed which will remain within the control of the person who has experienced the crisis and her carer).*

Additional Care Planning

When the crisis is noted to be in the final phase of resolution and the team prepare to withdraw, a final plan of care should be negotiated. Crisis theory suggests that for a crisis to be resolved effectively new coping mechanisms will have been learned which may be used if the crisis reoccurs (Aguilera, 1994). A final care plan will formalise this learning and focus upon how the person might identify precursors to crisis in the future and the steps they would need to take to deal with the situation (DoH, 2001).

Documentation

Keeping clear and coherent interdisciplinary documentation relating to assessment and planning of care is vital to effective intervention. Records must be contemporaneous and accessible to every member of the team and may be kept by the person (Scullion, 2001). Intensive home support requires every member of the team to have the same degree of familiarity with the plan and progress of care for each patient. A truly interdisciplinary approach including the use of one set of records will add coherence to the plan of care (Webster, 2002).

Because of the short duration of crisis interventions, clinicians do not act as care co-ordinators under the Care Programme Approach (CPA)(DoH, 1990). However, there is a responsibility to communicate with the care co-ordinators of those people already registered and become part of the joint planning process of care.

Time Frame

The objective of planning care for the person in mental health crisis is to promote a speedy/timely resolution of the crisis. The mental health issues should be addressed, along with any social issues that compound the crisis situation. Interventions are typically of five or six weeks' duration although some are longer and some considerably shorter (DoH, 2001; SCMH, 2001b).

Crisis resolution teams are in an ideal position to co-ordinate the input of a range of therapeutic services to address the holistic needs of the individual (Hopkins *et al.*, 2002). Journeying with the patient and their carers as they ride out the storms of the crisis puts the clinician in a position to establish problems and needs. The interdisciplinary and collaborative nature of such teams facilitates speedy attention to the areas requiring support. The evolving position of crisis services within the larger landscape of social and mental health services will ensure that close communication and fast track referral processes are part of the service they offer in order to provide seamless care.

Evidence Base

The research evidence to support the approach adopted by crisis resolution/home treatment teams is largely derived from studies carried out in the 1980s and 1990s and many teams are fashioned from these models (Stein and Test, 1980; Dean and Gadd, 1990). However, more recent published data consists of descriptive accounts of the functioning of individual services (Crompton, 1997; Bracken and Cohen, 1999; Harrison *et al.*, 1999; Niemiec and Tacchi, 2003). A systematic review of home treatment for mental health problems (Catty *et al.*, 2002) found only a weak evidence base for the approach. Future research which considers both statistical data on length of hospital admissions and cost of provision of services must run alongside research into the perspective of the users of home treatment services and their carers in order to develop locally sensitive services (Orme and Cohen, 2001).

Dissemination of Information

Sharing of information and managing confidentiality often poses clinicians with a delicate ethical dilemma. Clear and timely sharing of information, both with carers and other professional helpers is an important part of ensuring safety. This may be complicated by the need to obtain true informed consent to sharing information when the person is in the initial stages of crisis, and may be disorientated, frightened and vulnerable.

Reflective Practice

The pace at which crisis work takes place may leave little space and time for workers to reflect (Hawkes *et al.*, 2001). However, clinicians may use highly refined, rapid reflective approaches. Wherever possible, they should work in pairs to offer the possibility for debriefing after difficult situations and 'live' supervision. Formal supervision is an integral aspect of such teams, offering an opportunity to share 'clinical, organisational, developmental and emotional experiences with another professional in a secure, confidential environment in order to enhance knowledge and skills (Lyth, 2000, p. 728). Using the team approach to care for the patient provides a very important daily opportunity for reflection and live supervision of the ongoing process of planning and evaluating care in an interdisciplinary way.

Practice Development

Although as nurses we have always been adept at dealing with mental health crisis we have not previously been asked to do so in quite such an intense or formal way. This has some very specific implications for the development and maintenance of such teams. Although some training resources have been developed (SCMH, 2001a), the multi-dimensionality of the skills required are not, as yet, widely met by Higher Education Institutions. In order to plan holistic care that meets the multiple needs of the person in crisis, the development of a truly interdisciplinary team approach is a fundamental requirement (Onyet, 1999).

Conclusion

Planning care for the person in crisis requires not only the ability to engage and negotiate but also the ability to act calmly and to think and plan innovatively. Care planned in this way will not only be responsive to need but will be creative and flexible. It will consider the timely meeting of immediate needs whilst considering the horizon of recovery and the person's journey into the future.

Planned care of this kind is no more and no less enlightened than planned care has always been: however, crisis care is often done with immense rapidity at a time of great emotional stress. Planning of coherent care can only result if the team providing the care is clear about its philosophy and aims and can adopt a concerted approach to providing that care.

📖 Suggested Further Reading

Brimblecombe, N. (ed.) (2001) *Acute Mental Health Care in the Community: Intensive Home Treatment*, London: Whurr.

References

Aguilera, D. (1994) *Crisis Intervention: Theory and Methodology* (seventh edn), St Louis: Mosby.

Allen, K. (1999) What are crisis services?, in Tomlinson, D. and Allen, K. (eds), *Crisis Services and Hospital Crises: Mental Health at a Turning Point*, Aldershot: Ashgate, pp. 1–11.

Barker, P. and Cutcliffe, J. (2000) Creating a hope-line for suicidal people: a new model for acute sector mental health nursing, *Mental Health Care*, 3, 6: 190–3.

Bracken, P. and Cohen, B. (1999) Home treatment in Bradford, *Psychiatric Bulletin*, 23: 349–52.

Brimblecombe, N. (2000) Suicidal ideation, home treatment and admission, *Mental Health Nursing*, 20, 1: 22–6.

Brimblecombe, N. (2001a) Intensive home treatment for individuals with suicidal ideation, in Brimblecombe, N. (ed.), *Acute Mental Health Care in the Community: Intensive Home Treatment*, London: Whurr, pp. 122–38.

Brimblecombe, N. (2001b) Assessment in crisis/home treatment services, in Brimblecombe, N. (ed.), *Acute Mental Health Care in the Community: Intensive Home Treatment*, London: Whurr, pp. 78–101.

Brimblecombe, N., O'Sullivan, G. and Parkinson, B. (2003) Home treatment as an alternative to inpatient admission: characteristics of those treated and factors predicting hospitalisation, *Journal of Psychiatric and Mental Health Nursing*, 10: 683–7.

Caplan, G. and Felix, R.H. (1964) *Principles of Preventive Psychiatry*, New York: Basic Books.

Catty, J., Burns, T., Knapp, M., Watt, H., Wright, C., Henderson, J. and Healey, A. (2002) Home treatment for mental health problems: a systematic review, *Psychological Medicine*, 32: 383–401.

Coffey, M. (1998) Schizophrenia: a review of current research and thinking, *Journal of Clinical Nursing*, 7, 6: 489–98.

Cohen, M. (1998) Users' movement and the challenge to psychiatrists, *Psychiatric Bulletin*, 22: 155–7.

Crompton, N. (1997) Early intervention begins at home, *Nursing Times*, 93, 52: 27–8.

Cutcliffe, J. and Barker, P. (2002) Considering the care of the suicidal client and the case for 'engagement and inspiring hope' or 'observations', *Journal of Psychiatric and Mental Health Nursing*, 9: 611–21.

Dean, C. and Gadd, E. (1990) Home treatment for acute psychiatric illness, *British Medical Journal*, 301: 1021–3.

Department of Health (1990) *The Care Programme Approach for People with a Mental Illness Referred to the Specialist Psychiatric Services*, HC23, London: HMSO.

Department of Health (1998) *Modernising Mental Health Services: Safe, Sound and Supportive*, London: HMSO.

Department of Health (1999) *National Service Framework for Mental Health*, London: HMSO.

Department of Health (2000) *NHS Plan*, London: HMSO.

Department of Health (2001) *The Mental Health Policy Implementation Guide*, London: HMSO.

Farrow, T.L. (2003) 'No suicide contracts' in community crisis situations: a conceptual analysis, *Journal of Psychiatric and Mental Health Nursing*, 10: 199–202.

Faulkner, A. (1997) *Knowing Our Own Minds*, London: Mental Health Foundation.

Fulford, M. and Farhall, J. (2001) Hospital versus home care for the acutely mentally ill? Preferences of caregivers who have experienced both forms of service, *Australian and New Zealand Journal of Psychiatry*, 35: 619–25.

Hawkes, K., Hopkins, C. and Reed, A. (2001) Finding the centre of the cyclone: reflective family work in a psychiatric crisis service, *Mental Health Practice*, 5, 4: 14–17.

Harrison, J., Poynton, A., Marshall, J., Gater, R. and Creed, F. (1999) Open all hours: extending the role of the psychiatric day hospital, *Psychiatric Bulletin*, 23: 400–4.

Hill, B. and Michael, S. (1996) The human factor, *Journal of Psychiatric and Mental Health Nursing*, 3: 245–8.

Hopkins, C., Deltodesco, D. and Wasley, S. (2002) Intervening safely in a crisis, *Mental Health Nursing*, 22, 4: 18–21.

Hoult, J. and Reynolds, I. (1984) Community orientated treatment compared to psychiatric hospital orientated treatment, *Social Science and Medicine*, 8, 11: 1005–10.

Kolberg, C. (1999) Creating conversations in times of crisis, *Gecko*, 2: 10–17.

Leiba, T. (1995) Crisis intervention theory and method, in Tomlinson, D. and Allen, K. (eds) *Crisis Services and Hospital Crises: Mental Health at a Turning Point*, Aldershot: Ashgate, pp. 13–23.

Lyth, G. (2000) Clinical supervision: a concept analysis, *Journal of Advanced Nursing*, 31, 3: 722–9.

McGlynn, P. and Smyth, M. (1998) *The Home Treatment Team: Making it Happen*, London: Sainsbury Centre for Mental Health.

McNamee, S. (1992) Reconstructing identity: the communal construction of crisis, in McNamee, S. and Gergen, K. (eds), *Therapy as Social Construction*, London: Sage.

Marks, I., Connolly, J., Muijen, M., Audini, B., McNamee, G. and Lawrence, R. (1994) Home-based versus hospital-based care for people with serious mental illness, *British Journal of Psychiatry*, 165: 179–94.

Meltzer, H.Y. (2001) *Psychiatric Morbidity Among Adults Living in Private Households, 2000*, London: HMSO.

Mental Health Foundation and the Sainsbury Centre for Mental Health (2002) *Being There in a Crisis: a Report of the Learning from Eight Mental Health Services*, London: Mental Health Foundation.

Morgan, S. (2000) *Clinical Risk Management*, London: Sainsbury Centre for Mental Health.

Niemiec, S. and Tacchi, M-J. (2003) CRHT for inner city populations: the Newcastle and North Tyneside story, in Kennedy, P. (ed.), *More Than the Sum of All the Parts: Improving the Whole System with Crisis Resolution and Home Treatment*, Northern Centre for Mental Health, pp. 12–20. http://www.ncmh.org.uk

Onyet, S. (1999) Community mental health team working as a socially valued enterprise. *Journal of Mental Health*, 8, 3: 245–51.

Orme, S. (2001) Intensive home treatment services: the current position in the UK, in Brimblecombe, N. (ed.), *Acute Mental Health Care in the Community: Intensive Home Treatment*, London: Whurr, pp. 29–54.

Orme, S. and Cohen, B. (2001) Researching service providing IHT as an alternative to admission, in Brimblecombe, N. (ed.), *Acute Mental Health Care in the Community: Intensive Home Treatment*, London: Whurr, pp. 54–77.

Östman, M. and Kjellin, L. (2002) Stigma by association: psychological factors in relatives of people with mental illness, *British Journal of Psychiatry*, 181: 494–8.

Raven, J. (1999) Managing the unmanageable: risk assessment and risk management in contemporary professional practice, *Journal of Nursing Management*, 7: 201–6.

Reed, A. (2000) Manufacturing a human drama from a psychiatric crisis: crisis intervention, family therapy and the work of R.D. Scott, in Barker, P. and Stevenson, C. (eds), *The Construction of Power and Authority in Psychiatry*, Oxford: Butterworth Heinemann, pp. 151–61.

Rosen, A. (1998) Crisis management in the community, *The Medical Journal of Australia*. <URL: http://www.mja.com.au/> © 1998 Medical Journal of Australia. (accessed 1/6/03).

Sainsbury Centre for Mental Health (2001a) *The Capable Practitioner*, London: SCMH.

Sainsbury Centre for Mental Health (2001b) *Mental Health Topics: Crisis Resolution*, London: SCMH (www.scmh.org.uk).

Scott, R.D. (1980) A family oriented psychiatric service to the London Borough of Barnet, *Health Trends*, 12: 65–8.

Schnyder, U. (1997) Crisis intervention in psychiatric outpatients, *International Medical Journal*, 4, 1: 11–17.

Scullion, P. (2001) Home treatment service – a philosophy with impact, *Primary Health Care*, 11, 5: 21–2.

Simmons, S. (1990) Family burden – what does psychiatric illness mean to the carers?, in Brooker, C. (ed.), *Community Psychiatric Nursing: A Research Perspective*, London: Chapman Hall, pp. 45–71.

Stein, L. and Test, M. (1980) Alternatives to mental hospital treatment, *Archives of General Psychiatry*, 149: 137–44.

Sutherby, K. and Szmukler, G. (1995) Community assessment of crisis, in Phelan, M., Strathdee, G. and Thornicroft, G. (eds), *Emergency Mental Health Services in the Community*, Cambridge: Cambridge University Press, pp. 149–73.

Taylor, B. (1994) Ordinariness in nursing as therapy, in Taylor, B. *Being Human: Ordinariness in Nursing*, Edinburgh: Churchill Livingstone.

Webster, J. (2002) Teamwork: understanding multi-professional working, *Nursing Older People*, 14, 3: 14–19.

Whittle, P. and Mitchell, S. (1997) Community alternatives project: an evaluation of a community-based acute psychiatric team providing alternatives to admission, *Journal of Mental Health*, 6, 4: 417–27.

CHAPTER 8

Assertive Outreach/Assertive Community Treatment

Mike Fleet

Introduction

Assertive Outreach or Assertive Community Treatment (here after referred to as ACT) is a method of delivering treatment and care for people with serious mental health problems in the community (Thompson *et al.*, 1990). In essence, assertive outreach is a way of engaging services with people suffering mental illness that cannot, or do not wish to engage with those services. Despite the hype, assertive outreach is not a treatment in its own right. It is simply a vehicle by which evidence-informed treatment packages can be offered to clients.

It was first developed in the 1970s as an alternative to hospital admission (Stein and Test, 1978). The model of care has been further defined and validated, based upon the consensus of an international panel of experts (McGrew *et al.*, 1994, 1995).

ACT is a reasonably well-defined model of service delivery with relatively clear aims:

- to ensure people with serious mental health problems remain in contact with services;
- to reduce the extent of hospital admissions;
- to improve quality of life, social functioning and social inclusion.

Prevalence and Population

The vast majority of the evidence supporting the benefits of ACT is rooted in the care of people experiencing a serious mental illness in general, and schizophrenia specifically. Schizophrenia is a relatively common illness, the most common form of psychotic disorder. It has been suggested that people with schizophrenia, as a result of their illness, may be at a disadvantage in terms of social functioning, making it more likely that they will 'drift' into lower socio-economic circumstances, poor housing and unemployment (Jablensky *et al.*, 1992). [Editor: For further information on prevalence of schizophrenia, see Chapter 6.]

From its conception ACT has targeted those perceived as having the most intractable symptoms of serious mental illness, the highest level of functional impairment and hence a big drain on in-patient and community resources; the 'heavy service user'. Kent *et al.* (1995) describe the heavy service user as the 10 to 30 per cent of clients who use 50 to 80 per cent of resources.

Referrals

Primarily, ACT teams are a tertiary service accepting only referrals from the secondary service level, for service users more difficult to engage. Direct referrals from general practitioners and self-referrals are not the norm. As a result, the service users within ACT are usually well known to services. They tend to have a relatively long-term history of service use (such as those experiencing rapidly cycling bipolar affective disorder or schizophrenia). Referral to ACT services is usually made by the community mental health team (CMHT) during a periodic review. The Care Programme Approach (CPA) care co-ordinator will then write a letter of referral to the ACT team, including a comprehensive summary of the persons presenting problems and contact with services. This referral is then discussed amongst the ACT team at a referrals meeting. The decision to assess with a view to acceptance is then made. This decision is taken in light of the explicit acceptance criteria of the ACT team in question.

On the whole, the entry criteria for ACT teams should match the target client profile determined by the Department of Health (DoH, 2001). This profile determined that ACT should be a service:

- Provided to adults aged 18 to 65 with a severe and persistent mental illness (schizophrenia or a major affective illness).
- With a history of high use of inpatient or intensive home based care (two or more admissions in two years or more than six months inpatient care in two years).
- There should have been difficulty in maintaining contact with services.
- There should be multiple complex needs such as a history of violence, risk of persistent self-neglect, co-morbid substance use etc.

The ACT team then assess in order to determine the appropriateness of offering assertive outreach services to the service user. This is a clinical decision (Burns and Firn, 2002) based on the capacity and capability of the ACT team to offer a viable service to the referred person.

Theoretical Framework

There is some evidence that programmes more faithful to the ACT model have superior outcomes (McGrew *et al.*, 1994; McHugo *et al.*, 1999; Teague *et al.*, 1998). A measure of model fidelity has been developed, which is the 'Dartmouth Assertive Community Treatment Scale' (Teague *et al.*, 1998). This measure considers several factors indicative of high fidelity in an ACT team (see Box 8.1).

The services themselves should be *in vivo* with a no dropout policy and assertive engagement. Provision should be as much as is needed with frequent contact. Also, working with the service users support system, offering individualised substance abuse treatment and dual diagnosis treatment groups where necessary. [Editor: See also Chapter 13.] Ideally service users can and are employed as members of the treatment team. Thus providing a sensitive and insightful approach through a full commitment to those using services.

Many programmes that claim to be ACT services deviate from these standards in some way. Burns *et al.* (2001) suggest that a significant influence of national, or even local, culture is evident both in the acceptability of the service and in approaches to research and delivery. While these specifications are important, authors disagree on the relative importance of different components (McGrew and Bond, 1995; Schaedle and Epstein, 2000). A major bone of contention is 24-hour care by a dedicated team. This may be seen as both superfluous and an expensive luxury (a duplication of service when alternative crisis services are available). Additionally, in early implementations of ACT, avoidance of office or clinic visits was pursued pedantically. Avoidance of office visits may be better thought of as an outcome of assertive outreach, rather than an end in itself.

The need to have one team member as a care co-ordinator heading up a team approach is often considered a more important structural element of ACT programmes (McGrew and Bond, 1995).

Box 8.1 Dartmouth Assertive Community Treatment Scale

1. Staffing and resources: small, shared caseload (ten or fewer clients per case manager).
2. Team meetings at least four times per week, with a practising team leader and psychiatrist, substance abuse specialist and vocational specialist in the team.
3. Organisationally there should be explicit admission criteria and a low intake rate.
4. The team has full responsibility for treatment services, crisis services (24-hour coverage) and hospital admissions.
5. The team has responsibility for discharge planning with no time limit on services.

(Teague *et al.*, 1998)

Principles and Skills

While the challenges faced by people with serious and enduring mental illness are similar to those faced by anyone else in the twenty-first century, the social, political and clinical agenda has changed over recent decades. Approaches to helping people who are experiencing mental health problems have taken the form of cure-based approaches, skills-based approaches and needs-based approaches. With some approaches having more negative effects than others (Perkins and Repper, 1996).

The limitations of the cure-based approach have included the fact that people with enduring problems have often experienced cure-based strategies but their disabilities remain. Continuing attempts to effect a cure can prove demoralising for the client and staff leading to hopelessness. While a focus on a 'cure' as the only way that life can be meaningful implies that life with a disability is not worthwhile and can lead to devaluation of support and care. Modern, client-centred approaches are the needs-based approaches. Although there has been some criticism that 'needs' is just a euphemism for 'problems' (Perkins and Repper, 1998). People with serious mental illness differ from others in terms of their ability to meet their needs with the ordinary resources available. While, simultaneously, people with serious mental illness are often deprived of the means to meet their needs. Such means as work, an adequate income, home and family, relationships and social activities all contribute. The primary role of the mental health nurse is to assist people to access the ordinary activities, facilities and relationships through which most people meet their needs.

The purpose of working with people with serious mental illness is multifaceted. Factors and skills include:

- Minimising symptoms and the distress they cause people.
- Managing relapse in the least restrictive setting possible.
- Increasing independence from services.
- Optimise social functioning.
- Improve quality of life.
- Increase skills by accessing facilities, activities and relationships in the community.

Assertive Community Treatment is not a treatment in its own right, but rather a vehicle by which evidence-informed treatment packages can be offered. There are several interventions with variable quantities of evidence available. These interventions can be either (1) pharmacological or (2) psychosocial, or an ideal combination of both.

(1) Neuroleptic medication is the most evidence-based intervention on offer in the mental health arena. Whilst there is a significant minority of people for whom medication has little or no beneficial effect (Curson *et al.*, 1988) there is no doubt that some clients experience a great deal of benefit

from the medication available. For people who have 'treatment resistant schizophrenia', clozapine is the only medication with proven efficacy, improving the quality of life for many clients (Kane *et al.*, 1988; Meltzer *et al.*, 1989, 1990). Even the most efficacious medication has its negative aspects. Whether these are negative 'side' effects or the short time span in which non-adherence leads to the need to re-titrate the dose (in the case of clozapine a pitiful 48 hours).

(2) Psychosocial interventions (PSI) are not merely a collection of tools and skills to employ with those experiencing serious and enduring mental health problems. These interventions demand an attitude and disposition of the practitioner that does not merely place the client or the carer at the centre of all interventions. A real partnership should be developed and maintained that is collaborative, as opposed to giving lip service to the concept. [Editor: For further information on PSI please refer to Chapter 6.]

The Working Alliance in ACT

The skills necessary to develop a working alliance and deliver the evidence-based interventions could be viewed as being on three levels. The first level includes the ability to think creatively to create and utilise opportunities for engagement (therefore not necessarily skills developed as part of a professional training package). The goal of engagement is to form a trusting relationship or working alliance that will enable the nurse to support the client through treatment. Voluntary engagement in treatment may take place if the client sees that affiliation with ACT team can be of benefit.

A number of interventions may aid the process of engagement such as: practical assistance, empathic interviewing, crisis intervention, forming an alliance with the family or other social network members and ensuring that legal constraints are sensible (Sainsbury Centre for Mental Health, 1998).

To form this working alliance the use of the skills identified in motivational interviewing can be very beneficial. These skills include: acceptance, expressing empathy, listening carefully, reflecting the client's views back and understanding the client's conceptualisation of their situation in life (see Miller and Rollnick, 1991).

The second level of skills could be viewed as those basic skills developed within pre-registration training programmes and by appropriate life experience; effective communication skills, empathy and listening skills. The third 'higher level' skills are more specific in the utilisation of assessment tools, experience in assessment formats and the delivery of evidence-informed practices (Burns and Firn, 2002).

Several factors why service users do not wish to engage with services include:

(a) poor past history of service contact
(b) personality disorder

(c) racism
(d) dual diagnosis
(e) lack of trust.

Assessment

Approach and Process

The first element in any assessment process must be the development of the therapeutic alliance. Otherwise any information is not collaborative and second hand. Before any assessment can be undertaken there must be some level of engagement between the service user and the ACT service.

Assessment should be an ongoing dynamic process. Individual assessment tools provide only a 'snapshot' of the service user's life and experiences. This ongoing assessment should be part of a greater process seeking to engage the person with services and provide the most appropriate care.

Assessment should be a collaboration that focuses on identifying the person's strengths, goals and aspirations (DoH, 2001). This approach aids engagement and the ongoing relationship between the client and the ACT team. The assessment of needs for health and social care for people with serious mental illness must be comprehensive, addressing medical, physical, psychological, social, occupational, economic and cultural issues (NICE, 2003).

The purpose of assessment in ACT is to develop a hypothesis upon which it is possible to base care and deliver care, thus retesting the hypothesis. Therefore, a collaborative care plan can only be as good as the information it is based on (Richards and McDonald, 1990).

Assessment is multi-format, looking at:

- mental health issues
- social functioning
- accommodation
- financial issues
- risk assessment
- needs assessment (including exploration of desired goals in areas such as work and recreation).

Information Gathering

Whilst it is always best to gather information from the primary source (the service user), this is not always possible. The 'target service user' for ACT is usually difficult to engage and therefore less likely to supply the necessary information.

Information could be gleaned from the referral letters, mental health notes, clinicians and carers who 'know' the person. However, these are not always the best sources. If the person was easy to engage and assess, why are they referred to the ACT service?

Assessment is necessary to provide a comprehensive care package. However, it is not always possible for the traditional, logical process of assessment (followed by planning and implementation) to be undertaken. Basic assessments such as risk assessments may be undertaken to increase safety but more informative assessments will have to wait until the person is more engaged with the service. Once engagement is established, more comprehensive assessments can then take place.

Tools Used

The use of standardised tools for the comprehensive assessment of the service user's needs is paramount. There are many useful tools for measuring symptomatology (see Box 8.2).

Risk Priorities

A risk assessment must also be used. However, there has been a trend to produce risk assessment documents in terms of checklists and tick boxes covering predetermined risk factors. On the whole these are of little use to individual service users (Morgan, 1994). Risk assessments must be dynamic, not static, they must be done on an individual basis using a tool covering broad areas such as the history of risk and current factors which increase risk. Naturally the

---

Box 8.2 Useful tools for ACT

Brief Psychiatric Rating Scale (Overall and Gorham, 1962). Used as a baseline assessment scale for general use across all mental health settings.

Manchester Symptom Severity Scale (Krawiecka *et al.*, 1977). This helps to test the experience of illness and prioritise unmet needs.

These can point to the direction of further assessment, such as:

PSYRATS (Haddock *et al.*, 1999). To measure dimensions of hallucinations and delusions.

Beck's Depression Inventory (Beck *et al.*, 1961). Helps to indicate the severity of depressive symptoms.

Also:

Social Functioning Scale (Birchwood *et al.*, 1990). To assess social and daily living skills.

Camberwell Assessment of Need (Slade *et al.*, 1999). Assessment of basic needs, health needs, social needs, functioning needs and the need for services.

priorities identified by the risk assessment will be individually determined. Risks such as suicidality, self-neglect, vulnerability to exploitation by others or risk of violence are all individual. Thus prioritisation depends on need.

Care Planning

How Plan is Determined

Grech (2002) has identified four broad areas of care planning in ACT. These areas are the initial engagement phase; assessment and planning; environmental interventions such as family work and developing independent living skills; and finally crisis intervention and monitoring.

Persistent, constructive engagement will be the foundation of effective assertive outreach services/ACT (Sainsbury Centre for Mental Health, 1998). However, people do not engage with services *per se*, they engage with other people; valuing relationships which are 'authentic' (Beesforth *et al.*, 1994).

A major feature of a service user's life, especially where social networks have been damaged, is the worker–client relationship (the working alliance). The working alliance can be a predictor of outcome (Priebe and Gruyters, 1995). Peplau (1952) identified four phases of this relationship. See Box 8.3 for details.

Burns and Firn (2002) offer several activities, which may accomplish both initial engagement (Grech, 2002) and Peplau's (1952) orientation and identification phases. These activities may be referred to as being a constructive approach to engagement. These include activities such as befriending and collaboration. With 'home-based' interventions, the focus is on the client's strengths rather than their deficits. Further to this focus on strengths there is the preference for mainstream activities to promote social inclusion. Practical assistance and problem solving such as with financial benefits assistance should be offered. Support and problem solving for families and carers and preserving accommodation will enable the worker to be of immediate benefit. Hence, demonstrating the potential benefit of affiliation with the ACT service.

Informative approaches (observation and monitoring) are possible, but are more open to conflict with the client's views on autonomy. Restrictive approaches such as the use of statutory powers (supervised discharges etc) are possible. These approaches as the name implies, rely on restricting the personal freedom of an individual. It requires the team to make what can be very difficult ethical decisions. Attempting to resolve conflict between the client's right to decide to refuse services and the expectations of society, employers and the political agenda (Ford and Repper, 1994).

Engagement is often viewed as a means to an end. Indeed, in this chapter it is referred to as a vehicle to deliver other interventions. However, engagement activities such as social and recreational activity can have a positive effect on both mood and the client's quality of life (Beesforth *et al.*, 1994).

Box 8.3 Four phases of a working alliance (Peplau, 1952)

Orientation Phase

The service user may be anxious. They may not have totally understood their situation and will need space, time and information. They need to be able to ask questions, the answers to which provide information and a greater insight into the situation. By enabling the achievement of some degree of control in a difficult situation, Peplau claims, the worker and the service user learn to work in a co-operative manner to resolve difficulties.

Identification Phase

The service user identifies with those workers experienced as being useful to them. They engage with, and places trust in, staff doing the things they say they will do. The goal of engagement is to form a working alliance that will enable collaborative support through treatment. Engagement will only take place if affiliation is seen as a benefit. The relationship is initially built on helping the service user to achieve ends identified as important. Simpson (1991) suggests that service users identify with workers who are open and honest in their approach and who provide information for them.

Exploitation Phase

This is the main 'working' phase for both, within ACT. As the informed service user gains a clearer picture of the situation, identification of needs begin. This service user makes full use of the resources available, both physical and human resources. The relationship is at a potentially meaningful level. In this phase *care planning* and implementation can be a co-operative process. Ideally this is a dynamic phase of growth from dependency to a situation in which both worker and service user identify and exploit areas of independence and interdependence.

Resolution Phase

The service user begins to take steps to live a healthier life in their own environment. The handover of care needs to be planned carefully, with preparation for their next situation (the 'freeing process').

Entering the exploitation phase allows the environmental interventions (Grech, 2002) to be undertaken collaboratively. These interventions include family work (Pharoah *et al.*, 2002) and developing independent living and coping skills (Tarrier *et al.*, 1998), enabling clients to improve both their quality of life and their ability to manage relapse of their illness.

The final phase, the 'freeing process' may be an unattainable goal in ACT. In fact most clients are likely to require some form of continuing care from services. However, by appropriate development, utilisation and termination of the working alliance, the benefits of the work undertaken in ACT can be carried through into other, less specialist services.

Additional Care Planning

For many years there has been a significant population of service users for which appropriate and realistic care planning has been lacking. Those clients experiencing both a serious mental illness and a co-morbid substance use problem have received a poor response from services (Royal College of Psychiatrists, 2000). Previous service provision has been either sequential (one service provided before another) or concurrent parallel services, both proving imperfect (Drake *et al.*, 1993b; Crome, 1999).

ACT services are well geared to providing a service to these clients. In fact one model for developing services for dual diagnosis clients, the New Hampshire model (McHugo *et al.*, 1999), incorporates many of the elements of ACT. Elements such as assertive engagement, attention to basic needs and harm-reduction are some of the principles of treatment in dually diagnosed clients (Drake *et al.*, 1993a).

Case Examples

Case 1

Christabel has a diagnosis of paranoid schizophrenia. She has a long history of contact with the mental health services, including several admissions after being involved in incidents of self-harm by overdosing herself with benzodiazapines. Each incident had been preceded by abstinence from antipsychotic medication, including depot medication.

After her last admission Christabel was prescribed clozapine, which she was eager to take to improve the symptoms of her illness. Unfortunately, owing to her forgetfulness, Christabel was unable to administer her medication unsupervised.

By offering daily visits it was possible for Christabel to self-administer the clozapine and remain well. Naturally, this could not always be done by the key worker, owing to annual leave or sick days. By developing a cohesive team approach, Christabel could be visited by people she had developed a relationship with, even though not at the depth she had developed with her key worker.

Case 2

Quentin, a middle-aged man of European origin, has had twice-yearly admissions to hospital for approximately eight years. Each admission was under a section of the Mental Health Act (1983). During hospital admissions Quentin would develop a relationship with ward-based nurses but on discharge from hospital he would then refuse contact with his key worker.

During a formal admission to hospital he was referred to an ACT team. During in-reach sessions Quentin developed a relationship with his key worker from the ACT team, Sebastian.

During this period Sebastian discovered information from Quentin that he had an interest in fishing that he had never been able to fulfil. Sebastian offered to take Quentin and his friend on a fishing trip to the coast.

This trip enabled Quentin and Sebastian to engage at a befriending level. This relationship was further developed by *in vivo* collaborative working, allowing Sebastian to spend time with Quentin discussing relapse management. The relationship enabled Quentin to initiate his own hospital admission, on a non-compulsory basis with the result of increased self-esteem for Quentin and admissions of a much shorter duration.

Documentation

Owing to the fact that from its conception ACT has targeted those perceived as the 'heavy service user' all ACT clients will be registered on 'enhanced' CPA (DoH, 1990), with the allocation of a 'care co-ordinator'. The role of the 'care co-ordinator' is to ensure that the care programme is current, co-ordinated and carried out.

In order to fulfil this role several core records are used. Records such as standard CPA forms detailing demographic and service history of clients; risk assessment and needs assessment (Slade *et al.*, 1999). Carers are also offered an assessment of their needs (DoH, 1999a), however how and by whom their needs are to be met is open to debate.

Following from this a care programme will be developed identifying how each need is to be addressed and which clinician will be responsible for this care delivery. This care programme is not a *secret*. The client must be party to the proposed care delivery and the responsible clinician (DoH, 1999b), and therefore be offered a copy of their agreed care programme.

In addition to these standard documents, a specific record may be a 'contingency plan'. The current UK health system offers 24-hour care through GPs, Emergency Departments and Mental Health Liaison services. Imagine a very anxious person or someone complaining of distressing voices turning up at a hospital at 3 a.m. What are the emergency clinicians to do? The 'safest' option would be to admit the person to hospital. However, one aim of ACT is to prevent needless admission to hospital. In order to meet this aim it is possible to provide the relevant services with an up-to-date plan, agreed by the team, which details both the risks involved for the person and other options such as reassurance that a member of the ACT team will see the person later that day, or appropriate targeted medication (Burns and Firn, 2002).

Time Frame

Discharge from ACT is not an issue that has been examined in sufficient detail to specify rigid criteria. In practice, clinical judgement is based on:

- the nature and type of supports available to the person;
- a knowledge of the cyclical nature of the person's illness, stability of insight and symptoms;
- agreement and concordance with aftercare and relapse management plans;
- the person's wishes.

All determine the propriety of discharge.

Life is by its very nature a journey of growth and maturation. A number of people grow beyond the need for ACT, while for others the need is ongoing. However, given the relapsing nature of serious mental illness, most clients are likely to require some type of follow-up from mental health services. The essence of discharge would not be a 'cure'. Rather it is an acceptance that, while the illness is not terminated, the need for mental health services has been reduced to the point where standard care can be appropriately offered. This transfer to standard care must be collaborative. Abrupt withdrawal of ACT can amount to an abrupt withdrawal of a key, and often only form of stabilising support acting as a buffer to life's stressors.

The so-called 'revolving door client' is a major feature of those clients initially referred to ACT. The factors in reducing this recidivism have been described as community support, collaborative aftercare and the responsiveness of the services in place (Klinkenberg and Calsyn, 1996). Assertive outreach by its very nature increases the provision of aftercare and helps to bolster community support for the person, by either advocating with the necessary supporter or by direct provision where needed. ACT should be responsive not only to gross changes in mental health status, but to the changing and developing needs of the person on a daily basis. Indeed, these factors must be of central concern to any mental health system, not just a dedicated team.

However, if recidivism is reduced by collaborative aftercare there is an obligation for the client to collaborate. If this is not possible, if the client still does not engage with the ACT service, then there will arrive a time when the service cannot continue to attempt to engage. Sometimes a whole year of engagement activities is attempted with no success (Burns and Firn, 2002). However, those clients who succeed in not engaging with ACT services are, on the whole, the more able clients anyway (McGrew *et al.*, 1995).

Evidence Base

Marshall and Lockwood (2001) identified five key elements of ACT. These elements are:

(1) A multidisciplinary team-based approach.
(2) Provided exclusively for people with serious mental illness.

(3) Team members share responsibility for clients, providing all psychiatric/ social care.
(4) As far as practicable this care is provided at home or in the work place.
(5) Treatment and care is offered assertively to reluctant service users.

Assertive outreach is a well evaluated mental health intervention. However, this evidence is mixed and dependent on the definitions of the terms under consideration. A Cochrane Review (Box 8.4) concluded that there is little doubt that assertive outreach/ACT is helpful in reducing hospitalisation, improving housing stability, and possibly contributes to modest improvements in quality of life and symptomatology. However, the research evidence does not make clear what elements of ACT contribute to improvements or whether improvements are sustained over time once ACT services are withdrawn (Mueser *et al.*, 1998).

Dissemination of Information

The leading drivers for the development of ACT in the UK have been both clinical and political need. Lack of clear and coherent services have been cited as detrimental in many cases (Ritchie, 1994). The comprehensive approach of ACT teams to providing as much health and social care as is possible (NICE, 2003) decreases the need to disseminate information but does not remove it completely. Information sharing with GPs and other professionals, as well as with carers and families remains necessary. Access to client notes remains under the aegis of the Data Protection Act (DoH, 1998). In order to meet the objectives of ACT to reduce unnecessary admissions to hospital, it may be necessary to share information with third parties, such as Emergency Departments, Mental Health Liaison and potential in-patient units. Within areas of real risk of physical harm, the public interest outweighs the client's right to confidentiality (Noffsinger and Resnick, 1999).

Box 8.4   ACT conclusions

- Compared to standard community care, people allocated to ACT were more likely to remain in contact with services and when admitted to spend less time in hospital.
- More likely to be living independently and likely to have found employment.
- More satisfied with the service they receive.
- ACT is a more attractive way of working for professionals.
- There were no differences between ACT and control treatments on mental state or social functioning.

(Marshall and Lockwood, 2004)

Reflective Practice

As in all community mental health services there is a need to engage in some form of team support and reflective practice (Leiter, 1988). This need is arguably greater in ACT teams owing to the need for 'developing flexibility and a degree of role-blurring' (Burns and Firn, 2002, p. 280), requiring the team member to feel secure in their role and within the organisation.

While there will be ample scope for the discussion of client issues within CPA meetings, there will remain a need for more formal, one-to-one discussions and reflection.

Supervision is a major vehicle for enabling team members to engage in reflective practice; developing competent practitioners, supported and understood by the system in which they work (Nursing Times, 2000).

Supervision can take two forms, management supervision and clinical supervision. Management supervision is provided by a team member's line manager. This form of supervision provides identification, feedback and monitoring of areas such as training needs, sickness, performance, problem-solving weaknesses and developing strengths.

Clinical supervision provides for reflection on complex care packages and challenging client care; evaluation and improvement of clinical skills; and support while developing skills such as psychosocial interventions.

While many clinical areas undertake both management and clinical supervision by the same person, this could be difficult owing to the issues of confidentiality and trust when dealing with a 'clinical supervisor' who has a managerial/disciplinary function (King's Fund, 1994).

Practice Development

Owing to the holistic nature of ACT, and the need for professionals to perform outside of their assumed professional roles, there are many areas for practice development. There may be a need for training in aspects of welfare rights, housing issues and cultural and racial awareness. To promote evidence-informed interventions there is a need for training in the use of standardised assessment tools. Many of these tools have been in existence for many years. However their use has not generally been accepted as part of the regular workload of staff. Practice development should also include a 'marketing' focus to raise awareness of the ACT service, its target clients and way of working.

Finally, there is little formal accredited training in assertive outreach available in the realms of higher education.

Conclusion

Assertive outreach/ACT is a well-validated intervention for the care of people suffering serious mental illness. It has been developed specifically for clients whose experiences have led them to be ambiguous or even antagonistic towards services. Research shows that assertive outreach can deliver evidence-informed practices to these clients and can be of benefit to them. However, engagement is the key. A number of interventions described in this chapter can facilitate engagement. Without such, there is no realistic possibility of delivering evidence-informed interventions.

To assist in achieving this aim, the development of a therapeutic relationship that involves a working alliance is necessary. How this relationship develops will depend on the skills, attitudes and personality of the ACT nurse and the extent to which they believe in the value of the service.

📖 Suggested Further Reading

Burns, T. and Firn, M. (2002) *Assertive Outreach in Mental Health*, Oxford: Oxford University Press.
Onyett, S. (1998) *Case Management in Mental Health*, Cheltenham: Stanley Thornes.

References

Beck, A.T., Ward, C.H., Mendelson, M., Mock, J.E. and Erbaugh, J.K. (1961) An inventory to measure depression, *Archives of General Psychiatry*, 4: 561–71.
Beesforth, M., Conlan, E. and Grayley, R. (1994) *Have We Got Views for You: User Evaluation of Case Management*, London: Sainsbury Centre for Mental Health.
Birchwood, M., Smith, J., Cochrane, R., Wetton, S. and Copestake, S. (1990) The social functioning scale. The development and validation of a new scale of social adjustment for use in family intervention programmes with schizophrenic patients, *British Journal of Psychiatry*, 157: 853–9.
Burns, T. and Firn, M. (2002) *Assertive Outreach in Mental Health*, Oxford: Oxford University Press.
Burns, T., Fioritti, A., Holloway, F., Malm, U., and Rossler, W. (2001) Case management and assertive community treatment in Europe, *Psychiatric Services*, 52, 5: 631–6.
Crome, I. (1999) Substance misuse and psychiatric comorbidity: towards improved service provision, *Drugs: Education, Prevention and Policy*, 6, 2: 151–74.
Curson, D.A., Patel, M. and Liddle, P.F. (1988) Psychiatric morbidity of a long-stay hospital population with chronic schizophrenia and implications for future community care, *British Medical Journal*, 297: 819–22.
Department of Health (1990) *The Care Programme Approach for People with a Mental Illness Refered to the Special Psychiatric Services*, Joint Health/Social Services Circular HC (90) 23/LASS (90) 11, London: Department of Health.
Department of Health (1998) *Data Protection Act*, London: HMSO.
Department of Health (1999a) *National Service Framework for Mental Health: Modern Standards and Service Models*, London: HMSO.
Department of Health (1999b) *An Audit Pack for Monitoring the Care Programme Approach*, London: HMSO.
Department of Health (2000) *NHS Plan*, London: HMSO.

Department of Health (2001) *The Mental Health Policy Implementation Guide*, London: HMSO.

Drake, R.E., McHugo, G.J. and Noordsy, D.L. (1993a) Treatment of alcoholism among schizophrenic outpatients: 4-year outcomes, *American Journal of Psychiatry*, 150, 2: 328–9.

Drake, R.E., Bartels, S.J., Teague, G.B., Noordsy, D.L. and Clarke, R.E. (1993b) Treatment of substance abuse in severely mentally ill patients, *Journal of Nervous and Mental Disease*, 181: 606–11.

Ford, R. and Repper, J.M. (1994) Taking responsibility for care, *Nursing Times*, 90, 31: 54–6.

Grech, E. (2002) Case management: a critical analysis of the literature, *International Journal of Psychosocial Rehabilitation*, 6: 89–98.

Haddock, G., McCarron, J., Tarrier, N. and Faragher, E.B. (1999) Scales to measure dimensions of hallucinations and delusions: the psychotic symptoms rating scales (PSYRATS), *Psychological Medicine*, 29: 879–89.

Jablensky, A., Sartorius, N., Ernberg, G., Anker, M. Korten, A., Cooper J.E., Day, R. and Bertelsen, A. (1992) Schizophrenia: manifestations, incidence and course in different cultures. A World Health Organisation ten-country study, *Psychological Medicine Monograph Supplement*, 20: 1–97.

Kane, J., Honigfeld, G., Singer, J. and Meltzer, H. (1988) Clozapine for the treatment-resistant schizophrenic. A double-blind comparison with chlorpromazine, *Archives of General Psychiatry*, 45: 789–96.

Kent, S., Fogarty, M. and Yellowlees, P. (1995) A review of studies of heavy users of psychiatric services, *Psychiatric Services*, 46, 12: 1247–53.

King's Fund (1994) *Clinical Supervision in Practice*, London: King's Fund.

Klinkenberg, W.D. and Calsyn, R.J. (1996) Predictors of receipt of aftercare and recidivism among persons with severe mental illness: a review, *Psychiatric Services*, 47, 5: 487–96.

Krawiecka, M., Goldberg, D. and Vaughn, M. (1977) A standardised psychiatric assessment scale for rating chronic psychotic patients, *Acta Psychiatrica Scandinavia*, 55: 299–308.

Leiter, M.P. (1988) Burnout as a function of communication patterns: a study of a multidisciplinary mental health team, *Group and Organisational Studies* 13, 1: 11–28.

Marshall, M. and Lockwood, A. (2004) Assertive community treatment for people with severe mental disorders (Cochrane review), in the Cochrane library, issue 3, Chichester, UK: John Wiley & Sons Ltd.

McGrew, J.H. and Bond, G.R. (1995) Critical ingredients of assertive community treatment: judgments of the experts, *Journal of Mental Health Administration*, 22, 2: 113–25.

McGrew, J.H., Bond, G.R., Dietzen, L. and Salyers, M. (1994) Measuring the fidelity of implementation of a mental health program model, *Journal of Consulting & Clinical Psychology*, 62, 4: 670–8.

McGrew, J.H., Bond, G.R., Dietzen, L., McKasson, M. and Miller, L.D. (1995) A multisite study of client outcomes in assertive community treatment, *Psychiatric Services*, 46, 7: 696–701.

McHugo, G.J., Drake, R.E., Teague, G.B. and Xie, H. (1999) Fidelity to assertive community treatment and client outcomes in the New Hampshire dual disorders study, *Psychiatric Services*, 50, 6: 818–24.

Meltzer, H.Y., Burnett, S., Bastani, B. and Ramirez, L.F. (1990) Effects of six months of clozapine treatment on the quality of life of chronic schizophrenic patients, *Hospital & Community Psychiatry*, 41: 892–7.

Meltzer, H.Y., Bastani, B., Young Kwon, K., Ramirez, L.F., Burnett, S. and Sharpe, J. (1989) A prospective study of clozapine in treatment-resistant schizophrenic patients: I. Preliminary report, *Psychopharmacology*, 99 (Suppl.): 68–72.

Miller, W. and Rollnick, S. (1991) *Motivational Interviewing: Preparing People to Change Addictive Behaviour*, New York: Guilford Press.

Morgan, G. (1994) The assessment of risk, in Jenkins, R. *et al.* (ed.), *The Prevention of Suicide*, Department of Health, London: HMSO.

Mueser, K.T., Bond, G.R., Drake, R.E. and Resnick, S.G. (1998) Models of community care for severe mental illness: a review of research on case management, *Schizophrenia Bulletin*, 24, 1: 37–74.

NICE (2003) *Schizophrenia: Core Interventions in the Treatment and Management of Schizophrenia in Primary and Secondary Care*, London: National Institute of Clinical Excellence. http://www.nice.org.uk/pdf/CG1NICEguideline.pdf

Noffsinger, S.G. and Resnick, P.J. (1999) Violence and mental illness, *Current Opinion in Psychiatry*, 12, 6: 683–7.

Nursing Times (2000) Open learning: clinical supervision; make your experience work; cross-disciplinary supervision, *Nursing Times* 96, 7: 47–50.

Overall, J.E. and Gorham, D.R. (1962) The brief psychiatric rating scale, *Psychological Reports* 10: 799–812.

Peplau, H.E. (1952) *Interpersonal Relations in Nursing*, New York: Putnam.

Perkins, R.E. and Repper, J.M. (1996) *Working Alongside People with Long Term Mental Health Problems*, Cheltenham: Stanley Thornes.

Perkins, R.E. and Repper, J.M. (1998) *Dilemmas in Community Mental Health Practice: Choice or Control?*, Oxford: Radcliffe Medical Press.

Pharoah, F.M., Mari, J.J. and Streiner, D. (2002) Family intervention *Cochrane Database of Systematic Review*, 4.

Priebe, S. and Gruyters, T. (1995) Patients' assessment of treatment predicting outcomes, *Schizophrenia Bulletin*, 21, 1: 87–94.

Richards, D. and McDonald, B. (1990) *Behavioural Psychotherapy: a Pocket Book for Nurses*, Oxford: Heinemann.

Ritchie, J.H. (1994) *The Report of the Inquiry into the Care and Treatment of Christopher Clunis Presented to the Chairman of the North East Thames and South East Thames Regional Health Authorities*, London: HMSO.

Royal College of Psychiatrists (2000) *Drugs: Dilemmas and Choices*, Gaskell, London: RCP.

Sainsbury Centre for Mental Health (1998) *Keys to Engagement*, London: Sainsbury Centre for Mental Health.

Schaedle, R.W. and Epstein, I. (2000) Specifying intensive case management: a multiple perspective approach, *Mental Health Service Research*, 2, 2: 95–105.

Simpson, H. (1991) *Peplau's Model in Action*, London: Macmillan.

Slade, M., Thornicroft, G., Loftus, L., Phelan, M. and Wykes, T. (1999) *Camberwell Assessment of Need*, London: Gaskell.

Stein, L.I. and Test, M.A. (1978) An alternative to mental hospital treatment, in Stein, L.I. and Test, M.A. (eds), *Alternatives to Mental Hospital Treatment*, New York: Plenum Press.

Tarrier, N., Yusupoff, L., Kinney, C., McCarthy, E., Gledhill, A., Haddock, G. *et al.* (1998) Randomised controlled trial of intensive cognitive behaviour therapy for patients with chronic schizophrenia *British Medical Journal*, 317, 7154: 303–7.

Teague, G.B., Bond, G.R. and Drake, R.E. (1998) Program fidelity in assertive community treatment: development and use of a measure, *American Journal of Orthopsychiatry*, 68, 2: 216–32.

Thompson, K.S., Griffity, E.E.H. and Leaf, P.J. (1990) A historical review of the Madison Model of community care, *Hospital and Community Psychiatry*, 41: 625–34.

CHAPTER 9

Acute Inpatient Care

Trevor Lowe and Nancy Bunch

Introduction

Acute inpatient care remains an important part of the service response in case of crisis, representing about 25 per cent of the total health and social care budget for mental health (Sainsbury Centre for Mental Health (SCMH) 2002). This may be because there are few satisfactory alternatives.

Pressures on acute inpatient care have increased as a result of reductions in hospital beds and consequent increased occupancy, as well as the increased acuity of the inpatient population and the drain of experienced staff to the community. Despite the development of crisis resolution teams, there remains a group of service users who are too distressed or in such disadvantaged social circumstances that they have to be cared for in hospital. Although it is accepted that long stays in hospital are damaging, it is also argued that care can be offered which is safe, supportive and therapeutic (SCMH, 2002). The possible benefits of hospitalisation include: *stabilisation of the person's condition, providing a safe haven, a break from everyday stresses* and the *opportunity for the underlying causes to be addressed* in a supportive environment (Higgins *et al.*, 1999).

It should also provide a range of therapeutic activities in a pleasant environment, with the aim of supporting recovery and facilitating return to the community as quickly as possible. The SCMH (1998) identifies three key components of hospital treatment for people with psychotic illness including: comprehensive individualised care, a relaxed and secure environment and a multi disciplinary and evidence based approach to care. The National Service Framework (NSF) for Mental Health (Department of Health (DoH), 1999a) outlines the need for inpatient treatment to be seen as part of a system of care, including crisis resolution teams, day hospitals, community mental health teams and 24-hour staffed accommodation. Central to this should be the care programme approach, risk management and therapeutic engagement with calls for greater service user involvement and multi disciplinary planning (DoH, 1999a).

Prevalence and Population

There are 14,000 acute beds in England and Wales, in 521 wards. These wards take around 138,000 admissions per year and employ over 12,000 nurses and 15,000 staff in total (SCMH, 2002). The main difficulties that are likely to be presented include, *schizophrenia, depression, hypomania, alcohol and drug misuse, specific problematic issues,* for example, *suicidal intent.* Also, other presentations might include *personality disorders* and *anorexia nervosa.*

A survey by Ford *et al.* (1998) found that:

- Bed occupancy was 109 per cent in inner London and 111 per cent in outer London (although concluding that some pressure was due to the practice of trial leave for persons detained under a section of the Mental Health Act, with the consequent unpredictability about when they might return).
- The majority of admissions for emergency treatment tend to be for the relapse of an existing illness.
- More than 10 per cent are admitted for respite care or social reasons.
- 30 per cent of inpatients were detained, rising to 44 per cent in inner London.
- Women made up 53 per cent of inpatient admissions in all areas.

Bartlett *et al.* (1999) surveyed 23 consultant psychiatrists and reported that 179 out of 543 inpatients were regarded as inappropriately placed. Of these 112 were deemed to have been suitable for alternative care settings, had these been available.

Referrals

Referrals usually come by telephone and are most likely to come from secondary services. They may also come from GPs, or through the Accident and Emergency Liaison Service of the local general hospital. In the case of an emergency, referral may come from the emergency duty team, which has made an assessment under the Mental Health Act (DoH, 1983), or from the consultant psychiatrist.

The referral pathway is likely to be through the bed manager and senior nurse on call. The senior nurse will monitor the bed state and check availability. If there is no available bed on the unit to which the patient would normally be admitted, a search further afield would be required and it is sometimes necessary for extra contractual referrals to be made to other areas.

Theoretical Framework

Evans (2001) argues that over the years a more medical model has emerged within acute inpatient nursing, including Cognitive Behavioural Therapy (CBT)

Box 9.1 Beneficial elements for in-patient services

- A good quality environment
- Therapeutic activities, including sport and meaningful daytime activities;
- Psychological therapies, including cognitive behavioural therapy based interventions and counselling techniques;
- Medication management;
- Solving of problems around housing benefits and employment;
- Prevention of relapse;
- Psychosocial interventions.

---

and monitoring of medication. However there has also recently been a reaction against the 'observation culture' that has existed in many hospitals. The National Service Framework for Mental Health (DoH, 1999a) states that wards must be organised as therapeutic units and as one component of a continuum of care. The implications are that therapy and the therapeutic milieu should be more prominent. Barker and Rolfe (2000) argue that nurses can ally themselves too much with a medical model of care and suggest that engagement is a realistic alternative to over control.

There is a general agreement that inpatient care needs to be more active and less focused on containment (SCMH, 2002). It should develop a strategy to deliver a more therapeutic approach without compromising safety. Inpatient treatment should contain the elements described in Box 9.1.

Psychosocial Interventions
Baker (2000) argues that the psychosocial approaches can be adapted to acute inpatient care and identifies a number of key elements to the psychosocial approach, including medication and educating patients and their carers about medication management, as well as cognitive behavioural therapy and enhancing coping skills. [Editor: For further information see Chapter 6.]

Medication Management
Medication has a proven effectiveness in the treatment of psychosis and the prevention of relapse. Recent research into attempts to improve concordance with prescribed medication has focused on CBT and motivational interviewing techniques (Gray *et al.*, 2002). In inpatient settings it is particularly important to suggest a range of options to the client, rather than attempting to elicit all strategies and insights from them. Medication management is based on:

- A collaborative approach to working with service users;
- A careful assessment of the service user's beliefs and experience of treatment with antipsychotic medication;
- Giving service users information about their illness and treatment;

- Tailoring medication regimes to suit the service user;
- Use of motivational interviewing and cognitive behavioural techniques.
  [Editor: For further information see Chapter 6.]

Cognitive Behavioural Therapy and Coping Skills

CBT is a psychological intervention best known for its efficacy in treating depression but also used in the management of delusions and hallucinations. It can help people to come to terms with such experiences and learn to manage them (Drury *et al.*, 1996a).

For example a number of coping strategies for hearing voices have been documented by Buccheri *et al.* (1996). These include *Self monitoring, Reading aloud, Talking, Watching TV, Saying 'stop', Music with headphones, Relaxation tapes with headphones, Humming a single note.* According to Buccheri *et al.* (1996) sufferers found at least one of these strategies helpful.

Working with beliefs may involve helping people to be less preoccupied with distressing beliefs, thus lessening the conviction with which they are held. Coping strategies include spending time with others, preferably engaged in distracting activities (Mills, 2000). Studies by Drury *et al.* (1996a, b) indicate that CBT principles can make a positive contribution to the management of acute psychosis. Nelson (1997) states that CBT techniques can be used in inpatient settings and Allen and Kingdon (1998) argue that staff on acute units should use the opportunities afforded by regular nurse–patient contact on the wards to provide therapeutic interventions.

Solution-focused Therapy

Solution-focused Therapy (SFT) is another approach which enables nurses to help their patients to focus on finding solutions, resulting in increased hope and support for their strengths (Webster *et al.*, 1994). Vaughn and Webster (1995), adopting a model based on SFT (de Shazer, 1988) and the nursing theory of modelling and role modelling (Erikson *et al.*, 1988) found that the approach reduced length of stay in hospital. They suggest that SFT will improve the satisfaction that nurses find in their interactions with clients and increase patient satisfaction. Stevenson *et al.* (2003) found good patient satisfaction ratings with the introduction of SFT training for inpatient nurses. The purpose of solution-focused groups, as described by Vaughn and Webster (1995), is to identify how a particular problem developed and to find solutions. The emphasis is on how to apply solutions to the real world in the future. As a result, therapeutic interactions within the hospital milieu become less important, in keeping, according to the authors, with the shorter hospital stays now current.

Principles and Skills Required

Gamble (2000) puts forward a strong argument for the need for professionals to challenge their assumptions about mental illness and to review their own personal attitudes, knowledge and beliefs. Pointing out that professionals respond differently to some service users than to others and using the concept of expressed emotion (Leff and Vaughn, 1985).

It is important therefore that staff *learn to accept illness as genuine, lower their expectations appropriately, remain calm and empathic, focused and objective*. They should also try to be adaptive, to adopt a problem-solving approach and be non-intrusive and non-confrontational (Gamble, 2000, p. 118). Engagement is important and the nature of even the informal interactions between nurses and inpatients has been shown to affect well-being and self-esteem (Emrich, 1989).

Similarly, Rosenthal and McGuinness (1986) suggest that nurses consider their own comfort zone when working with people who express delusional beliefs. It is important not to agree with the delusion and yet it is also inappropriate to argue the point, as this can be frustrating as well as increasing the anxiety associated with the experience. Establishing a trusting relationship is crucial and as with hearing of voices, feelings can be acknowledged whilst neither arguing nor agreeing. Rosenthal and McGuinness (1996) suggest looking for the element which is true within the delusional ideas expressed and supporting this. Another suggestion is to discuss the delusional content at a different time when it is not actually being experienced.

The therapeutic relationship remains the key to establishing a successful admission. Establishing a successful therapeutic relationship requires a number of qualities from the staff member, such as:

- ability to display empathy,
- being a good listener,
- being a good communicator,
- providing emotional support,
- being available for patients and valuing them as individuals,
- mastering self-awareness.

Working in an inpatient environment, nurses are encountering people in crisis, with all the attendant uncertainties and unpredictabilities. This can be demanding for nurses and may lead them to question their ability to respond. One possible reaction in such circumstances is to try to control the environment (Simpson and Wright, 2003).

Physical Intervention

In the UK, the dominant model of physical intervention is known as Control and Restraint (C & R) (Parkes, 1996). Developed by the UK Prison Service, it was exported to Health and Social Care in the mid-1980s. Control and Restraint involves the use of techniques attempting to contain violent or potentially violent situations in a safe manner. The actual techniques have been modified over time and variants such as C & R General Services have emerged, in response to concerns over the aversive nature of C & R and its suitability for non-forensic settings (Gournay, 2000). Gournay (2000) states that the main benefit of C & R approaches is that they increase staff confidence but concluded that whilst it is a relatively effective method, it remains controversial because of the use of holds which use pain to control behaviour. Bonner *et al.* (2002) argue for a move away from aversive techniques and emphasise the need for engagement, prediction and prevention in training on the management of aggression.

Assessment

Approach

Acute care can be said to consist of three phases, the onset of the crisis and admission, the inpatient phase and the discharge and follow-up. Assessment should be continuous and begins from the point of referral. The first 72 hours post admission are crucial to the establishment of the therapeutic relationship and will dictate the person's feelings about the crisis and their attitude to the admission. The decision to admit is often also taken in conjunction with the patient and their family. Admission to hospital can in itself be stressful. The person may question the need to be in hospital and feel that it is an injustice or that they have been rejected or betrayed by family or others.

Admission Interview

The key nurse should introduce themselves and explain their role, empathise with the person's situation, seek the person's own view of their circumstances and what may help them.

The interview should be as collaborative as possible and should aim for a situation in which the patient becomes a willing and constructive partner. The nurse should try to respond to individual needs, allow choice and promote autonomy. Although there is a need to record and go through a formal process the style should be as informal as possible and should avoid a distant and bureaucratic approach. The interview should proceed at the service user's pace and time allowed for breaks. Rules of confidentiality should be explained. The service user needs to feel that this will be respected but also that information relevant to their treatment will be passed on to members of the team involved in their care. Recording should as far as possible be collaborative, allowing the service user to express their view and comment on conclusions drawn and plans developed.

Barker (1997, p. 43) states that the initial interview provides an opportunity to:
(a) Develop a relationship with the person;
(b) Establish trust;
(c) Promote professional closeness and collaboration;
(d) Start to identify problematic patterns in the person's actions;
(e) Identify how the person's personal resources might help the person to overcome distress.

It should be borne in mind that patients are likely to be confused and distressed on arrival and should be taken to a quiet place within the unit for the initial period. Assessment should therefore focus on the person's specific complaints rather than make assumptions about the character of the disorder. A diagnosis of any illness may encompass a range of symptoms and behaviours, which vary from person to person.

A complete assessment should include:

- information about the person's perception of himself,
- the person's goals or expectations of himself,
- the person's strengths and potential,
- the person's manifest mood state,
- the person's available and potential support systems.

(Barker 1997, p. 168)

During the initial interview, the patient may be unwilling or unable to provide the information needed. However, it is useful at the outset to provide an outline of the nurses' intentions and to put forward ideas in the form of suggestions, adopting a collaborative approach from the beginning. If the person is finding it difficult to answer, it may be necessary to take a more active direct approach, asking closed questions that are short and well punctuated. Also, you can try rephrasing or changing the topic.

Chadwick *et al.* (1996) suggest that it should be assumed that a potentially threatening situation like an assessment interview may exacerbate a client's psychotic symptoms and that they are likely to be active. Voices may comment on the interviewer and paranoid traits may be accentuated. This can be raised at an early stage by direct enquiry and it may be useful to say that this is not an uncommon experience. The person may feel unsafe and the development of trust could be hindered if this went unrecognised.

Mills (2000) points out that the process can be an opportunity to work collaboratively, to examine the way that stress precipitates the symptoms, to look at the way vulnerability factors such as poor social support affect the problem and to promote a normalising rationale for the symptoms.

Process

Assessment should if possible take place on admission but if the patient's condition makes this impossible, should take place within 72 hours. It might initially involve an assessment of the patient's mental state, their psychological condition, their social circumstances, physical well-being and spiritual needs. The initial reception of a new patient is usually a nursing responsibility although it is best if the admission procedure is carried out together with a doctor in order to avoid too much repetition of basic information. The admission procedure is likely to last at least one hour and should include the allocation of a named nurse (Barker, 1997).

Maintaining a safe environment is another important issue in acute inpatient units. Balancing the need for freedom and tolerance against the safety of patients and staff is highly relevant and involves assessment of what is acceptable or unacceptable risk. Issues for this client group whilst an inpatient include:

- Many patients feel unsafe
- There is a lack of basic amenities
- Frequent readmissions
- A lack of therapeutic activities and interventions
- Restrictions of movement and behaviour.

(SCMH, 1998)

It is important to try to create as welcoming a situation as possible in the circumstances. This will include finding a private place in which to talk, offering refreshments, finding a place and time for the patient to smoke if desired, showing them around including own room, toilet and bathroom, basic information about times of meals or visiting and generally putting them at ease. Information regarding the patient's Mental Health Act status should be available and if the admission is formal, their rights should be explained fully and written information given. The general philosophy or approach of the unit should be explained along with information regarding male and female areas, the availability of quiet areas, areas for smoking or non-smoking and general arrangements at night time. The roles of the different staff and the skill mix should be explained.

The above information must be offered in a format that is accessible and at a level appropriate to the person's mental state at the time. It should not be assumed that, once the information is conveyed, there will be no need to revisit it. Someone who is distressed and preoccupied will not necessarily take in everything they are told. Even people who have been admitted several times in the past may be confused on admission or forgotten some of what they knew about the unit. It is useful for information to be available in written form as well, in the form of a booklet.

Information Gathering

The initial information should include information from relatives or anyone who has accompanied the patient. It may be necessary to see friends or relatives separately from the patient in order to get a complete picture of events. Community Mental Health Nurses or other professionals involved are other possible sources of information.

Information is obtained from as many sources as possible and may also include the General Practitioner, Social Worker and Doctor/Psychiatrist. Existing notes can be helpful in filling in previous history and background information. Information is expanded upon through the skills of assessment including observation (level of observation and frequency depending on Trust policy), interviewing, teamwork, professional knowledge and experience and facilitating the service user's self-assessment.

Tools Used

Information gathering can be aided by the use of appropriate assessment tools. Some that might be of use are detailed below:

Brief Psychiatric Rating Scale (BPRS) (Overall and Gorham, 1962)   The most commonly used rating scale for schizophrenia. It contains 16 symptom constructs, which are rated on a 7 point scale from not present to extremely severe. It is based on a 20-minute interview. The BPRS has a high degree of reliability but there is little evidence of construct validity. It is easy to use, but relies on the interpersonal skills and judgement of the interviewer. It is widely used in research and in clinical practice.

Beck Depression Inventory (BDI) (Beck *et al.*, 1961)   The BDI covers 21 items, each presented as 4 statements and the timeframe used is the previous 3–7 days. The respondent circles the number corresponding to the statement which applies to them for each item. The inventory covers items such as feelings (of shame, sadness, guilt etc) but also rates biological features. A total score is obtained which provides an indication of whether the respondent is suffering from depression and this is graded according to whether it is likely to be mild, moderate or severe. The BDI is simple to use and takes a few minutes.

Hospital Anxiety and Depression Scale (HADS) (Zigmond and Snaith, 1983) The HADS is a self-report questionnaire containing 14 items, 7 each for anxiety and depression, each rated on a 4 point scale. It is easy to complete and acceptable to patients. It is regarded as valid for out patient settings and may also be valid for other groups.

Liverpool University Neuroleptic Side Effect Rating Scale (Day, 1995)   The LUNSERS is a 51 item, self-report questionnaire covering psychological, neurological, autonomic, hormonal and miscellaneous side effects. The questionnaire also includes 10 red herring items. Each item is rated by the patient on a 0–4 rating scale from 'not at all' to 'very much'. Day (1995) found that the LUNSERS demonstrated good reliability and validity.

The Drug Attitude Inventory (DAI) (Hogan *et al.*, 1983)   The DAI 30 has 30 items scoring true or false. The results are predictive of compliance or non-compliance. There is a shorter version, the DAI 10. The DAI is a useful tool to aid in discussion about the service user's beliefs and concerns about medication and in encouraging them to think about the evidence for and against these beliefs.

Positive And Negative Symptom Scale (PANSS) (Kay *et al.*, 1987)   The PANSS rates the positive and negative features of schizophrenia. It has strong validity and reliability. It consists of 30 clearly defined items (7 positive, 7 negative and 16 general psychopathological items) rated on a 7 point scale from 'absent' to 'extremely severe'. Ratings are based on a 40-minute structured interview.

Risk Priorities

Risk assessment should be suitable and appropriate to an acute unit. It should be clear if the service user is at risk, what observations are required, whether they have been informed that they are being observed and why. Reasons should be given for any actions or judgements.

   Consideration of risk posed will need to take into account the circumstances of the individual and how they see their situation. It should not be concerned solely with a general assessment of dangerousness. Self-harm, suicide and harm to others are the main risk related concerns of staff on inpatient acute units. Clinical risk assessment is concerned with making judgements on a daily basis about the relative risk of such events as well as other changes in the health status of patients (Ryrie, 2000). Each organisation has its own tools for the assessment of risk and these are useful adjuncts to clinical judgement. Of greater importance is the establishment of a collaborative alliance through understanding of the patient's needs and their subjective view of their circumstances (Keirle, 1997).

Suicide   The Department of Health (1993) suggests a lifetime risk of suicide amongst psychiatric diagnostic groups of: schizophrenia 10 per cent, affective disorders 15 per cent, personality disorders 15 per cent and alcohol dependence 15 per cent. Specific risk factors include depressed mood and feelings of worthlessness and hopelessness. Indicators may include verbalising suicidal ideation or a plan or expressions of the futility of trying, giving away one's possessions or making a will, or refusing to sign a 'no harm' contract. They may also include sudden improvements in mood and energy, or the display of a calmer, more peaceful manner. Conversely, Linehan *et al.* (1983) found that the reasons most frequently given for *not* attempting suicide were: concern for the impact on children, religious belief and fear of pain.

   The degree of risk of suicide should be identified through direct questions about the patient's intentions, as well as through observations of other indicators described above. The risk should be re-evaluated when mood changes are observed, when medication is changed or if the patient seems more withdrawn. It should also be thoroughly reviewed prior to and immediately after discharge.

Observation of patients at risk are instituted to prevent potentially suicidal, violent or vulnerable patients from harming themselves or others, or from being harmed by others. They are also an important opportunity for the observing staff to interact in a therapeutic way with the patient on a one-to-one basis. Observing a patient who is distressed is an important task which calls for empathy, engagement and readiness to act in the best interests of the patient. The Standing Nursing and Midwifery Advisory Committee's guidelines (DoH, 1999b) recognise four levels of observation:

Level 1   (general observation),
Level 2   (intermittent observation),
Level 3   (within eyesight),
Level 4   (within arm's length).

Formal observation of service users in acute inpatient facilities is extremely common. As Bowles *et al.* (2002) point out, it uses high levels of nursing staff, makes considerable demands on them and focuses resources on to a relatively small group of inpatients. Other criticisms of the use of nursing observations are that a significant proportion of the suicides committed by inpatients occur during observation (DoH, 1999b, 2001b) and that many inpatients dislike the experience and find it intrusive (Jones *et al.*, 2000; Bowles and Dodds, 2001). However, Jones *et al.* (2000) found that, if inpatients were observed by nurses who they knew, trusted and were willing to talk to, the practice was found to be more helpful and therapeutic.

Harm to Others   It can be provocative to seek information directly through closed questions about the patient's past behaviour. They may be more inclined to share information through discussion around a more reflective and empathic approach in which they can share their experiences of anger and frustration.

Previous instances of violent behaviour provide useful information about the specific context in which it may occur in a particular individual. Previous instances may also provide clues as to how the risk might be minimised. Ryrie (2000, p. 106) provides a functional analysis for determining this in Box 9.2. Risk factors for violence may include psychotic symptoms such as delusions and hallucinations. Indicators may include a lack of development of trust or inappropriate interpersonal relationships, perceptions of threat, irrational, threatening or assaultive behaviour. In Bonner *et al.*'s (2002) study of the effects of restraint, patients reported feeling upset, distressed and ignored prior to incidents.

Also, it is worth pointing out the need to assess relapse indicators. These can detail the person's susceptibility to the risk of recurrence and establish a pattern for their presentation. Some relapse indicators include:

• Refusing or stopping medication
• Isolating self from family and friends

> **Box 9.2**   Functional analysis for determining risk (Ryrie, 2000)
>
> Assessment of intent following violent behaviour
>
> Antecedents   Circumstantial factors that motivated client
>   Provocation
>   Drug or alcohol intoxication
>   Treatment status
>
> Behaviour   Was behaviour planned or impulsive?
>   Was behaviour directed at a specific individual?
>   Were weapons used?
>   How was the behaviour stopped, and by whom?
>
> Consequences   Degree of resultant harm or damage
>   Victim empathy
>   Positive reinforcers for past behaviour
>   Current perception of past behaviour

- Increased levels of negative or paranoid thoughts
- Feeling picked on or persecuted
- Hallucinations, such as hearing voices
- Changes in normal routine – staying in bed and refusing to go to work and college.

Care Planning

How Plan is Determined

Care plans should be a partnership between the nurse or key worker and the patient. Patients should be encouraged to keep copies of their care plans for personal reference (DoH, 1999a). Understanding of the purposes of care plans should apply to everyone involved in direct patient care, whether trained or untrained. According to Young (2002) care plans should be viewed as simple routes of care, outlining the individual needs of patients and how those needs are to be met. Care plans should also clarify the interventions required.

Regular evaluation should take place and the outcome documented.

A care plan should include:

- The reason for admission
- Presenting problem
- Structured assessment
- Measurement rating scales/ charts used
- Educational needs

- The patients' view of problems/needs
- Status under the Mental Health Act (DoH, 1983)
- A medication management plan, particularly if admitted as a result of non-concordance
- Specific statements regarding interventions
- The purpose of any assessment tools used
- Specific statements about the development of therapeutic relationships.

Practical Application

Each person should be engaged in a programme of activity for each day of their stay, reflecting their wishes and involving genuine choice. A range of activities should be available which could also involve volunteers and outreach to settings such as leisure centres. The Mental Health Nursing Review Team (Butterworth, 1994) emphasised the individual needs of patients being involved in the development of care plans that are person-centred and needs led. For details of how interventions could be formulated, see Box 9.3. Tunmore and Thomas (2000) warn against the use of care plan clichés, such as 'Assess mental state, Maintain a safe environment, Establish one to one, Orientate to ward environment, Give medication prescribed, Monitor signs and symptoms, Allow patient to ventilate feelings, Develop a therapeutic relationship.'

It is important for the plan to be specific about what is intended. For example, what does the statement, 'maintain a safe environment' involve? It should be what problem leads to the need for a safe environment, whether the risk assessment has been completed, whether the patient is a danger to themselves or others, or other specific safeguards.

Box 9.3   A Formulation model for interventions

- **Specific.** Apply to the needs and problems identified, state the assessment tools used and state what is required, the level of frequency and who is responsible for carrying out each intervention.
- **Measurable.** Be clear what is being attempted and how this will be measured.
- **Achievable and appropriate.** How will the intervention be achieved and is it appropriate to the needs of the specific individual?
- **Realistic and required.** Is it realistic to expect the results documented and is it what the patient requires and agrees to.
- **Timescale.** Achieved within a realistic time frame.

The example used below is not based on real events, but an amalgamation of experience. Any resemblance to specific information or events is coincidental.

Case Example

Background

Frank is aged 40 and has a long history of suffering from schizophrenia. He has been admitted to the unit after a long period of concern during which he spent days in bed and neglected all areas of personal hygiene. Frank has increased paranoid ideation and is hearing voices telling him to kill himself. He has in fact attempted to jump in front of a bus causing an accident in the High Street. Frank does not believe that he is ill and feels there is nothing wrong. He has been refusing to take his medication or see his community care co-ordinator. He was assessed under the Mental Health Act (DoH, 1983) in the community and it was decided that he requires a period of admission for a thorough assessment of his needs. He is therefore detained under Section 2.

Admission and Care Plan

From admission, a baseline assessment needs to take place by the admitting nurse. This will help establish need, influencing factors and a basic rapport. The care plan will be made up of three – five statements for attention. Agreement will be attempted through a process of engagement. Each plan will have a statement of need identified with Frank and must be signed by both the key worker/named nurse and Frank himself.

Initial care planning must take account of the immediate legal requirement to inform Frank of his rights. The care plan will also need to record his level of understanding at this time. The procedure should be repeated within 72 hours if not understood and 7 days if understood. A standard appeal form will be provided if he chooses to appeal against his detention. Longer term, he should have a full understanding of his rights under the act and the plan would include provision to accept treatment and receive it as an informal patient. It will also aim at giving Section 17 leave when appropriate and putting into place a community care plan prior to discharge.

Discharge

Before discharge is considered, a number of issues at home need to be addressed. These are: (a) home cleaned and tidied, (b) carpet and bed

> contaminated with urine need to be replaced, (c) arrange home care to coincide with discharge, (d) electricity to be reconnected, (e) finances to be arranged through benefits agency.
>
> - Frank will continue with current medication to help prevent relapse and will be encouraged to explore his feelings and beliefs about medication. He will be given a two-week supply.
> - Has agreed to maintain contact with his community care co-ordinator.
> - Will continue to maintain current sheltered employment.

Example of a care plan statement:

Statement for attention
Inability to sleep

Goal statement
Short term Gain baseline information on sleeping pattern
Long term Patient sleeps well and feels that he does

Intervention (with rationale)
Patient to monitor sleep pattern for one week
Staff to do the same
Patient and staff to compare

Further interventions
Explain the approach, offer education, consider food intake, reading, watching television etc, monitor activities. Make sure all interventions are SMART.

Signature of nurse and patient
Note and explain if not signed.

Evaluation
Where possible, agree how often to be evaluated. Notes should be brief.

Documentation

Documentation of the needs, problems and interventions for the patient should be clear and unambiguous. There should be no abbreviations, jargon or irrelevant information and the format should be consistent.

Documentation should be a single set of records encompassing a multidisciplinary approach to care and should be accessible to all members of the team (Tunmore and Thomas, 2000).

All registered nurses should adhere to the Nursing and Midwifery Council (NMC, 2002a) guidelines for records and record keeping. The quality of record keeping is a reflection of the standard of professional practice. The best record is the result of consultation and discussion, which has taken place at local level between all members of the multidisciplinary health care team and the client/service user. Good record keeping is the result of good teamwork and an important aspect in promoting high quality health care.

Tunmore and Thomas (2000) state that reports from inquiries often comment on the lack of clarity over who is responsible for what in relation to the records. Each professional would often make assumptions about what other professionals were going to record and this could lead to repetition and/or omission of information. How frequently entries are made into the care plan and the key people involved and other appropriate assessment tools and other documentation that may be associated with the care plan should be considered, as well as any other local standards that govern the care planning process (Tunmore and Thomas, 2000).

Prior to or on discharge all service users are subject to the Care Programme Approach (CPA) (DoH, 1999a, 2000) which emphasises the need for planned and co-ordinated delivery of multidisciplinary care. CPA provides the framework for effective mental health care with the principles of assessment, care planning, care co-ordination and reviews that put the service user at the centre of the process. All service users are entitled to a care co-ordinator who is responsible for ensuring close contact with the service user, advising members of the care team of any changes in the care plan or circumstances of the service user. Care plans and documentation should be audited to ensure they reach the minimal desired standard.

Time Frame

Discharge planning is essential to the success of an admission and maintains continuity between the inpatient and community services. It is important that the length of an admission should be as short as possible for the well-being of the patient and to conserve resources and ensure that beds are made available for new admissions. It is also essential that all the resources that are needed to ensure that people remain well once discharged, such as housing, finance, and social support, are all in place at the time of discharge and that there are no omissions in the plan which might hamper the maintenance of recovery. Discharge should therefore be planned for from the time of admission. The length of stay will depend on the individual and the needs identified.

It is important whilst the client is an inpatient to include them in all aspects of their care, and to encourage them to have as much control over their life as they would normally, building on their strengths and weaknesses to enhance their social standing, acceptability and inclusion (Repper and Perkins, 2003). Families/friends and carers can be involved positively in support and care, as continued contact is often a critical part of recovery (Repper and Perkins, 2001) and makes it easier to be accepted socially back into the community.

Evidence Base

Some of the recent research on various aspects of acute inpatient care is imbedded in the material presented elsewhere in this chapter and includes psychosocial interventions, as well as challenging behaviour, observations and engagement.

A recent review by Marshall *et al.* (2003) shows that treatment in day hospitals was feasible for between 23 and 38 per cent of patients currently admitted to hospital and that there was evidence for increased satisfaction for patients. Home based care is the preferred alternative to inpatient care at present and would be feasible for about 55 per cent of patients who would otherwise be admitted. An American based review (Horvitz-Lennon *et al.*, 2001) found that outcomes for partial hospitalisation were no different from those for inpatients but acknowledged that it is not an option for all patients requiring intensive services. Fulford and Farhall (2001) found that the proportion of carers in Victoria who preferred community care over hospital care for acute psychosis was smaller than had been thought.

Dissemination of Information

Thought needs to be given as to how information is disseminated throughout the multidisciplinary team. The service user needs to not only have a copy of their care plan but to understand what it contains, why and to sign it. They also need to know who else will receive this information and the reason why.

Registered nurses are bound by the NMC (2002b) Code of professional conduct guidelines on confidentiality. If information is passed on to other people it should be because they have a genuine need for it. Information can be given to relatives, carers and friends once consent is obtained from the client. If other people or agencies require information then this should be discussed with the client and consent obtained to do so, unless required by law. The service user has a legal right to see their records and consent must be obtained from the client in writing for permission for another person, for example, a solicitor, to see a copy of their records.

Reflective Practice

Reflective practice is achieved in a variety of ways, both formally and informally, for example, through discussions generated during handovers, debriefing sessions, multidisciplinary team meetings and staff meetings. Care plan meetings are a useful way of ensuring that care plans and interventions are discussed fully. Clinical supervision was highlighted in the Health of the Nation report (DoH, 1993) defining it as a formal process, offering professional support and education, leading to enhancements in quality of care.

Most units have a teaching slot in the timetable and many have group supervision led by an independent facilitator. The need for support can conflict with the organisation's requirements for accountability and a frequent difficulty can be cancellation of supervision activities on the basis of staff shortage and workload.

Practice Development

Over the next few years, changes are expected in how mental health care will be delivered. There is an emphasis on creating a demand for alternatives to hospital admissions including short stay units and half way houses. With the advent of home treatment and crisis resolution teams offering 24-hour assessment and support acute inpatient admissions are expected to be reduced.

However there are limitations to home treatment and inpatient care should be seen as an option for care and treatment rather than as a 'failure'. Rotation of staff between teams can maximise resources, expertise and knowledge and offer high levels of consistent and appropriate care and shorter stays. Although there may be a reduction in inpatient beds, inpatient services seem certain to remain an essential part of an integrated mental health service. Simpson and Wright (2003) argue that changing the emphasis of mental health services will lead to a more user led service which is dictated by what service users need and is more likely to promote respect and active engagement, offering choice, information and continuity of care. The implication is that this will in turn have a humanising effect on inpatient services, making them more responsive and less based on notions of custodial care.

The NHS is undergoing a period of significant change and is required (Middleton and Roberts, 2002, p. 3) to examine new approaches to care which:

- focus on the client/service user's journey through the care process;
- are capable of creating alternatives to existing functional and organisational relationships;
- are open to testing and validation;
- are capable of developing process-based performance measures and clinical outcome measures;
- and integrate care across professional and organisational boundaries.

There is substantial support for the need for specialist training for nurses who work in acute care settings (DoH, 1999a, 2001a, 2002; Jones and Lowe, 2001). Jones and Lowe (2003) found that nurses recently qualified tend to favour training in practical nursing skills, including care planning, whilst more experienced nurses prefer information updates. The components considered most important by nurses who work in acute inpatient settings were risk assessment, violence and aggression and psychosocial interventions.

Conclusion

In recent years there has been a considerable amount of criticism of acute inpatient care as poor in quality and environment, lacking choice and information for service users, being custodial and lacking in therapeutic direction. Despite, or perhaps because of this, there is now an increasing amount of research and policy guidance on which to base improvements. Work in acute settings is difficult and demanding and reliable, supportive supervision is important. Although psychopharmacology remains important, with proven effectiveness, the nursing virtues of holistic and humanistic care have been threatened by adherence to a 'sometimes simplistic' medical model. However the traditional values of engagement and therapeutic alliance have recently been re-emphasised. At the same time, psychosocial techniques are becoming established and promise ways of ensuring that more effective interventions are available to inpatient nurses. Provided that the planning and implementation of care can become more responsive and collaborative, acute inpatient care should once again be acknowledged as an interesting, satisfying and highly valued part of a continuum of care.

📖 Suggested Further Reading

Barker, S. (2000) *Environmentally Unfriendly: Patients' Views of Conditions on Psychiatric Wards*, London: Mind.

Schultz, J.M. and Videbeck, S.L. (2002) *Lippincott's Manual of 'Psychiatric Nursing Careplans'*, Philadelphia: Lippencott.

References

Allen, J. and Kingdon, D. (1998) Using cognitive behavioural interventions for people with acute psychosis, *Mental Health Practice*, 1, 9: 14–21.

Baker, J. (2000) Developing psychosocial care for acute psychiatric wards, *Journal of Psychiatric and Mental Health Nursing*, 7: 95–100.

Barker, P.J. (1997) *Assessment in Psychiatric and Mental Health Nursing*, Cheltenham: Stanley Thornes.

Barker, P.J. and Rolfe, G. (2000) Therapeutic nursing care in acute psychiatric wards: engagement over control, *Journal of Psychiatric and Mental Health Nursing*, 7: 179–84.

Bartlett, C., Evans, M., Holloway, J., O'Connor, S. and Harrison, G. (1999) Markers of inappropriate placement in acute psychiatric inpatient care: A five hospital study, *Social Psychiatry & Psychiatric Epidemiology*, 34, 7: 367–75.

Beck, A.T., Ward, C.H., Mendelson, M., Mock, J.E. and Erbaugh, J.K. (1961) An inventory to measure depression, *Archives of General Psychiatry*, 4: 561–71.

Bonner, G., Lowe, T., Rawcliffe, D. and Wellman, N. (2002) Trauma for all: A pilot study of the subjective experience of physical restraint for mental health patients and staff in the UK, *Journal of Psychiatric and Mental Health Nursing*, 4, Aug. 9: 465–73.

Bowles, N. and Dodds, P. (2001) Eye for an eye. Improvements in nurse-patient relations and therapeutic care due to ending formal patient observation on an acute psychiatric ward, *Open Mind*, 108, Mar./Apr.: 18–19.

Bowles, N., Dodds, P., Hackney, D., Sunderland, C. and Thomas, P. (2002) Formal observations and engagement: a discussion paper. Comparison of formal observation and engagement for acute psychiatric patients at risk, *Journal of Psychiatric and Mental Health Nursing*, 3, Jun, 9: 255–60.

Buccheri, R., Trystad, L., Kanas, N., Waldron, B. and Dowling, G. (1996) Auditory hallucinations in schizophrenia: Group experience in examining symptom management and behavioural strategies, *Journal of Psychosocial Nursing and Mental Health Services*, 34: 12–25.

Butterworth, A. (1994) Working in Partnership: a collaborative approach to care. The review of mental health nursing, *Journal of Psychiatric and Mental Health Nursing*, 1, 1: 41–4.

Chadwick, P., Birchwood, M. and Trower, P. (eds) (1996) *Cognitive Therapy for Hallucinations, Delusions and Paranoia*, Chichester: Wiley.

Day, J.C. (1995) A self rating scale for measuring neuroleptic side effects: validation in a group of schizophrenics, *British Journal of Psychiatry*, 166: 650–3.

Department of Health (1983) *The Mental Health Act*, London: HMSO.

Department of Health (1993) *The Health of the Nation: Key Area Hand Books, Mental Illness*, London: Department of Health.

Department of Health (1999a) *National Service Frameworks for Mental Health: Modern Standards and Service Models*, London: HMSO.

Department of Health (1999b) *Report by the Standing Nursing and Midwifery Council, Mental Health Nursing: Addressing Acute Concerns*, London: HMSO.

Department of Health (2000) *Effective Care Coordination in Mental Health Services: Modernising the Care Programme Approach. A Policy Booklet*, London: HMSO.

Department of Health (2001a) *Adult Mental Health: National Service Framework (and the NHS Plan) Workforce Planning, Education and Training. Underpinning Programme: Adult Mental Health Services: Final Report by the Workforce Action Team*, London: HMSO.

Department of Health (2001b) *Safety First. Five Year Report of the Confidential Inquiry into Suicide and Homicide by People with Mental Illness*, London: DoH.

Department of Health (2002) *Mental Health Policy Implementation Guide: Adult Acute Inpatient Care Provision*, London: HMSO.

De Shazer, S. (1988) *Clues: Investigating Solutions in Brief Therapy*, New York: Norton.

Drury, V., Birchwood, M., Cochrane, R. and Macmillan, F. (1996a) Cognitive therapy and recovery from acute psychosis: a controlled trial. I. Impact on psychotic symptoms, *British Journal of Psychiatry*, 5, Nov., 169: 593–601.

Drury, V., Birchwood, M., Cochrane, R. and Macmillan, F. (1996b) Cognitive therapy and recovery from acute psychosis: a controlled trial. II. Impact on recovery time, *British Journal of Psychiatry*, 5, Nov., 169: 602–7.

Emrich, K. (1989) Helping or hurting? Interacting in the psychiatric milieu, *Journal of Psychosocial Nursing and Mental Health Services*, 27: 26–9.

Erikson, H., Tomlin, E., and Swain, M. (1988) *Modeling and role- modeling: A theory and paradigm for nursing*, Lexington, NC: Pine Press.

Evans, R. (2001) Therapeutic directions in acute inpatient psychiatric nursing, *Nursing Standard*, 12, Dec., 5–11, 16: 33–6.

Ford, R., Duncan, G., Warner, L., Hardy, P. and Muijen, M. (1998) One day survey by the Mental Health Act Commission of acute adult psychiatric inpatient wards in England and Wales, *British Medical Journal*, 7168, Nov., 317: 1279–83.

Fulford and Farhall (2001) Hospital versus home treatment for the mentally ill? Preferences of caregivers who have experienced both forms of treatment, *Australian and New Zealand Journal of Psychiatry*, 5, Oct. 35: 619–25.

Gamble, C. (2000) Using a low expressed emotion approach to develop positive thera-peutic alliances, in Gamble, C. and Brennan, G. (eds), *Working with Serious Mental Illness*, London: Bailliere Tindall.

Gournay, K. (2000) *The Recognition, Prevention and Therapeutic Management of Violence in Mental Health Care: A Consultation Document*, London: UKCC.

Gray, R., Wykes, T. and Gournay, K. (2002) From compliance to concordance: a review of the literature on interventions to enhance compliance with antipsychotic medication, *Journal of Psychiatric and Mental Health Nursing*, 9: 277–84.

Higgins, R., Hurst, K. and Wiston, G. (1999) *Psychiatric Nursing Revisited: The Care Provided for Acute Psychiatric Patients*, London: Whurr.

Hogan, T.P., Awad, A.G. and Eastwood, R. (1983) A self-report scale predictive of drug compliance in schizophrenics: reliability and discriminative validity, *Psychological Medicine*, 13: 177–83.

Horvitz-Lennon, M., Normand, S-l.T., Gaccione, P. and Frank, R.G. (2001) Partial versus full hospitalisation for adults in psychiatric distress: A systematic review of the published literature (1957–1997), *American Journal of Psychiatry*, 5, May, 158: 676–85.

Jones, J. and Lowe, T. (2001) The post registration education and training of mental health nurses working in acute inpatient psychiatric settings, *Mental Health Practice*, 4, 5: 8–11.

Jones, J. and Lowe, T. (2003) The education and training needs of qualified mental health nurses working in acute adult mental health services, *Nurse Education Today*, 23, 8 (November): 610–19.

Jones, J., Ward, M., Wellman, N., Hall, J. and Lowe, T. (2000) Psychiatric inpatients experience of observations – a U.K perspective, *Journal of Psychosocial Nursing and Mental Health Services*, 12, 38: 10–20.

Kay, S.R., Fiszbein, A. and Opler, L.A. (1987) Positive and negative syndrome scale, *Schizophrenia Bulletin*, 13: 261–76.

Keirle, P. (1997) Psychiatric inpatient violence: assessment and management of risk, *British Journal of Community Health Nursing*, 2: 191–4.

Leff, J. and Vaughn, C. (1985) *Expressed Emotion in Families*, New York: Guilford.

Linehan, M., Goodstein, J., Nielsen, S. and Chiles, J. (1983) Reasons for staying alive when you are thinking of killing yourself: the reason for living inventory, *Journal of Consulting and Clinical Psychology*, 51: 276–86.

Marshall, M., Crowther, R., Almaraz-Serrano, A.M., Creed, F., Sledge, W.H., Kluiter, H., Roberts, C., Hill, E. and Wiersma, D. (2003) Day hospital versus admission for acute psychiatric disorders, *Cochrane Database Systematic Review 2003*, 1 CD004026.

Middleton, S. and Roberts, A. (2002) *Integrated Care Pathways: A Practical Approach to Implementation*, Oxford: Butterworth Heineman.

Mills, J. (2000) Dealing with voices and strange thoughts, in Gamble, C. and Brennan, G. (eds), *Working with Serious Mental Illness*, London: Bailliere Tindall.

Nelson, H. (1997) *Cognitive Behavioural Therapy with Schizophrenia: A Practice Manual*, Cheltenham: Stanley Thornes.

Nursing and Midwifery Council (2002a) *Guidelines for Records and Record Keeping*, London: NMC.

Nursing and Midwifery Council (2002b) *Code of Professional Conduct*, London: NMC.

Overall, J. and Gorham, D. (1962) The brief psychiatric rating scale, *Psychological Reports*, 10: 799–812.

Parkes, J. (1996) Control and restraint training: a study of its effectiveness in a medium secure psychiatric unit, *Journal of Forensic Psychiatry*, 7: 525–34.

Repper, J. and Perkins, R. (2001) Mental Health Nursing and Social Inclusion, *Mental Health Practice*, 4, 5: 32–9.

Repper, J. and Perkins, R. (2003) *Social Inclusion and Recovery: A Model for Mental Health Practice*, London: Bailliere Tindall.

Rosenthal, T. and McGuinness, T. (1986) Dealing with delusional patients: discovering the distorted truth, *Journal of Mental Health Nursing*, 8: 143–54.

Ryrie, I. (2000) Assessing risk, in Gamble, C. and Brennan, G. (eds), *Working with Serious Mental Illness*, London: Bailliere Tindall.

Sainsbury Centre for Mental Health (1998) *Acute Problems*, London: SCMH.

Sainsbury Centre for Mental Health (2002) *Adult Acute Inpatient Care for People with Mental Health Problems*, London: SCMH.

Simpson, A. and Wright, J. (2003) Admission to a psychiatric unit, in Barker P. (ed)., *Psychiatric and Mental Health Nursing: The Craft of Caring*, London: Arnold.

Stevenson, C., Jackson, S. and Barker, P. (2003) Finding solutions through empowerment: a preliminary study of a solution-oriented approach to nursing in acute psychiatric settings, *Journal of Psychiatric and Mental Health Nursing*, 10: 688–96.

Tunmore, R. and Thomas, B. (2000) Nursing care plans in acute mental health nursing, *Mental Health Practice*, 4, 3: 32–7.

Vaughn, K. and Webster, D. (1995) Brief inpatient psychiatric treatment: Finding solutions, *Issues in Mental Health Nursing*, 16: 519–31.

Webster, D., Vaughn, K. and Martinez, R. (1994) Introducing solution-focused approaches to staff in inpatient psychiatric settings, *Archives of Psychiatric Nursing*, 8: 254–61.

Young, A. (2002) Improving care planning and communication, *Mental Health Practice*, 5, 7: 8–10.

Zigmond, A.S. and Snaith, R.P. (1983) The hospital anxiety and depression scale, *Acta Psychiatrica Scandinavia*, 67: 361–70.

PART IV

Specialist Services Outside of Generic Mental Health

Child and Adolescent Mental Health Services (CAMHS). Taking Care of Business on the Unit!

Dean-David Holyoake

> I've got a care plan, but no one ever looks at it, or does what's in it …
> Me too … it's somewhere under the bed …
> (Personal correspondence from a focus group with young people while preparing to write this chapter.)

Introduction

Child and Adolescent Mental Health Services (CAMHS) is an umbrella term. It is used to describe the range of services delivered by statutory, independent and voluntary agencies to children, young people and their families who are experiencing mental health difficulties. There are, two commonly agreed distinct groups: *Children* (6–12) and *Adolescents* (12–16). I do think it is worthy of note that young people who fall into the age group 16–19 are, always have been, and continue to be a 'difficult to place' group within the specialism. Some services consider them too old for CAMHS, but too young for Adult services. In more recent years, this persistent gap in services has been partly filled by fragmented attempts at providing limited regional services. A roll the dice and keep them crossed approach to service planning.

All CAMHS are organised within the tradition of the ubiquitous Tier framework. The best way for me to explain the breakdown is through the use of Figure 10.1.

There are approximately 80 adolescent Tier 4 services in England and Wales (QNIC, 2001). However, the number of professionals working in these services have not been calculated for the public sphere.

Tier 1   Primary or Direct Contact Services

● Consists of GPs, Teachers, Health Visitors, Social Workers, School Nurses, Voluntary Workers, Juvenile Justice Workers.

● Usually the first point of contact.

Tier 2   Individual Specialist Mental Health Workers

● This is the core of CAMHS. Services are delivered by individual professionals, supporting Tier 1 professionals through training and consultancy.

● Professionals include: Clinical Psychologists, Educational Psychologists, Community Mental Health Nurses, Psychotherapists, Pupil Support Teachers, Specifically Tasked Social Workers, Teachers.

Tier 3   Interventions Offered by Teams of Staff from Specialist CAMHS

● Usually a Multi-Disciplinary Team headed by a Consultant Psychiatrist and Community Psychiatric Nurses. Other professionals include Social Workers, Psychologists and other professionals involved in joint working.

Tier 4   Very Specialised Interventions and Care

As noted by Richardson and Joughin (2000) this tier provides for highly specific and complex problems that require considerable resources. These include:

● inpatient psychiatric provision for adolescents (adolescent units).

● secure provision and other specialised service provision.

Figure 10.1   The CAMHS Tier framework (HAS, 1995)

Prevalence and Population

This chapter is concerned with those adolescents (12–16) in Tier 4 services. There are other types of specialised services for young people aged 6–12 which include both community and inpatient facilities. As with adolescent CAMHS these services are regionally co-ordinated and therefore differ from place to place. This can mean frustrating long waiting times for access to community teams and Consultant Child Psychiatrists.

Amongst the child and adolescent population as a whole, rates of mental health problems vary, but the frequently quoted figure of one in five young people reflects a significant level of disturbance (Lindsey, 2000). Similarly the Audit Commission (1999) emphasised that besides the substantial number of young people requiring specialist types of service; there is also difficulty in providing enough resources for CAMHS to meet the needs of the population. As noted by FOCUS (2000) in 1996 it was estimated that only 20–30 per cent children who had significant psychological problems received specialist professional help.

The main illnesses treated in adolescent units are in my opinion arguably different from those suggested diagnoses often cited as being predominant among the average CAMHS population. However, they include:

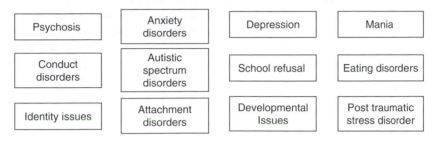

Defined conditions that can either help or hinder young people making sense of their well-being. Some young people can be treated at home for their condition, but it seems that it is the intensity and degree of severity that signifies admission into an adolescent unit. Unfortunately, it can be a lack of resources (professional personnel and beds) that determines what is available. This means that safety, risk and self-harm are key issues in determining admission and referral patterns. Statistics concerning different specific illnesses blur the issue of resources for this age group, through diagnostic grouping, see Figure 10.2.

Referrals

In practice, the Audit Commission found that National Health Service (NHS) clinicians provide the main referral route to specialist CAMHS. More than half the referrals came from GPs (52 per cent) and 15 per cent from Paediatricians, with the remainder being varied between Trusts (Audit Commission, 1999).

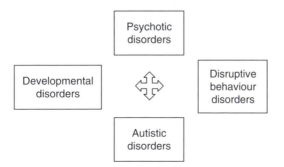

Figure 10.2 Simplistic spectrum of child and adolescent mental illness

The referral process is a theoretical process involving numerous groups of multidisciplinary professionals working together to provide a seamless service. In reality, another referral process emerges. A referral is made to a specialist child and adolescent consultant and community team. The waiting time can be anything up to 18 months for an assessment and then treatment, which could mean referral to the regional adolescent unit (due to a general shortage of beds young people are rarely referred out of their own region).

Admission could then take up to another 6 months until a bed becomes available. Most direct referrals are made via Accident and Emergency department and thus the whole theoretical referral process is leapfrogged as consultants have to calculate the risk and needs of young people presented before them. Indeed, it has been found that health authorities differ in the range and scope of measures used to evaluate such needs (Audit Commission, 1999). In addition, health authorities vary in the extent to which they 'work closely' with other agencies to identify needs.

Theoretical Frameworks

There are a number of theoretical frameworks for the nurse working with children. The most relevant are familiar for their exploration of childhood experience. These include the extensive work of Bowlby (1980) through attachment theory and issues of bonding for children. Also, the work of Piaget (1952) determined a framework for cognitive development. This assists in providing further understanding of the child's viewpoint. Erikson (1968) identified a life cycle, which is navigated. The mental health nurse can utilise this framework when gaining recognition of the trials a person experiences in order to progress. Young people move through various stages in most of these developmental models, such as; 'Industry vs. Inferiority', 'Identity vs. Role Confusion' and 'Intimacy vs. Isolation' (Erikson, 1968).

For adolescents and particularly those in adolescent units, there is a focus on the types of theoretical knowledge postulated by these developmental models, but also on models that incorporate the use of Milieu Therapy which attempts in some ways to construct a safe environment that includes stable and consistent relationships for all the young people (see Association of Therapeutic Communities, 2001; Charterhouse group, 2000). Also, the use of Systems Theory for understanding family relationships and the dynamics at work between people is an important driver in most adolescent unit's philosophy (see Dallos and Draper, 2000 and for Family Theory: Bloch *et al.*, 1981).

In line with psychodynamic theories and systems theory the philosophical foundations consider the way individuals function within groups and learn about themselves, others and daily experiences. It is usually the intention to aid a type of reframing process and an understanding of dynamics between the interplay of peer relationships. Through a consideration of cognitive and emotional need as with most therapy, the variety of interventions include play therapy, recreation, creative music, drama and so on. Each group having its own defined therapeutic objectives, which can be seen to 'bleed' into many activities.

Most adolescent units adopt a hybrid approach to treatment provision.

Principles and Skills

There are many principles required for working with young people. The influence of a power relationship is exaggerated, with the nurse being an adult as well as therapist. Awareness of this important factor is necessary. The focus on the child/young person warrants specialist skills and a level of respect, tolerance and understanding. Some of the skills required are:

- A respect for children and their needs.
- Ability to establish a therapeutic relationship with children and young people.
- Communication skills to build essential rapport with families and significant others.
- Confident working within a multidisciplinary context.
- Child orientated flexibility to engage in relationships.
- Role modelling.
- Maintaining appropriate boundaries and role responsibilities.
            (Adapted from Soppitt and Vostanis, 2000; Croom, 2003)

Assessment

Approach

Most young people show their distress. That is, significant adults begin to notice that they are not their usual self. S/he may be more aggressive, missing dad, quiet in school, wetting the bed, not coping well with exams, being bullied, isolating themselves, lost interest in usual habits and routines. Assessment by professionals will then begin to explore the nature of family dynamics and relationship issues, as well as physical investigations. It may be that the child/young person is presenting a risk (self-harm, threatening others, suicidal, risky behaviours including drug use, not responding to authority). If this is the case, there are a number of significant risk assessment tools (see Tunmore, 2000).

In practice, assessment usually takes place during a pre-admission and or during the first meeting by the young person and the professional team. It is a chance for the key professionals and the young person to 'check one another out'. In this sense, the initial assessment is about starting a relationship, which will progress into a care planning partnership. For the professional, there is also the need to assess the level of understanding and maturity of the young person so that the future care planning can be needs led.

The primary assessment tool is the 'use of self'. That is, over time, the nurse attempts to build a relationship and provide conditions that allow the young person to discover him/herself and expose their hurt. This is what adolescent units do particularly well. They enable a holding environment to occur, thus allowing young people to feel contained and safe. Adolescent units provide the opportunity for groups of young people to be *observed*. It is this surveillance that is another primary source of assessment in helping clarify and assess young people's needs.

All assessments in CAMHS will take into consideration issues pertaining to the Children Act (1989) (DoH, 1991). In particular, the principle that young people and their families should be fully involved in the strategies impacting on their welfare. This means that the days of 'doctor knows best' are long gone. Young people are expected to be full participants in the development of their own care planning with a full multidisciplinary team (MDT).

The young person is always regarded as part of a family and unit milieu, as well as the notion of being a unique individual person (which is often the focus of modern care planning theory). It is now considered best practice to involve the young person regardless of age in all parts of the assessment. This often means that a young person will be present during the dialogue with parents. Issues to do with confidentiality will always be observed if the young person is over 16 and or able to make informed decisions for themselves. This means, that if a young person wants certain information unknown to their parents, then this will be discussed and adhered to.

Process

The moment a young person enters CAMHS there is the usual requirement that some type of assessment takes place. This will usually include a *risk assessment* and sometimes more specific tests to try and ascertain cognitive abilities, educational levels and the like. This primary phase of any care plan development is the stage in which young people and their families are introduced to the team they will be working with and informed of the value of their input. This includes explaining that involvement in care planning is expected.

The assessment is usually directed by the considerations shown in Figure 10.3: environmental, family, support systems, cultural and spiritual factors. It is usual that individual adolescent units have set assessment criteria, which are now beginning to take the views of young people into account.

Assessing mental illness in children and adolescents can be a difficult process due to the developmental turmoil that is part of growing up. We all know about (or think we do) the temperamental teenager phase, but mental health issues are never a simple matter.

Information Gathering

In the first place, most information gathering is done through an interviewing type process in which professionals will ask questions about problem areas. Forms and risk assessment tools will be used, but as the young person settles into the unit the process becomes one that is ongoing. The process mentioned earlier means the nurse has to make a therapeutic use of self, but this doesn't mean all information gathering has to be 'dull'. In fact it is important that young people are seen in a variety of settings within the unit, for example, groups, individually, school, having fun and socialising with others. It is from these observations that care plans are formulated with the young person. In addition, the use of play provides many opportunities for professionals to gather information such as:

- Is the young person able to trust?
- Is the child too trusting?
- Is the child sociable?
- Can they take criticism?
- Can they respond to instruction?

Tools Used

Some Recognisable Assessment Tools Used in CAMHS:

Marital Satisfaction Index (Azrin *et al.*, 1973)
Goldberg's General Health Questionnaire (Goldberg, 1978)
A brief index of social support (SSI) (Brown and Harris, 1978)
Bene–Anthony Family Relations Test (Bene, 1978)
Children's Depression Scale (Lang and Tisher, 1978)
Eyberg Child Behaviour Inventory (Robinson *et al.*, 1980)
Culture-Free Self-Esteem Inventory (Battle, 1981)
The Parent/Child Game (Forehand and McMahon, 1981)
The McMaster Family Assessment Device (Epstein *et al.*, 1983)
The Family Grid (Davis and Rushton, 1991)
The Parenting Stress Index (Abidin, 1992)
Darlington Family Assessment System Package (Wilkinson, 1993)
The Family System Test (Gehring and Marti, 1993)
Adolescent Coping Scale (Frydenberg and Lewis, 1993)
Millon Adolescent Personality Inventory (Millon, 1993)
'Bag of feelings drawing task' (Binney and Wright, 1997)

Risk Priorities

As with other specialities in health care there are a number of risk priorities encountered in most CAMHS. Principally, these centre on the young person attempting to 'harm themselves'. There are a number of typical behaviours that will be recognisable in most CAMHS. These include self-harming by cutting self, attempting to commit suicide by hanging, poisons (over dose) and drowning. Other dangerous behaviour includes throwing oneself in front of cars and placing oneself in risky situations, for example, high buildings. In addition, there are other risk issues such as the use of harmful chemicals and drugs, anti-social behaviour, physical harm to others, fire setting and even vulnerability. Units sometimes use checklists to ensure that all facets of risk are considered as an ongoing process.

Care Planning

How Plan is Determined

If we move beyond the care plan as a structure it is possible to see that one of the most important things for young people and staff alike is the process involved in care planning. That is, the fact that nowadays, young people contribute to their care plans and subsequent evaluations and reviews. They are no *longer done to, but rather part of*. For good or ill, this framework usually takes the form of regular meetings with a *Key Nurse* or *Care Co-ordinator* to 'go through the care plan and check that it is up-to date'. On the face of it, this does not appear to be rocket science, but the process demonstrates more than the outcome driven objectives of the care plan ethos. In fact the process brings the humanness to the whole affair. So, a young person like Joe (see Case Example) could expect to have a Care Co-ordinator, but that doesn't mean that there will be a standardised care plan or care pathway. I would argue that regardless of how honourable this ideal would be that in practice it does not happen, because different nurses bring different things to the care planning process. As we see in the case example, assessment and treatment can be dependent on the relationship with the care co-ordinator.

There is no set formula than one that fosters the young person's imagination (or the relationship). This is particularly true when care plans incorporate a more 'behavioural' management approach. For example, some young people need the use of charts, stars and or point systems to help pinpoint change behaviours. This 'when/then' approach to care planning is peculiar to working with young people, for example:

> *When* Joe has attended 10 hours (per week) of education classes, *then* he will be able to attend the local shops with peers.

Some of the pertinent issues related to the Case Example have already been alluded to, but there may be a number of overlapping criteria that motivate the professional parts of the care plan and the process. Some of these may include:

- The focus needing to be *contextual*. That is, about the individual young person within the context of the family system.
- Family system behaviour represents the most effective *level of functioning* at that given point in time.
- For some: individual symptoms and behaviours are *defence mechanisms* designed to maintain ego integrity and reduce anxiety.
- Support and empathy are necessary to establish a relationship that provides for effective *problem resolution*.
- Behaviour of one of the family system affects all of the family and there is always a *reciprocal response*.
- Interventions should be directed towards alleviating symptomatic behaviour and *assisting parents* in providing more effective strategies of parenting.
- Professionals need to recognise their own *emotional responses* to parents and children.

We should never underestimate the importance of *allowing time* and showing *attention*. I have known many good Key Nurses fail to capitalise on novel care planning opportunities because they have cancelled meetings with young people or generally given the message that other things are more important than 'sorting the care plan'. The necessity to establish the developmental needs of the young person by providing *age appropriate* approaches also moves us further away from the traditional adult approaches to care planning.

The special considerations above provide the backdrop that professionals in Tier 3 and Tier 4 CAMHS generally consider when attempting to plan care with young people and their families.

Practical Application

We establish and agree what it is we think the young person needs. We determine and agree what is a reasonable health target, ones that are achievable. We wrestle and think through all of the typical nursing interventions that we can put in place in order to allow 'change' to happen. We break it all down into stages or the traditional short- and long-term goals. We consider contingency plans and feel relieved when we sign, date and close the folder with the firm conviction that we will evaluate it (the plan) within a week. Two weeks later we justify that 'well two weeks isn't bad'. There are no professional guidelines as to how this overall process should occur. It is about negotiation with the young person and in most cases, being a responsible adult providing boundaries to ensure that the care planning actually takes place.

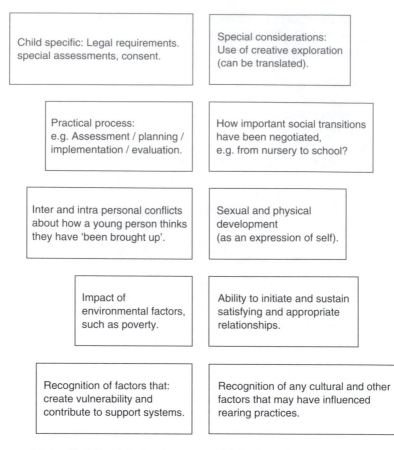

Figure 10.3 Building blocks: factors to think about (special considerations)

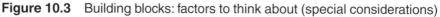

The above satirical look at care planning is a recognisable one, but we know that nowadays the young person will be involved in devising the care plan. Joe (Case Example) had his own, signed copy. But this brings with it a mass of inherent practical difficulties:

First: the nature of the language used.
Second: the typical topography (layout) of the traditional care plan (e.g. date, objective, action, evaluation and signature).
Third: the central importance of the plan in the overall big picture, which to a teenager always feels far removed from the current discomfort they currently experience.

Whatever the practical issues that attempt to limit the notion and usefulness of care planning *per se*, it seems (in my opinion at least) that young people usually need lengthy and detailed work to unravel their (often hidden) needs. This unravelling usually involves their peers (social aspects of the care plan including attendance in all group work and encouragement to interact), a detailed listening to their stories (weekly 1 : 1 psychotherapy and regular meetings with Key Nurse to evaluate care plan) and consistent support for their family and other significant relationships (access to talk about family issues, parenting groups, attendance at family therapy and structured psycho-education groups). All of these are pertinent to the care many young people would have discussed and signed for in their care plan. This might be encapsulated in a typical line such as: *Joe will attend all groups and individual therapy*, but care planning does not have to be this predictable.

One advantage of actually having a young person as an inpatient is that observation and therefore assessment, planning and implementation of a care plan is made more simple, consistent and immediate. In addition, treatment and the milieu can be more easily controlled. So, in theory the care plan can be in a constant process of validation.

Young people and their families require different things from care planning. I would suggest that the medium best suited for a young person to understand, enjoy and participate fully should always be employed. This may mean using drawing, paint, crayons, movement and even sand which can be formally translated into 'written adult' and then checked by the young person. I'm not suggesting that drawn pictures should replace the formal and legal requirements of the care plan, but rather, a child-centred emphasis to its development. When I worked with Joe, we tried an *experiment*. He wanted to write his own clinical notes. We explored the possibility with the wider team and came up with an agreeable solution (see Case Example).

Some of the special considerations that I have found important include the use of *praise* (positive *feedback*) as a simple yet astonishingly effective tool for motivating young people. Young people are quite capable of being proud of their care planning and even more robust at ensuring nudging their Key Nurses complete the weekly evaluation. In addition to praise, following the young person's *lead* allows for the savouring of opportunity and trust to complete set tasks. It is also important to breakdown into chunks (*chunking*) so that the process doesn't become too overwhelming. To do this the Key Nurse might want to ensure that there is an overall *time frame* which helps make the young person feel *contained* with a safety net.

The inherent need to ensure boundaries are maintained is always an ongoing commitment, but for some this type of care planning is very effective.

In addition to rewarding appropriate behaviour there is sometimes also the need to *ignore, distract* or make *clear commands* within the care plan. For example, for Joe this often meant that he would not be able to go out in the evening unless chores had been completed. In his care plan this included possible sanctions. The primary one being what we began to term: 'being blanked'. In professional speak it could be likened to '*reflective time out*'. In short, he'd be expected to spend 10 minutes writing down or drawing the consequences of his actions for the given behaviour. This would then be given as feedback to me.

Additional Care Planning

Often there is a co-morbidity within CAMHS. Children will present with other disorders as well as the dominant feature. Thus, additional care is required and a plan of action necessary. The agreement of the child is paramount (Soppitt and Vostanis, 2000). Certain disabilities and other developmental needs will require additional care planning. For example a young person who requires specialist education may need to have weekly trips to specialist language facilities. Also young people who are still physically developing sometimes require multiple trips to a dentist, optician and other specialist health services. All of which have to be considered in the holistic approach to the care planning process, because they can't go alone (see Figure 10.3).

Case Example

Background

Joe (13) was referred by his GP to the Adolescent Unit 50 miles away from his home because there were no local Tier 4 services in his region. Prior to admission he had become increasingly more withdrawn at home and school. After his parents had taken him to see his GP he was initially referred to his local Tier 3 child and adolescent consultant who prescribed him medication to help with what his mother described as: 'his concentration problems'. In addition to antipsychotic medication Joe was also referred to a community nurse. Due to demands in the overall service, his treatment plan amounted to meeting only twice in the three-month period prior to admission. During his admission Joe's mother reported that his treatment plan had been virtually non-existent during this period. In her worry she'd taken to surfing the Internet to try and find out more about what she called Joe's 'complaint'. She spoke about 'joined up working', 'seamless service provision' and 'being client centred'. I looked over to Joe (who appeared embarrassed by his parents concerns – asking for them to 'just leave') and said that from now on Joe would be expected to be fully involved in all stages of his care planning. He looked down and sighed. He didn't know it, but he'd be in the unit for the next year of his life.

Admission Period

Joe had been in the unit for a couple of days before I arranged to get down to the 'serious business' of the care planning.

'The serious business?' I asked.
'Yeah, the others have told me that everyone has to have a care plan and that it's boring stuff … no one ever looks at it anyway, it's phoney.'

'We need to make sure that yours is different then don't we.'

'We do?'

'We need to take care of business.'

By gently interacting with Joe during the first few weeks I was able to begin building rapport and establish a care planning relationship. The notion of this 'process' as being the most important aspect is probably well driven home by now, but without it, the only 'objective' we could have met would have been one of ensuring a *phoney care plan* was in place. It was during this period that Joe undertook a number of assessments.

Joe was given a special space in his nursing notes which he would complete each day. These reflections were in addition to the ongoing nursing notes. After two weeks we began to compare. It was surprising how similar the entries were. In his care plan, we made it official: 'Joe will record in his notes on a daily basis'. This then led us to experiment even more. Joe suggested that he record his feelings and I said we could also grade his positive behaviour towards other people. So, sure enough, over the next two weeks we found that our scoring was remarkably similar. We were able to implement this type of *collaborative care planning* through the full support of the MDT.

Both Joe and I decided that there should be three rules about our care planning relationship (this kept to the idea that young people work better with brief instruction and logical plans). First, that all care should have stages. Second, all care should be engaging and try and be fun. Third, Joe was to match my input. In short, this transpired into us meeting at least weekly (sometimes for care planning walks) specifically to discuss the care plan and start taking care of business. The primary interventions centred on Joe's attendance in therapy groups, 1 : 1 therapy work and an increase in the amount of educational work expected of him. In addition other interventions included negotiated free time, which could include recreational activities with single staff members and peers.

Discharge

Recognising the fact that most of my well made intentions were often scuppered in the 'real world' I was very proud of Joe when his day came to be discharged. We'd agreed a plan that he'd have an *integrated* return back home and into a special educational school. This meant that for four weeks he'd attend the unit twice a week so that I could 'keep an eye on him'. The partnership had worked and although he often complained: 'I can't get away with anything while you're around!' he went on to maintain his progress through his own success.

Documentation

There is nowadays a recognition that multidisciplinary notes are the most useful way to ensure that care is more consistent and 'joined up'. Therefore, most young people have shared notes between all professionals. Access to these notes by the young person is usually allowed, but this may be 'negotiated access', in that professionals need to ensure that any information doesn't upset the young person. Having access to notes by the young person is seen as being an important part of the empowering partnership of care planning. Access to notes by parents is an issue that will usually involve discussion with the young person regardless of age. Seeking approval and ensuring confidentiality is central to building trust. Young people are also made aware that there are no secrets between members of the team.

The Care Programme Approach or CPA model is also another framework more familiar to those working in adult specialities. There is at present no legal or professional responsibility to use this in CAMHS. However, some adolescent unit teams choose to use the CPA framework to structure the overall care planning process.

Time Frame

There is an expectation in most adolescent units that care plans will be evaluated at least weekly, but it is also understood that this standard is sometimes unrealistic in its intent, because sometimes things change rapidly (Psychosis) and for others change is very slow (e.g. Eating disorders). Having acknowledged this, most nurses will attempt to spend at least one hour a week care planning with each young person in their direct care. It is usually the case that the average admission to an adolescent unit is substantially longer than that experienced in acute adult services. A young person may stay anything between three months to a year in the unit depending on their needs. Interventions vary, but a long-term view will be taken in which there will be an expectation that community services will become more involved as the young person moves towards discharge. The process of discharge planning will involve assessing educational needs as well as any future psychiatric needs, so it will usually involve liaison with educational services, teachers and special needs personnel.

Evidence Base

There is now a considerable amount of evidence suggesting that young people and their families are best helped when they are fully involved in the planning of their own care (Audit Commission, 1999). Nowhere else is this better shown than in legislation pertaining to the welfare of young people. This is specifically true for 'looked after young people'. In addition to the *Mental*

Health Act (DoH, 1983), young people have the umbrella protection of a number of other acts, having some bearing on the way care planning is considered. The two primary pieces of legislation are the *UN Convention on the Rights of the Child* (1989) and *the Children Act* (1989). Both of these afford young people rights in addition to those applicable to adults. Therefore, the *welfare of the child is the paramount consideration* in court proceedings.

This has implications for health professionals working with young people who have been involved in family disharmony. It means that wherever possible children should be brought up and cared for by their families and be informed of what is happening to them.

Parents continue to have parental responsibility for their children, even when they are no longer living with them. They should be kept informed about their children and participate when decisions are made about their children's future. So when a care plan is being devised in all of its various stages these issues need consideration.

Issues related to the *consent, confidentiality, cultural diversity* and the need to be kept *informed* begin to make certain issues very complex.

Dissemination of Information

It is usual that most young people are quite able to make decisions regarding the nature of their own care. With the partnership of a Key Nurse, the care planning process can quite easily tackle issues regarding both consent and confidentiality. This important point is related to what is known as the Gillick Principle:

> A person under the age of 16 shall have the legal capacity to consent to any surgical, medical or dental procedure or treatment where, in the opinion of a qualified medical practitioner attending him, he is capable of understanding the nature and possible consequences of the procedure or treatment. (Taken from Spender *et al.*, 2001, p. 24)

The issue of confidentiality is central if professionals are to begin and sustain trusting relationships with young people. If a young person has the capacity to consent and understand their wishes regardless of their age it is an important consideration for all professionals. This includes doctors, nurses, teachers, social workers and parents. It is usually the practice that any sharing of information has the consent of the young person and usually in their presence if they choose.

The same principle applies to all assessments and treatments. Some young people have specific issues that they want to be kept private from their parents such as matters to do with sexual health. For others, issues to do with their parents are central to why they are in the service. The need for professionals to foster good working relationships with the entire family while maintaining a young person's confidentiality can be a tricky task. In practice, it is very difficult to conduct a mental health assessment without a young person's consent, so every effort should be made to obtain this as well as parental consent (Spender *et al.*, 2001).

Reflective Practice

It is considered best practice for all practitioners to partake in clinical supervision and it is usually the case that most do. In addition to individual supervision in which clinical issues are discussed many units also have large group type supervision. The purpose of this is to allow the MDT staff group space to explore clinical issues that occur within the therapeutic environment. This may be related to care planning issues as well as matters to do with relationship dynamics between staff members and young people. Having acknowledged the importance of supervision, it is usually the case that practitioners have to ensure time is made in order to have supervision.

Practice Development

During the last ten years it has been recognised that CAMHS has to grow, change and adapt if it is to best provide for the population it serves (HAS, 1995; Audit Commission, 1999; QNIC, 2000). This has meant that a number of developments including the emergence of new roles such as the Primary Care Worker and new interfaces and subspecialities (16–19 age group) will more than likely symbolise the next 10 years.

At present there are no regulated or set qualifications nurses need to work in CAMHS. Therefore, the speciality is able to attract a wide range of interested practitioners and is not limited to a certain core group. It is also the case that in some regions it is becoming increasingly clear that a good skill mix in the staff team helps maintain a professional balance within the team. Therefore, more and more units are considering the role of specialist children's nurses, general nursing qualifications and all other specialist practitioners. Some nurses choose to continue their education and take a post-registration qualification (usually at degree level). In the long term, these provide them with more advanced skills, confidence and the chance to help advance a young yet expanding speciality.

Conclusion

The clinical responsibility for the nursing care plan always lies with the Key Nurse. It is the Key Nurse who has to cajole the young person, try and find them in the unit and try and motivate them to think about the issues that are important for them. The stage of planning and implementing interventions relies on the establishment of some sort of data collection process in order to provide prompt and effective treatment to restore individuals and their families to optimum levels of functioning. In the long term the same planning will progress and evolve into a discharge-planning phase, which will assess community resources and educational needs. It is at this point that it is easy to recognise the benefits of CPA principles in attempting to plan for seamless care between services, stuff like training for staff, supervision and joint care planning.

The world is a fast changing place. Young people of today expect ready-made objects and why should care plans be any different? They desire good service and they want it now! Care planning within this speciality is about being prepared to stay the distance for the whole journey, no matter what it takes. But in this postmodern world there is never any substitute for promoting the therapeutic relationship so that you can just simply take care of business.

📖 Suggested Further Reading

Barwick, N. (2002) *Clinical Counselling in Schools*, London: Routledge.
House, A. (2002) *The First Session with Children and Adolescents*, London: Routledge.
Spender, Q., Salt, N., Dawkins, J., Kendrick, T. and Hill, P. (2001) *Child Mental Health in Primary Care*, Oxon: Radcliffe Medical Press.
Wilkinson, I. (2002) *Child and Family Assessment*, London: Routledge.

References

Abidin, R. (1992) The determinants of parenting behaviour, *Journal of Clinical Child Psychology*, 21: 407–12.

Association of Therapeutic Communities (2001) *Kennard-Lees Audit Checklist II*, London: Association of Therapeutic Communities.

Audit Commission (1999) *Children in Mind: Child and Adolescent Mental Health Services (National Report)*, Oxon: Audit Commission Publications.

Azrin, N., Naster, B. and Jones, R. (1973) Reciprocity counselling: a rapid learning-based procedure for marital counselling, *Behaviour Research and Therapy*, 11: 365–82.

Battle, J. (1981) *Culture-Stress SEI (self-esteem inventories) for Children and Adults*, Seattle: Special Child Publications.

Bene, E. (1978) *The Family Relations Test: Children's Version*, Windsor: NFER-Nelson.

Binney, V. and Wright, J. (1997) The bag of feelings: an ideographic technique for the assessment and exploration of feelings in children and adolescents, *Clinical Child Psychology and Psychiatry*, 2, 3: 449–62.

Bloch, S., Crouch, E. and Reibstein, J. (1981) Therapeutic factors in group psychotherapy *Archives of General Psychiatry*, 38: 519–26.

Bowlby, J. (1980) *Loss: Sadness and Depression*, Vol. 3 *of Attachment and Loss*, Harmondsworth: Penguin.

Brown, G. and Harris, T. (1978) *Social Origins of Depression: A Study of Psychiatric Disorder in Women*, London: Tavistock Press.

Charterhouse Group (2000) *Standards and Criteria for Therapeutic Community Childcare, Health and Education*. Charterhouse Group.

Croom, S. (2003) Groupwork with Children and Adolescents, in Barker, P. (ed.), *Psychiatric and Mental Health Nursing: The Craft Of Caring*, London: Arnold.

Dallos, R. and Draper, R. (2000) *An Introduction to Family Therapy: Systemic Theory and Practice*, Buckingham: Open University Press.

Davis, H. and Rushton, R. (1991) Counselling and supporting parents of children with developmental delay: a research evaluation, *Journal of Mental Deficiency Research*, 35: 89–112.

Department of Health (1983) *The Mental Health Act*, London: HMSO.

Department of Health (1991) *The Children Act 1989: An Introductory Guide for the NHS*, London: HMSO.

Epstein, N., Baldwin, L. and Bishop, D. (1983) The McMaster family assessment device, *Journal of Marital and Family Therapy*, 9: 171–80.

Erikson, E. (1968) *Identity: Youth and Crisis*, London: Faber.

FOCUS (2000) A collaborative approach to care, in (eds), *The Mental Health Needs of Looked After Children*. [Richardson, J. and Joughin, C.] The Royal College of Psychiatrists, London, pp. 11–14

Forehand, M. and McMahon, R. (1981) *Helping the Non-compliant Child: A Clinician's Guide to Parent Training*, London: Guilford Press.

Frydenberg, E. and Lewis, R. (1993) *Adolescent Coping Scale*, Melbourne: ACER.

HAS (1995) *Child and Adolescent Mental Health Services: The Commissioning Role and Management of Child and Adolescent Mental Health Services*. An NHS Health Advisory Service Thematic Review, London: HMSO.

Gehring, T. and Marti, D. (1993) The family system test: differences in perception of family structures between nonclinical and clinical children, *Journal of Child Psychology and Psychiatry*, 34, 3: 363–77.

Goldberg, G. (1978) *Manual of the General Health Questionnaire*, Windsor: NFER-Nelson.

Lang, M. and Tisher, M. (1978) *Children's Depression Scale*, Windsor: NFER-Nelson.

Lindsey, C. (2000) Why focus on the mental health needs of looked after children?, In Richardson, J. and Joughan, C. (eds), *The Mental Health Needs of Looked After Children*. (Ed: Richardson, J and Joughin, C.) The Royal College of Psychiatrists, London. pp. 7–10.

Millon, T. (1993) *Millon Adolescent Clinical Inventory*, Minneapolis: NCS.

Piaget, J. (1952) *The Origin of Intelligence in the Child*, London: Routledge & Kegan Paul.

QNIC (2001) Quality Network for In-patient CAMHS Child and Adolescent Units in England and Wales: Unit Directory (first edn), London: Royal College of Psychiatry.

Richardson, J. and Joughin, C. (ed.) (2000) *The Mental Health Needs of Looked After Children*, London: The Royal College of Psychiatrists.

Robinson, E., Eyberg, S. and Ross, A. (1980) The standardization of an inventory of child conduct problem behaviours, *Journal of Clinical Child Psychology*, 9: 22–9.

Soppitt, R. and Vostanis, P. (2000) Children's and adolescent's difficulties, in Newell, R. and Gournay, K. (eds), *Mental Health Nursing: An Evidence-based Approach*, London: Churchill Livingstone.

Spender, Q., Salt, N., Dawkins, J., Kendrick, T., and Hill, P. (2001) *Child Mental Health in Primary Care*, Oxon: Radcliffe Medical Press.

Tunmore, R. (2000) *Practitioner assessment skills*. In (eds) (Thompson. T and Mathias, P.) *Lyttle's Mental Health and Disorder* (third edn), London: Bailliere-Tindall, pp. 482–504.

UN (1989) *UN Convention on Rights of the Child 1989*, London: HMSO.

Wilkinson, I. (1993) *Family Assessment*, London: Gardner Press.

CHAPTER 11

Older People with Mental Health Problems

Jayne Sayers

Introduction

Many of the developments to close the large Victorian Asylums from 1950 onwards reflected suspicion about the standards of care in mental hospitals and concern for abuse (Muijen, 1995). Traditional services were often seen as reinforcing the stigma and marginalisation of older people. Subsequently, this resulted in a shift towards the development of care at home or more misleadingly, community care services, within a 'mixed economy of care' (DoH, 1989).

The problems associated with the care of older adults with mental health issues are very different from those experienced by younger people. Carers are often in advancing years themselves and left with critical responsibilities, coupled with increasing reduction in NHS continuing care beds. In addition, the increase in the numbers of older people who need care coincides with a decrease in the number of family members who are able to care for them.

Thus, the success of an older person with mental health problems, particularly a dementing illness remaining in the community, depends fundamentally on the range of accommodation and services available.

The clinical settings for providing care continue to grow fuelled by the NHS Plan (DoH, 2000) and The National Service Framework for Older people (DoH, 2001). They now include intermediate care provisions in order to prevent unnecessary admission to hospital, supporting timely discharge and maximising independent living. This chapter will mainly focus on the care of older adults in the community setting.

Prevalence and Population

England has an increasing ageing population: one-fifth is aged over 60 years and 8 million people are aged over 65 (DoH, 2001). This is largely because throughout most of the twentieth century survival prospects have improved,

Table 11.1   Prevalence of dementia according to age

Age	Percentage
65 years	5
80 years	20

mainly because of decline in infant mortality and increasingly due to reductions in mortality in late middle age and early old age.

Between 1995 and 2025 the number of people over 90 will double (DoH, 2001). The absence of physical ill health and psychological problems is crucial to enjoying life at this stage. Whilst mental health decline is not an automatic feature of ageing, psychiatric epidemiological studies have shown that mental health problems are common in older people, especially depression and dementia (Copeland *et al.*, 1987; Evans and Katona, 1993).

The prevalence and incidence of dementia rises with age. Approximately 600,000 people in the UK have dementia and it is estimated that by 2026 there will be 840,000 rising to 1.2 million by 2050 (DoH, 2001). In addition approximately 17,000 people below the age of 65 have dementia, although this figure is likely to be more of an estimate than an accurate reflection, as often younger people face years of investigations in the NHS before a diagnosis is made (see Table 11.1).

Actual estimates of prevalence of depression in older people vary, but at any one time, around 10–15 per cent of the population aged over 65 will have depression severe enough to merit clinical intervention. Less common are more severe states of depression affecting 3–5 per cent of older adults. Mania can also occur in later life with no history of mood disorders although again is not as common as depression and usually occurs in the context of either depression or mania, that is bipolar affective disorder. However, many older people have anxiety disorders or misuse alcohol (Copeland *et al.*, 1987).

Schizophrenia in people over the age of 65 occurs in 2 population groups: those people who were diagnosed in early adulthood and have lived with the illness throughout life; and those who receive a diagnosis in old age. Late onset schizophrenia is termed 'paraphrenia' and is considered to be very rare (Naguib and Levy, 1992).

Complex Population

Mental health issues in older people are often not detected and remain untreated due to the complex relationship between physical and mental health (psychiatric disorders associated with physical disease are less likely to be acknowledged as needing treatment in their own right). Further complicating factors include:

• The impact of life events on an older person,
• Current socio-economic status,
• Lack of specialist knowledge in primary care and acute hospitals,

- Ageist assumptions with resultant impact on care practices and service provision.

Indeed, GPs need to be suitably trained if they are to recognise mental health problems in older people. However many feel ill prepared to deal with them (Audit Commission, 2000).

Black and Ethnic Minority Elders

Older people from black and ethnic minority groups may face additional problems of hostility and racism as well as loneliness, isolation and declining physical health. The number of black ethnic minority elders in the UK compared to numbers of older people is still small. However, progressive ageing of the minority ethnic population is anticipated in the future. Furthermore, it is often assumed that minority ethnic groups 'look after their own' which is a dangerous assumption. Fennell *et al.* (1988) indicate that although many ethnic older people live in multi-generation homes, they may not be receiving adequate or appropriate care. Traditionally, women have provided the expected level of care but second and third generations of women may choose to or be compelled to work outside the home.

It is however, generally accepted that the NHS has been less responsive to the needs of black and ethnic minority groups as well as older people (Henley and Schott, 1996). Therefore, one of the most challenging issues for mental health services is to provide culturally sensitive mental health services for older people. Guidelines are laid down by the Patient's Charter (DoH, 1991) and include issues such as the need for diversity training for staff, the right for individuals to expect sensitivity to their past life experiences, using interpreters with care and research to underpin food habits and customs in more depth.

> **?** *Point of Reflection:* How would you ensure effective and therapeutic communication with an older client whose first language isn't English?

Referrals

Due to more formalised, specialised and complex referral systems, referrals are generated from a multitude of clinical settings and passed on to the most appropriate discipline. For efficiency and effectiveness, the scope of practice, referral criteria, agreed goals and progress reports from those to whom older people are referred, are the minimum standards that should be expected. Typically, an older person will be referred by a GP, a concerned neighbour or calls to emergency services following a crisis. Box 11.1 represents a whole systems approach to referrals and demonstrates the range of professional disciplines that potentially may be the first point of contact.

Box 11.1   Whole systems approach

- Primary Health Care Team
- Private and Voluntary Sector
- Housing Agencies
- Acute Hospitals
- Social Services
- Intermediate Care
- Liaison Mental Health Worker/Nurse
- Community Mental health Nurse

Theoretical Framework

It is important to point out that older people are not a homogenous group but numerous independent individuals with rich biographical histories. Thus, any framework for practice must be underpinned by a positive approach to mental health care for older people, which place the person at the heart of service provision rather than on the margins. Evidence pointing towards older people as untreatable is usually found in the minds of therapists rather than in empirical studies. Powerful forces of counter transference and cultural prejudice are at work. These include personal fear and despair over ageing and death. Therapeutic pessimism and nihilism are inappropriate, invalid and inhumane (Butler *et al.*, 1991).

Counselling

Counselling in later life is important, as problems addressed are not age specific. Sadly, counselling in older age tends to be under used. Yet there is no reason why it cannot be as effective at this stage of life than any other. It enables people to become involved in a process whereby they can be helped to reflect in and become aware of their current situation and the complexity of their own needs. Humanistic psychology embraces understanding of the older adult in a positive way, emphasising strengths and development along the life continuum rather than highlighting weaknesses and limitations.

Person centred therapy developed by Rogers (1970) sits within this framework and is rooted in the central truth that the client knows best. It is the client who knows what is hurting and in the final analysis it is the client who knows how to move forward. The relationship between the client and therapist should be one in which the client is afforded unconditional positive regard with a clear shift in power relations away from therapist and towards the client. In later life, counselling often still remains associated with loss and bereavement and can do much to improve quality of life. There are many losses associated with this period of life including loss of role, partner and social network, financial status, health and independence.

The application of person centred counselling for people with dementing illnesses has provoked great debate. Raising the question that someone whose cognition no longer enables them to engage with the here and now, let alone the future, cannot surely be deemed to know what is best? By failing to understand or enter into the feelings and experience of people with dementia we deny the validity of their subjectivity.

Validation Therapy

Such invalidation can be rectified if there is a genuine attempt to understand their perspective on the world. The origins of Naomi Feil's Validation Therapy (VT) can be traced back to 1963. Feil was the first person to take the apparently confused and disorientated speech and behaviour of dementia sufferers seriously in their own right. She believed that disorientation is not just about making poor judgement about time, place, person but a process where the self loses contact with reality and retreats in to an inner subjective world. If the therapist could view this subjective world through the eyes of the client then the seemingly unintelligible speech and confused behaviour would have meaning. All behaviour, no matter how bizarre, has a rational explanation (Feil, 1967). Thus, it is our lack of ability to see the world of the person who has retreated to their subjective world that leads to labelling individuals as 'confused'. Hence, there was a dramatic shift towards feelings and emotions and a realisation that there might be genuinely therapeutic psychological outcomes in dementia, thus leading to the experiences of people with dementia being taken more seriously.

Resolution Therapy

Stokes and Goudie (1989) took this one step further by developing resolution therapy. The focus is on the emotional distress accompanying dementia, with emphasis on empathy and communication. The role of the therapist is to employ person-centred counselling techniques by attempting to overcome the communication barrier. This can be achieved by identifying the meaning behind seemingly confused speech and uncover the underlying needs and meaning behind it. Thus, there is commonality between validation and resolution with the aim to improve the emotional well-being of the person by establishing contact, displaying empathy and searching for meaning in communication.

Personhood

Kitwood and Bredin (1992) propose that a prerequisite for helping people with dementia is to maintain 'personhood' by continuing to see and treat them as fellow human beings. Kitwood rejected the medical model as being too simplistic. He proposed that in reality, there is a complex interplay between neurological factors and the social milieu in which the dementia sufferer finds themselves. Thus, personhood is unlikely to survive in the prevalence of highly negative and stigmatising attitudes, which in turn influence the delivery of care; any may ultimately worsen the dementia. Kitwood argued that this leads to malignant social psychology (see Box 11.2), which may rob sufferers of their self-esteem, confidence, sense of worth leading to disempowerment and loss of agency. Care should be based on a respect of individuality and adopting a strengths perspective rather than a focus on deficits or limitations.

Box 11.2	Malignant social psychology (Kitwood, 1997)
Treachery	Using forms of deception in order to distract or manipulate, or force into compliance.
Disempowerment	Not allowing a person to use the abilities that they do have; failing to help them to complete actions they have initiated.
Infantilisation	Treating a person very patronisingly as an insensitive parent might treat a young child.
Intimidation	Inducing fear in a person, through the use of threats or physical power.
Labelling	Using a category such as dementia, or 'organic mental impairment' as the main basis for interacting with a person and explaining behaviour.
Stigmatisation	Treating a person as if they were a diseased object, an alien or an outcast.
Outpacing	Providing information, presenting choices at a rate too fast for a person to understand; putting them under pressure to do things more rapidly than they can bear.
Invalidation	Failing to acknowledge the subjective reality of a person's experience, and especially what they are feeling.
Banishment	Sending a person away, or excluding them – physically or psychologically.
Objectification	Treating a person as if they were a lump of dead matter: to be pushed, lifted, filled, pumped or drained, without proper reference to the fact that they are sentient beings.
Ignoring	Carrying on (in conversation or action) in the presence of the person as if they were not there.
Imposition	Forcing a person to do something, overriding desire or denying the possibility of choice on their part.
Withholding	Refusing to give asked for attention, or to meet an evident need.
Accusation	Blaming a person for actions or failures of action that arise from their lack of ability or their misunderstanding of the situation.
Disruption	Intruding suddenly or disturbingly upon a person's action or reflection; crudely breaking their frame of reference.
Mockery	Making fun of a person's 'strange' actions or remarks; teasing, humiliating, making jokes at their expense
Disparagement	Telling a person that they are incompetent, useless, worthless, etc., giving them messages that are damaging to their self-esteem.

The Life Cycle

The work of Erikson (1950) discusses ideas about developments in old age. His theory is very sophisticated, attempting to describe personality development across the life cycle. Developments at one point in the life cycle can only be understood with reference to earlier developments. He argued that successful negotiation of life events depends on understanding the way in which earlier tasks were experienced and dealt with and the impact this had on later development. It is therefore crucial to understand older people in the context of their life history. Erikson described the last developmental crisis of the life cycle as '*ego integrity versus despair*'. Thus, to him adjustment in later life is not simply a case of coming to terms with physical ill health, the life that has been lived to date, relationships and the loss of friends and loved ones but also coming to terms with discontinuities between the past, the present and the likely future.

 Point of Reflection: What would you consider the best theoretical framework for engaging older people with dementia?

Principles and Skills

The skills required for working in services for older people with mental health problems, include the ability to

- Strike up good interpersonal relationships with older people, their carers.
- An understanding of the roles and contributions of other professional disciplines.
- Influence decision making by challenging barriers and overcoming obstacles in order to enhance service provision for older people.
- Acknowledge and understand the complex link between physical and mental health in later life.
- Skills to carry out accurate, comprehensive assessments based on a sound knowledge base of both physical and mental health issues.
- Work in ways that are innovative and creative in order to raise the profile of mental health in later life.
- Place the older person at the heart of service provision rather than on the margins.

Assessment

Approach

Assessments are carried out for the main purpose of understanding the nature and extent of an individual's problems/needs. Their perception of the issues and that of the carer are also sought, exploring the extent to which a referral is required to mobilise professional intervention.

Any assessment of an older person must be conducted with the utmost sensitivity to the needs and wishes of the individual. In addition, collaboration with the informal carer or family unit is necessary. The length of the interview will depend on the presentation of the individual and the risk involved to self or others. It is essential, therefore to establish a rapport by ensuring effective communication, which matches the time and pace of the client and allows for frailty, tiredness and confusion.

A variety of different professional disciplines may be called upon to carry out an assessment, which in turn will affect where the assessment is carried out and the depth of the assessment process. Older people often complain about the number of assessments they complete for different agencies (Sutherland, 1999). This has been recognised within the NSF for Older People explicitly stating that:

> NHS and social care services treat older people as individuals and enable them to make choices about their care. This is achieved through the single assessment process, integrated commissioning arrangements and integrated provision of services, including community equipment and continence services. (DoH, 2001)

Process

A single assessment process is much needed and since April 2002 local trusts have been working to agree between different disciplines, as to which assessment tool will be used. Whether a single individual can accomplish this is unlikely. Thus, the level of assessment needs clarification that is, will it be a generic screening and then passed to the most appropriate person or a series of specialised assessments? For the single assessment process to be effective, mutual education, trust and respect must occur across all professional disciplines.

Assessment of the mental health needs of older people should be comprehensive and can be affected by a complex interplay of many factors (see Box 11.3). Failure to assess fully may result in planning care based on the presenting clinical signs and symptoms, leaving any other contributing factors inadequately addressed. Rushed, inadequate assessments lead to ineffective care planning, resulting in considerable long-term cost to all involved.

In 1989 the World Health Organisation (WHO) recommended the following framework for assessment of older people. It can be utilised in conjunction with a range of screening tools specifically designed for more in-depth assessment of older adult mental health needs.

Information Gathering

Information should be gathered over a period of time to ensure that the assessment is comprehensive and inclusive of all the needs of the older person in relation to physical, psychological, social and spiritual well-being, The process of gathering information may vary but will include an interview with

---

Box 11.3 Assessment of older people (WHO, 1989)

Activities of Daily Living (ADL)
- Physical activities of Daily Living for example, communicating, eating, self-care
- Mobilising
- Instrumental activities of Daily Living that is, participating as a functional member of society and involved in domestic tasks

Mental health functioning
- Cognitive
- Presence of psychiatric symptoms

Psychosocial functioning
- Emotional well-being in a cultural context

Physical health functioning
- Self-perceived health status
- Physical symptoms and diagnosed health conditions
- Health service utilisation
- Activity levels and measures of incapacitation

Social resources
- Accessibility of family, friends and a familiar/professional, voluntary helper
- Availability of resources

Economic resources
- Income as compared to an external standard

Environmental resources
- Adequate and affordable housing
- Siting of housing in relation to transport, shopping and public services.

---

the older person often accompanied by the main carer, possible liaison with other professionals who may have been involved and via reports/ referral letters from the primary care team.

Tools Used

Various tools can be used to assist in identifying mental health needs:

- Abbreviated Mental Test (Hodkinson, 1972)
- Care Giver Strain Questionnaire (Robinson, 1983)

- Geriatric Depression Scale (Sheik and Yesavage, 1986)
- Hospital Anxiety and Depression Scale (HADS) (Zigmond and Snaith, 1983)
- Middlesex Elderly Assessment of Mental State (MEAMS) (Golding, 1989)
- Mini Mental Status Examination (MMSE) (Folstein *et al.*, 1975)*
- Cambridge Mental Disorders of the Elderly (CAMDEX) (Brayne and Calloway 1989)*

* Further training is required in the use of these tools.

Risk Priorities

Risk assessment is an essential component of every accurate assessment. Legal and safety issues such as risk of harm to self and others, the ability to manage own affairs, vulnerability of attack or exploitation and consequences of concurrent/untreated disease should be addressed.

Key areas for further exploration in assessing risk are:

- Documentation of past history of self-harm or violence
- Suicidal ideation, including any previous attempts and method
- Past history and evidence of hostility to others
- Client's perception of risk
- Reports from significant others, that is, family, carers, concerned neighbours, police
- Reports, observations from professional carers (GP etc).

It should also be noted that where an older person has severe mental illness, they will require the packages of care set out in the Care Programme Approach (DoH, 1990) with the same standards that apply for working age adults in the National Service Framework for Mental Health (DoH, 1999).

 Point of Reflection: How would you ensure you have gained all of the necessary information, yet not overwhelmed the client and carer/family member?

Care Planning

How Plan is Determined

Once the assessment has been completed a plan of care can be drawn up. Wherever possible, it must be in collaboration and negotiation with the older person and their carer. It should always begin with prioritising immediate needs. Care plans must be specific, measurable, achievable, realistic, framed within a time scale (SMART) and acceptable to the individual. Due to complex needs it is not possible for one service to meet all the required needs. Therefore, a multidisciplinary approach has lead to the development of integrated care pathways as part of the response to calls for evidence based, equitable, comprehensive, systematic and outcome orientated care, outlined in standard seven of the National Service Framework for Older Adults (DoH, 2001).

A care pathway is based on guidelines and evidence where available which has been determined by locally agreed interdisciplinary practice. Positive outcomes include:

- Better informed patients and carers and early treatment interventions for the early stages of illness.
- Leading to treatment of symptoms, better community support and reduced burdens on carers in the middle stages.
- Resulting in a delay of illness progression, smoother transition into institutional care and a more dignified decline in the late stages of an illness.

Pathways should form all or part of the clinical written record. They are an essential component of care planning, where interdisciplinary input is paramount in providing care to people with problems resulting from multiple pathology. Care pathways exist for depression and dementia and to facilitate differential diagnosis with local trusts often adapting nationally recognised protocols (to obtain copies contact local Primary Care Trusts or Specialist Mental Health Services).

Practical Application

The two case examples offer further information for the practical application of care planning for a client with a depressive illness originating from the primary care setting and another with dementia. Care planning of vulnerable older people will be most supportive if individualised with supportive carers recognising the person as having a unique set of needs and wants, deserving of respect, with the right to be treated with dignity and to have a say in the assessment of need. Factors, which facilitate this process, include personal qualities of the mental health practitioner, what constitutes evidence-based practice, the skill mix and values of the team, supportive leadership and the management and rationalisation of resources. The latter often causes many obstacles as with cuts to funding, care providers are often left feeling that what they are able to provide doesn't match what they, the older person and the carer have agreed would meet their needs.

Case Example: 1

Mr Jones is a 73-year-old retired bank worker whose wife of 50 years died suddenly following a heart attack last year. As a devoted couple they had a tendency to keep themselves to themselves, so had a limited social network. His only hobby had been golf, which he gave up after his wife died. He rarely goes out of the house now, other than to pick up a few bits of grocery from the corner shop. His only son lives in Australia.

On recently attending his local surgery for his annual flu injection, the practice nurse noticed he had lost a considerable amount of weight since she last saw him. He had always been a very smartly dressed man, but on this occasion he presented at the surgery as unshaven, shabbily dressed and not his usual self. The practice nurse felt that Mr Jones could be depressed but was unclear as to whether this was part of his grieving process. With his agreement, she made arrangements for the primary mental health care nurse to visit later the same afternoon. The nurse visited Mr Jones, explained her role and asked if she could talk to him about how he is coping and whether there was anything that she could do to help.

It transpired that Mr Jones:

- Shut himself away since his wife's death with little social contact.
- Reluctant to visit his General Practitioner (GP) not believing in 'pills and potions'.
- Housework had become a real chore as his wife had always done it.
- Had never learned how to cook a proper meal or even use the washing machine.

The primary care liaison nurse explained that she thought he may be depressed and could benefit from the support of the community mental health team. Following discussion of the care options, Mr Jones agreed that some advice and support would be useful. A care plan was then drawn up based on identified needs:

Immediate problems

- Early morning wakening
- Weight loss
- Lethargy
- Loss of concentration
- Low mood

Plan

To assist in regaining control over clinical symptoms and to work through the grieving process.

Time Frame

The Immediate need, assisting the client and primary health care team to manage any problems with support from the community mental health nurse.

In the short-term:

- To negotiate with client and the GP to prescribe a course of antidepressant therapy, explaining the positive benefits, the chemical changes that take place within the brain, the need to ensure that the medication is taken regularly for the prescribed length of time, possible side effects and that they are not addictive.
- To help establish routine and structure to the day.
- To identify friends, past hobbies and establish which links would enable reintegration into social networks.
- To facilitate the opportunity to access bereavement counselling from the community mental health nurse/practice counsellor or a local organisation.

In the long-term:

- To enable client to accept his wife's death through successful negotiation of the grieving process.
- To enable client to become symptom free.
- To enable the development of essential cookery/house keeping skills.
- To reintegrate into society and find meaningful purpose in life.

With support and advice from the primary care liaison nurse Mr Jones was able to make sense of his situation and find hope in his life once again.

Case Example: 2

Mrs Clarke is a 66-year-old lady who lives at home with her husband. They have been married for 45 years and have two grown up daughters. Both live some distance away with their respective families, although they are in touch frequently by telephone and visit once a month. Mrs Clarke was a part-time librarian and her husband was a postman. They are on a fixed retirement pension and have no savings and until recently, had remained active in their local community via their association with the church. Unfortunately, two weeks ago, Mrs Clarke began to exhibit disturbing, bizarre behaviour, which has made it difficult for her husband to take her to church functions. Last year Mrs Clarke had a cerebral vascular accident, which has left her with right-sided weakness. Recently her husband has noticed that she has become tearful and increasingly more forgetful, exacerbated by a recent cough and cold. He no longer takes her out as he feels she is an embarrassment to him and doesn't feel that he can leave her alone in the house. She constantly wakes him during the night so he is exhausted and readily admits that he is frustrated with the situation and can no longer cope.

Last week she suddenly became verbally aggressive, incontinent of urine and now she doesn't recognise him. He finds this particularly traumatic. Finally, ashamed and embarrassed Mr Clarke reluctantly called the GP to do a home visit, stating that somebody has to do something as he feels a prisoner in his own home. The GP discussed with Mr. Clarke the option of immediate referral to the community mental health nurse. He agreed and an urgent home visit was requested. The nurse found Mrs Clarke in a distressed state and obtained as much information as possible from Mr Clarke who was relieved to have contact with someone who could help.

Immediate Problems

1. Recent increased forgetfulness, confusion and incontinence.
2. Carer burden through lack of support and awareness.

Plan

1. To establish the cause of the confusion, to stabilise and liase with GP to carry out blood tests/investigations.
2. To treat any underlying reversible causes.
3. To assess carer's needs separately.
4. To provide information on cognitive impairment and enhancing well-being through interaction and maintenance of existing skills.
5. To mobilise support mechanisms.

Time Frame

1. Investigations to be conducted within 24 hours.
2. Depending on the outcome of the investigations to return within a week to conduct a more in-depth assessment and use various tools such as MEAMS.
3. If dementia is diagnosed then it is important to identify potential cause in order to offer a range of treatment options.

In the short-term:

1. To establish the problems and needs as perceived by both client and carer.
2. To return client to optimum level of functioning before skills become lost and offer choices to empower client to make decisions about her future.
3. To monitor ongoing potential risk factors.

In the long-term:

1. To visit on a two weekly basis to monitor medication needs, ongoing change, offer practical advice and a range of therapeutic interventions acceptable to client and carer, including reminiscence therapy, life history work and relaxations sessions.
2. To liase with carer and other disciplines to ensure appropriate benefits are being claimed (housing, attendance allowance, council tax reductions) via social worker
3. Refer on to physiotherapist.
4. Provide an information pack and contact details for support agencies for carer (Alzheimer's Society).

Following the nurse's initial visit, the GP carried out blood tests including full blood count, Urea and electrolytes, Thyroid function Test, glucose and a Liver Function Test. The results revealed that Mrs Clarke has a chest infection and is mildly dehydrated. Antibiotic therapy was commenced immediately and fluid intake increased. Mr Clarke had reduced Mrs Clarke's fluid, as he couldn't cope with the incontinence, which had merely made the problem worse. Within 48 hours Mrs Clarke's confusion had reduced significantly which allowed the nurse to return to conduct the second assessment. This revealed possible mild vascular dementia linked to her previous stroke. After discussion with the GP, aspirin was prescribed on a long-term basis, to reduce the risk of other cardiovascular events such as myocardial infarction, stroke and trans ischaemic attacks. Aspirin lessens the chances of clots developing.

By assessing the problems perceived by Mrs and Mr Clarke, other professional agencies and support mechanisms were then arranged to enable Mrs Clarke to remain at home and function at her optimum level. Post-it notes, reminders and signs helped to remember things and enabled her to find her way around the house and gave her an element of choice and control over her daily routine. Since the recent episode with her chest infection she had reduced mobility and a course of physiotherapy enabled her to enjoy once again short walks up and down the garden. The liaison nurse arranged transportation through a local bus company for Mr and Mrs Clarke to begin attending their much-enjoyed weekly Sunday service, which they had expressed, was vital to maintaining their well-being.

Mr Clarke took advantage of the carer support networks, respite care services and the education, information and therapeutic interventions from the community mental health nurse which enabled them to cope with and understand the nature of Mrs Clarke's illness, thus, reflecting that good person-centred care, including the use of therapeutic approach enables people to regain and maintain their skills.

It is important to mention that depression and dementia are not mutually exclusive and to be aware that people in the early stages of dementia often have depressive symptoms. The value of a good assessment is evident in being able to determine the difference between them. These illnesses can present with similar features and misdiagnosis is common.

> **?** *Point of Reflection:* How can you ensure that the client's expressed wishes and needs have been properly addressed and that decisions are based on informed choice?

Documentation

Accurate, comprehensive and up to date record keeping is essential to ensuring that care is delivered effectively through the nursing process of assessment, planning, implementation and regular evaluation of the person's changing needs. In the community setting nursing notes remain the responsibility of the individual's key worker which may be a community mental health nurse or in the case of a carer an admiral nurse and are filed in a lockable cabinet with information being shared with other professionals where appropriate via written correspondence.

Time Frame

The length of involvement with mental health services will vary with each client and which aspect of the service is required. For older people with mild to moderate problems the mental health liaison nurse is often able to (with the person and primary health care teams) enable them to help restore the person to their effective level of functioning fairly quickly. For someone else with a past history of depression and a series of devastating life events then a community mental health nurse is likely to be involved for several months.

For someone with a diagnosis of dementia, specialist mental health services will be involved with the individual and the carer for duration of the illness until death and with the carer often for a considerable time afterwards. In this situation a range of mental health services will be involved including Psychiatrist, Community Mental Health Nurses, Memory Clinics, Inpatient Units and respite care services, Home Support and Intermediate Care, Admiral Nurses for the Carer, Social Services and Occupational Therapy.

Evidence Base

The UK has some of the best specialist services for older people in the world (NSF for older people, DoH 2001). Along with a solid evidence-base for their effectiveness, is evidence that timely intervention reduces long-term needs, especially in the early recognition and prompt treatment of depression (Lebowitz *et al.*, 1997), especially when coupled with psychological therapies (The British Psychological Society, 1994). This is also the case in dementing illnesses. The use of non-pharmacological management strategies may reduce the impact or slow down the progression of the disease (Kitwood, 1997) and delay the need for institutionalised care.

Dissemination of Information

Dissemination of the information required by other professional groups has been greatly enhanced by electronically held records and through the single assessment process and integrated care pathways. In some clinical areas there is a single set of notes that all professional groups contribute, but crucial to dissemination is the issue of confidentiality. However nurses are bound under the Nursing and Midwifery Council Code of Conduct (2002) with regard to confidentiality.

Reflective Practice

Professional quality is about considering the outcome and processes of a professional's work, using methods and techniques to measure the effectiveness and applying the results to practice. This is achieved personally by ensuring as mental health professionals that:

- Every action and encounter with older people sees the individual as a person first.
- Any agreed actions are carried out in collaboration with the person.
- Individual needs, preferences and life experiences are taken into account.

Reflecting enables the practitioner to identify room for improvement and to practice in a way that offers a greater range of evidence-based intervention. In addition, clinical supervision is a positive and enabling process (Graham, 1999). It offers the opportunity to bring the practitioner and skilled supervisors together to reflect on practice by identifying solutions to problems and increasing understanding of professional and clinical issues.

Practice Development

There is now a shift in attitude towards encouraging users of older adult mental health services and their carers to complain if service provision doesn't meet their expectations. This has lead to a clearer process of exploring the quality of provision, identifying areas for improvement and taking appropriate action. Furthermore, there is a drive for improved services through clinical governance and the development of practice alongside government policy. National Service Frameworks for Mental Health (DoH, 1999), for Older People (DoH, 2001) and the NHS Plan (DoH, 2000) provide guidelines for improving practice and recognition of the need for a suitably trained work force to meet the mental health demands of changing health care. This is achieved through research and forging stronger links with academic institutions. Also, strengthening inter-professional learning and working for all grades of staff in all clinical areas. The evidence for practice development can be seen in:

- The greater number of choices available to older people.
- The increased levels of satisfaction.
- The number of new, innovative services.
- The dissemination of research and best practice within this speciality.

Conclusion

Throughout the last century, interest in the study of older people has grown steadily resulting in a wealth of books, publications and the generation of research into social gerontology. The increase in the number of older people, as a proportion of the population, has resulted in the study of human ageing. This not only focuses on old age in general, but also the issues and challenges of later life, including mental health.

Services for older people have made significant strides over recent years placing older people with mental health needs centre stage. A range of effective therapies now exist, with contributions from reminiscence, reality orientation, validation therapy, resolution therapy, cognitive therapy and not least, through the work of Kitwood in dementia care. In addition, the demand for effective services to provide care is growing both from professionals and older people/ informal carers. This has been underpinned by a radical modernisation agenda for health services generally, though, there are still challenges ahead.

The benefits of inter-professional working are well established. However, much remains to be done if we are going to put rhetoric into reality; embracing and encouraging opportunities for shared learning amongst the many different professional disciplines. Meanwhile, working with older people with mental health problems remains an interesting, challenging, continually developing speciality area, with many opportunities for like-minded professionals to make a real difference.

📖 Suggested Further Reading

Keady, K., Clarke, C. and Adams, A. (2003) *Community Mental Health Nursing and Dementia Care*, Maidenhead: Open University Press.

Nolan, M., Davies, S. and Grant, G. (2003) *Working with Older people and their Families*, Maidenhead: Open University Press.

References

Audit Commission (2000) *Forget Me Not: Mental Health Services for Older People*, London: Audit Commission.

Brayne, C. and Calloway, P. (1989) An epidemiological study of dementia in a rural population of elderly women, *British Journal of Psychiatry*, 164: 396–402

The British Psychological Society (1994) *Psychological Well-Being for Users of Dementia Services*, Leicester: Briefing paper no. 2.

Butler, R.N., Lewis, M. and Sutherland, T. (1991) Ageing and mental health: positive psychological and biomedical approaches, *Psychiatry*, 29: 16–28.

Copeland, J.R.M., Gurland, B.J., Dewey, M.E., Wood, N., Searle, R., Davidson, I.A. and McWilliam, C. (1987) Range of mental illness among the elderly in the community:prevalence in Liverpool using the GMS-AGECAT package, *British Journal of Psychiatry*, 150: 815–23.

Department of Health (1989) *Working for Patients*, London: The Stationery Office.

Department of Health (1990) *The Care programme Approach for People with a Mental Illness Referred to the Specialist Psychiatry Services*, London: The Stationery Office.

Department of Health (1991) *The Patient's Charter*, London: The Stationery Office.

Department of Health (1999) *The National Service Framework for Mental Health*, London: The Stationery Office.

Department of Health (2000) *The National Health Service Plan*, London: HMSO.

Department of Health (2001) *The National Service Framework for Older People*, London: The Stationery Office.

Erikson, E.H. (1950) *Childhood and Society*, New York: Norton.

Evans, S. and Katona, C. (1993) Epidemiology of depressive symptoms in elderly primary care attenders. *Dementia*, 4: 327–33.

Feil N (1967) Group Therapy in a Home for the Aged, *The Gerontologist*, 7: 192–5.

Fennell, G., Phillipson, C. and Evers, H. (1988) *The Sociology of Old Age*, Milton Keynes: Open University Press.

Folstein, M.F., Folstein, S.E. and McHugh, P.R. (1975) 'Mini Mental state'; practical method for grading the cognitive state of patients for the clinician, *Journal of Psychiatric Resources*, 12: 189–98.

Golding, E. (1989) *The Middlesex Elderly Assessment of Mental State*, Suffolk: Thames Valley Test Company.

Graham, I.W. (1999) Reflective Narrative and Dementia Care, *Journal of Clinical Nursing*, 8: 675–83.

Henley, A. and Schott, J. (1996) *Culture, Religion and Childbearing in a Multiracial Society*, Oxford: Butterworth-Heinmann.

Hodkinson, H.M. (1972) Evaluation of a mental test score for assessment of mental impairment in the elderly, *Age and Ageing*, 1: 233–8.

Kitwood, T. (1997) *Dementia Reconsidered: The Person Comes First*, London: Open University Press.

Kitwood, T. and Bredin, K. (1992) Towards a theory of dementia care: the interpersonal process, *Ageing and Society*, 12: 269–87.

Lebowitz, B.D., Pearson, J.L. and Schneider, L.S. (1997) Diagnosis and treatment of depression in late life, *Journal of the American Medical Association*, 278: 1186–90.

Muijen, M. (1995) Scare in the community: part five: care of the mentally ill people', *Community Care* (7–13 September): i–viii.

Naguib, M. and Levy, R. (1992) Paranoid states in the elderly and late paraphrenia, in Jacoby, R. and Oppenheimer, C. (eds), *Psychiatry in the Elderly*, Oxford: Oxford University Press.

Nursing and Midwifery Council (2002) *Code of Professional Conduct*, London: NMC.

Robinson, B. (1983) Validation of a caregiver strain index, *Journal of Gerontology*, 38: 344–8.

Rogers, C.R. (1970) *On Becoming a Person: A Therapist View of Psychotherapy*, Boston: Houghton-Mifflin-Sentry Edition.

Sheik, J.I. and Yeasavage, J.A. (1986) Geriatric Depression Scale; recent evidence and development of a shorter version, in Brink, T.L. (ed.), *Clinical Gerontology: A Guide to Assessment and Intervention*, New York: Hawarth Press.

Stokes, G. and Goudie, F. (1989) Understanding Confusion, *Nursing Times*, 39: 35–7.

Sutherland, S. (1999) *With Respect to old Age: Long Term Care – Rights and Responsibilities*, A Report by the Royal Commission on long-term care, London: The Stationery Office.

World Health Organisation (1989) within World Health Organisation *International Classification of Impairment, Disability and Handicap*, The Netherlands: WCC World Health Organisation Collaboration Centre.

Zigmond, A.S. and Snaith, R.P. (1983) The hospital anxiety and depression scale, *Acta Psychiatrica, Scandinavica*, 67: 361–70.

PART V

Specialist Practice

CHAPTER 12

Eating Disorders

Tom Williams

Introduction

The field of eating disorders provides many challenges to those involved in service delivery. The field is diverse, and the needs of those diagnosed require skilled assessment and intervention at a number of different levels. Treatment can span primary, secondary and tertiary service provision and can occur in outpatient, day care and inpatient settings.

The term 'eating disorders' should be thought of as an umbrella term for several distinct conditions, some of which show both difference and a degree of overlap in presenting features. There are several different types of eating disorder, and these mainly fall under the broad diagnostic categories of anorexia nervosa restricting sub-type and purging sub-type, bulimia nervosa purging sub-type and non-purging sub-type (Silverman, 1997), binge eating disorder (APA, 1994), and atypical or eating disorders not otherwise specified (EDNOS), and some forms of obesity. It is likely these conditions will continue to change over time (Silverman, 1995).

Recent legislation suggests, most mild to moderately severe eating disorders can be treated in primary care (DoH, 1999; NICE, 2003). Likewise almost all cases of bulimia and binge eating disorder will be seen in an outpatient setting. There are some notable exceptions to this; such as where purging and/or acting out behaviours are so severe as to make an individual vulnerable to physical or psychological decompensation, as in cases of multi-impulsive bulimia (Lacey, 1992; Russell and Marsden, 1998).

These like any other severe eating disorder may ultimately require admission for reasons of complicating co-morbidity or a risk of suicide. The group most likely to require admission are those with severe anorexia nervosa (Palmer, 2000; RCP, 2000; NICE, 2004). It is this group who arguably pose the greatest challenge and generate most anxiety for clinicians when asked to intervene and alleviate symptoms. This chapter will consider only the adult population, and suggests the reader seek specialised texts when searching for approaches to child and adolescent populations.

Prevalence and Population

There are a number of difficulties in accurately mapping out the incidences of new cases, or the prevalence of existing cases at any point in time. In epidemiological research, prevalence studies vastly outnumber incidence studies (Hoek, 2002).

Estimated point prevalence for:

- Anorexia is 10–30 per 100,000 total population, with estimated incidence rates at 4–10 per 100,000 (Palmer, 2000).
- Bulimia might be around 100 per 100,000 per population, with an estimated incidence rate of 10–15 per 100,000 (Palmer, 2000).

It is fair to say there is wide variation in many of the studies carried out to date (NICE, 2004). Eating disorders are not evenly distributed across the general public, and most occur in young females between mid-teens and mid-twenties. There is approximately a ratio of 9 : 1 females to males affected (Copperman, 2000). It has been reported there is a reticence to identify males as having an eating disorder (Copperman, 2000).

There is poor recognition of eating disorders at a primary care level, leading to only a small proportion gaining access to treatment (EDA, 2000). Indeed the EDA (1995) state that there are approximately 60,000 diagnosed eating disorders involved with services at any one time but, claim the real figure in the population is likely to be closer to 1,100,000. This figure is significant when one considers the standardised mortality ratio for eating disorders is claimed to be higher than in depression, schizophrenia and alcoholism (RCP, 2000).

Referrals

It is likely that the existence of services and the way in which these are organised will influence the way referrals are processed. The Audit Commission (1997) has suggested the use of a 'Hub and Spoke' model to deliver services. This advocates the use of a centralised hub, containing experts or specialists, with distinct linkages to outlying services or 'spokes'.

The model relies on cases being identified in primary or secondary settings; with some of the milder cases receiving treatment or being filtered out, with only the most severe cases, or those who fail to improve, referred to the hub (Palmer and Treasure, 1999).

Recent legislation has called for the establishment of *'agreed protocols between primary care and specialist mental health services to ensure speedy access'*, and *'protocols to guide referrals for specialised services such as – eating disorders units'* (DoH, 1999, p. 105).

While this legislation is to be welcomed there are a number of inherent difficulties to be solved. In such a system it is vital decisions to re-refer are made within agreed timescales, and are based on perceived severity (DoH, 1999).

> **Box 12.1**   Stepped care model
>
> Care may commence in primary settings with the least intensive interventions and then increase in intensity, as referrals are moved along the pathway through secondary and tertiary settings towards increasingly specialist intervention. Referral to the next level is dependent on insufficient improvement being made at the previous one. It is suggested this prevents costly and often unnecessary interventions (Palmer, 2000).

One common way of doing this is to use a 'stepped care' model (RCP, 2000) that can span a number of care settings.

At times of high activity services may have insufficient capacity to accept referrals within agreed timescales. The severity of illness has a wide spectrum and can show significant change over time,

- Person arrives with a less severe presentation and quickly deteriorates,
- While others arrive in a very debilitated condition on their first presentation to services.

This can create a situation where cases must be held and managed for considerable periods of time, until provision can be made for referral and transfer to specialist services. Furthermore, it is not inconceivable for many to refuse treatment on the basis of distance alone (EDA, 2000). Where services are more available and accessible there can be a tendency to re-refer sooner, preventing non-specialist staff from gaining the experience required to deal with complex cases. Equally, significant numbers of cases will not show improvement at specialist level, and subsequently be discharged back to the referrer to be monitored and held.

Theoretical Framework

Any approach in the treatment of eating disorders must take into consideration the multi-determined nature of the conditions, and the concept of multi-component care (Garner, 1997). Some claim it is essential to have a multidimensional perspective if care is to be patient centred (Berg *et al.*, 2002). These authors suggest each discipline views the condition from a narrow perspective limited by their own professional ethos (Berg *et al.*, 2002). Others have claimed wide variations in treatment practices occur as a result of different views on the nature of the conditions (Parkin, 1995).

As in all other conditions aetiology is an important determinant to inform treatment plans. In the case of eating disorders there are no single universally accepted explanations of aetiology (Schmidt, 2002).

At the traditional end of the spectrum there are those who locate their beliefs in the concept of eating disorders as a pathological process, with distinct biological and psychological sequelae. There is always a need to manage the physical consequences of starvation, disturbed eating, and purging behaviours where these exist. Undoubtedly, sufferers will usually show improvement when physical consequences of the conditions are restored to healthier levels. However, there is invariably a need to treat the psychological and social factors for hope of a lasting recovery to be realised. Out of this position two of the most commonly used therapeutic stances emerge, these being psychodynamic and cognitive theories.

Psychodynamic Formulations

These cite the egosyntonic (Crisp, 1997) and egodystonic (Russell and Marsden, 1998) nature of anorexia and bulimia respectively, involving the use of primitive mental defence mechanisms. The main focus of these frameworks is to work through unknown and unresolved conflicts and uncover the symbolic meaning of symptoms, with the therapist interpreting or managing transference and working with counter transference (Hughes, 1997).

Cognitive Formulations

These identify patterns and use of distorted cognitions and/or rigid schema as maintenance factors. This has particular utility in the case of bulimia and binge eating (Fairburn *et al.*, 1993) although there are currently trials aimed at applying this approach to all eating disorders including anorexia (Fairburn *et al.*, 2003). Clinicians here do not search for unknown meaning, but focus on the thoughts that trigger behaviours, underlying core beliefs and perceived consequences of the behaviour.

Family and Systemic

In a different place on the aetiological spectrum there are those who contend that the pathologising language of the above models, and the use of the term eating disorders is incorrect. This view contends there are no disorders as such, and these descriptions exist as products of socially constructed discourse, in which the dominant narratives of psychiatry and psychology are privileged, over other possible and potentially more helpful descriptions (Hepworth, 1999; Duran *et al.*, 2000). Therapy from this perspective is likely to utilise the metaphor of language, the deconstruction of the dominant and constraining professional language and power and consist of narrative approaches aimed at externalising the problem (White, 1995; White and Epston, 1991). From this tradition contemporary systemic approaches have been advocated and family intervention is widely accepted as the treatment of choice, when there is a young age of onset.

It has been suggested the model chosen for working with those with eating disorder may be of less importance than the attitude and knowledge of the person delivering the care (EDA, 2000). Recent guidelines suggest whatever frameworks are used; there is a need for minimum periods of specific therapies, coupled with extensive follow up for some conditions, and ongoing research into the efficacy of approaches (NICE, 2003).

Principles and Skills

The creation of a *therapeutic alliance* is necessary but often tricky when combined with the responsibility for ensuring weight gain. There needs to be some form of dialogue, which both recognises and *respects the wishes* of the person seeking help, but also transparently reveals any constraints or agency demands placed on the helpers. Nurses in the field hold many *ideals and beliefs* related to eating, weight, exercise and body shape. To be *empathic* they are required to be aware of these and how they influence their *perception and attitude* towards their patient. For instance nurses may value thinness and practice restricted eating and yet insist their patient give up these ideals (Williams, 2000).

A lack of power or rather a perception of powerlessness is of prime importance in eating disorders (Katzman, 1997), this may be similar for both males and females. Therefore, there is a need to recognise the *power differentials*, the *sufferers desire to please the therapist*, and the *passivity inherent* in the marginalisation of women's experiences (Kayrooz, 2001).

The creation of some form of therapeutic contract is essential as, effective clinicians show empathetic understanding for patient's feelings of despair, defiance and mistrust (Yager, 2002, p. 345). A *therapeutic alliance* can only be said to exist when patient and professional have an *agreement* on desired change and the steps to achieve this change. 'Whatever the model of therapy used, the therapeutic alliance is an important mediator of change' (Connan and Treasure, 2000, p. 140).

Nurses rarely work in isolation from other disciplines and this issue will require some discussion and agreement if treatments are to be perceived as *helpful*. Some claim it is essential that *therapeutic congruence* be created with all involved clinicians operating from a shared philosophy rather than from their own perspective alone (Berg *et al.*, 2002).

At times of emotional difficulty an eating disorder can be experienced as a comfort and security and the person may cling to their symptoms. Other times they resent the way in which the disorder exerts control or influences their lives and wish they were free of its tyranny. Nurses must be *alert* to this and see these shifts as *windows of opportunity* to *explore the possibility of change* while *demonstrating sensitivity, concern* and *recognition of the fears* involved when trying to change.

Assessment

Approach

It has been suggested mortality rates may increase in areas that do not have specialist input (Crisp *et al.*, 1992). This gives weight to the argument that severe eating disorders should have access to specialist services close to home, as this offers the best prognosis (RCP, 2000). Even where these specialist services exist, it does not mean nurses in other settings will not need special skills and experience of assessing and managing these cases. It is likely nurses at all levels will be required to assess and possibly provide interventions at least for some part of the process, even when ultimately there is an intention to re-refer to another service. Of equal concern is that in the process of recovery, conditions can alter with some moving from one diagnosis to another that is, anorexia into bulimia (Lawrence, 2001) and vice versa.

There are at least four distinct goals in initial assessment that may occur in several different settings:

1. Recognition of the existence of an eating disorder,
2. Type and severity of the disorder,
3. Does the person wish to change,
4. Risk assessment focusing on and discussing the individuals' ability to take control of their symptoms.

The third and fourth point should be approached with openness, and attempts should be made to reach some agreement on what will happen if goals or targets are not achieved within an identified timescale for this to occur.

It has been suggested many eating disorders are often not detected within primary care settings (EDA, 2000). This is of concern as those who are detected early and are given specialist assessment generally do better than those who do not (EDA, 2000; RCP, 2000).

In essence a standard mental health assessment will uncover much of the information needed, however there are some additional enquiries that will prove useful. In all cases of eating disorder it is essential to seek to gain information in the following:

Weight

- Establish height and current weight to ascertain Body Mass Index (BMI).
- Taking a detailed weight history will prove useful. Starting from the earliest memory of weight (or clothes size) moving to the present time can help identify the rate of any precipitous weight loss and map out changes. This can be used to seek an understanding of reasons for these changes while making connections to life events.

Physical

- History of menstrual cycle.
- Current dietary intake, with attention to any restrictions or avoidance of particular food groups and the reasons for this.

Behaviour

- Weight or shape concerns and weighing behaviours.
- Details and frequency and severity of any binging or purging behaviours with reference to the degree of control or distress involved.

- Details of any compensatory behaviour such as purging, exercise, and usage of laxatives, emetics, appetite suppressants, slimming pills or amphetamines.
- A detailed behavioural assessment of the precipitants for such behaviours and an understanding of the sufferers perceived advantages or consequences of their behaviour would help guide initial interventions.

Formulation

- Create a psychological formulation including predisposing, precipitating and maintenance factors. The meaning and utility of the symptoms is crucial for interventions.

(Adapted from Birchall, 2002)

Where a person is seen is likely to influence the information provided. For many discussing their symptoms can involve intense emotional upheaval and create embarrassment, with many sufferers attempting to keep their behaviour hidden from others. At the outset, in most situations, it is desirable to request they attend a professional setting where the environment can be controlled; privacy ensured and then interview the person alone. If assessment reveals an eating disorder of significant severity then a physical assessment should be arranged to determine the current health status.

Process

The attitude and knowledge of the person first contacted is the most important variable in the engagement process (EDA, 2000). The gender of the interviewer is of less importance than attitude, and having a good understanding of the impact of eating disorders (Copperman, 2000). The interviewer should focus on helping the individual to discuss their behaviours in an open and honest manner. This can be difficult, as they may fear the consequences of revealing their actions. Some may assume judgemental responses and a loss of control, while others can have feelings of self-hatred, disgust or shame.

One way of creating a collaborative dialogue is by use of motivational interviewing (Miller and Rollnick, 2001), and this has been modified as a tool for helping to understand the desires of people with eating disorders and potential for change (Treasure and Ward, 1997). This model proposes reflective listening and empathic understanding to bridge the differences between beliefs of change and perceived ability to make these changes a reality.

Information should not be imposed but given in a way that allows the person to consider what is said, take an interest, and respond if they choose. Some contend motivation is not an internal state but is best viewed from a non-structuralist position as an intentional state that arises out of communication (Carey, 2003). For instance, Motivation is a malleable construct and can be modulated by interpersonal processes (Treasure, 2002, p. 10). This acknowledges that knowing an action may improve an aspect of your life is not the same as being able to carry this out. Resistance is best considered as 'a lack of matching between therapist intervention and patient readiness for change, and indicates need for a change in treatment strategy' (Connan and Treasure, 2000, p. 143). It may be helpful to remember, the problem is the problem not the person.

Information Gathering

As there are no prescriptive treatments that can be administered for eating disorders it is vital the individual is recruited into the treatment and an alliance at the earliest time. Secrecy and honesty are issues to be addressed as many will keep certain aspects of their condition hidden from significant others. In cases of anorexia fear will lead some to attempt to prevent accurate monitoring of their condition, by artificially massaging their weight to present as heavier, by use of tricks like, water loading and hiding weights on their person. It must be remembered that there is a big difference between 'seeking' and 'being taken' for help, and therefore it is possible to alienate the client if one insists upon involving relatives in the process. Relatives and carers can provide useful information but one should always be aware that their aspirations and desires might differ considerably from the sufferer. The client's perception of any involvement of carers can create suspicion and might not be conducive to the creation of a therapeutic alliance with the sufferer.

Permission will need to be sought for ongoing current accurate measurement of weight and BMI rather than relying on other sources. This permission can only be negotiated. Due to the secrecy involved in many cases of bulimia, the sufferer will be required to voluntarily reveal details of how the condition manifests.

Some information can be gleaned from medical case notes and from the patient's GP or other involved professionals. Previous case notes can reveal potential strengths to be mobilised and also areas of potential difficulty.

Baseline and ongoing information may be sought by making arrangements for some routine screening investigations to be carried out. Where distance is a problem this can often be arranged with the GP who may also weigh the client then communicate this to others involved.

These tests should routinely include,

- Full blood count
- Urea and electrolytes (Us & Es)
- Glucose
- Ionised calcium (++ where purging is a feature), magnesium, phosphate, zinc etc.
- Liver function tests (LFTs) (Gamma GT where alcohol usage is a feature)
- Thyroid function tests (TSH & FT4)
- Oestrogen, Progesterone, LH and FSH.

- ECG (particularly if Us and Es are abnormal).
- DEXA scan (if amenorrhoea has been a feature for a year or more).

Tools Used

There are a number of screening tools available to clinicians with good evidence of reliability in detection of eating disorder symptoms. These can be used when clinicians have concerns related to eating problems.

- Eating Attitudes Test (Garner and Garfinkel, 1979).
- Eat 26 (Garner *et al.*, 1982).
- Eating Disorders Inventory (EDI) (Garner *et al.*, 1983).
- The Bulimic Investigatory Test (BITE) (Henderson and Freeman, 1987).
- Scoff questionnaire (Morgan *et al.*, 1999).

This list is not exhaustive but is an example of some of the tools available. Where results exceed thresholds these should be followed up by a detailed interview with reference to diagnostic criteria. The establishing of a diagnosis is not an indication of treatability as this relies on acceptance of the diagnosis, perception of symptoms as a problem, and desire to engage in attempts to alleviate the symptoms.

Risk Priorities

In all instances there is the need to consider the balance between physical risk, psychological need and implications of any complicating co-morbidity. There are generally less physical complications in bulimia than anorexia (Winston, 2002) and those that are of concern are mainly connected to purging behaviours. In anorexia severity, measured by duration and BMI, is an indicator of risk in terms of both mortality and outcome (Treasure, 2002). It is claimed males with eating disorders show higher prevalence of homosexuality, stronger psychiatric co-morbidity and more suicidal behaviour than the general population (Bramon-Bosch *et al.*, 2000). Issues for consideration of risk include:

- Anorexia might best be considered by looking at physical complications, suicidality, weight and motivation (Palmer and Treasure, 1999).
- Body Mass Index is used as a proxy measure of risk, is better than weight alone (Treasure, 2002) and the thresholds for referral to specialist services should be low (Connan and Treasure, 2000).
- Blood chemistry results are of importance particularly where purging behaviours are a feature of the condition.
- Where there is precipitous weight loss the use of a medical admission for re-feeding should be considered.

- This should only occur in a specialist setting (Winston, 2002) as there is a risk of re-feeding syndrome which while rare can be fatal (Solomon and Kirby, 1990).

There have been recent attempts to validate a tool (RIBeD-8) for measuring risk in eating disorders (Waaddegaard *et al.*, 2003). Reference to physical risk criteria (Winston, 2002) can help identify the levels of risk associated with weight loss and changes in biochemistry, although I would argue supplementary discussion with medical colleagues should be considered essential.

Care Planning

How Plan is Determined

As a general guide many nursing interventions can be thought of as similar across all diagnostic groups that is, working with restrictive eating or purging behaviours. Management of the most severe eating disorders invariably requires skilled psychological intervention, coupled with informed management of any physical debilitation. A comprehensive service for those with eating disorder will likely require the involvement of several disciplines and models, each providing a different lens with which to view and meet needs. Indeed it could be argued no single discipline could possibly hope to provide a comprehensive package of care (RCP, 2000).

When considering how the care plan is to be determined, problems in the alliance can arise when goals are not shared (Connan and Treasure, 2000). However the ambivalent nature of the condition (Anderson *et al.*, 1997) is likely to influence any such agreement and threaten any alliance. Without an alliance nurses are placed in a custodial role and while 'attempts to empower patients are viewed as imperative – it has been argued that treating patients as partners is an unrealistic ideal' (Speedy, 1999, p. 62).

Attempt to form a therapeutic relationship and find common agreement on the way forward. Goals must be negotiated and unshared goals can affect the relationship, but equally so will collusion with inappropriate goals (Connan and Treasure, 2000). Sharing professional concerns is important to maintain trust. Outpatient work should cease if stability is threatened, for example, continuing weight loss. Seek agreement among the professionals on the criteria for measuring improvement and the timescale for re-referral if this not achieved.

Inpatient treatment of severe anorexia nervosa is a specialised task and requires an environment that provides clear structured approaches to encourage eating and weight restoration, consistency by all team members in the delivery of these approaches, containment to allow for the expression of difficult emotional responses, and high levels of support for all involved.

Skilled nursing interventions are central in the treatment of anorexia nervosa in inpatient settings (Crisp *et al.*, 1985; Treasure *et al.*, 1998). This is one area where nurses are most influential as agents of change, 'The core of the work undertaken during treatment is the work of the nurses, the main goals of which are: ... forming a therapeutic alliance and ... weight restoration' (Treasure *et al.*, 1998, p. 278). The alliance should be collaborative, kind, firm and consistent and issues of power, control and trust need to be recognised (Treasure *et al.*, 1998).

Treatments that rely on weight gain and the use of behavioural restrictions have been heavily criticised in the nursing literature as unethical, unnecessary, for the benefit of the carers in that it creates short-term improvement, and contributing to the continuing medicalisation of the conditions (Parkin, 1995; Clare and Cuthbertson, 1998). One of the difficulties facing nurses is the dearth of nursing contribution to the literature and the prescriptive nature of that which does exist. Much of the literature about nursing interventions is written by other professionals rather than by nurses for nurses (Treasure *et al.*, 1998). It is widely accepted strict behavioural plans are inappropriate (Connan and Treasure, 2000) however treatment invariably requires some restrictions. Care can be conceptualised as the management of the environment based on the demonstrable ability to take responsibility for one's self. This will require skilled interventions combining the practical application of some of the following.

Practical Application

Components of an Outpatient Care Plan

- Request the GP carry out routine blood tests and weekly weighing at the same time.
- Request the family read some of the available self-help literature (Crisp *et al.*, 1996; Treasure, 1997) for education regarding the disorder. This is likely to be of benefit to carers and by offering realistic hope of change.
- Provide psycho-education regarding the potential consequences of the disorder (Garner, 1997). Some suggest this forms a main part of engagement and later treatment before using more intensive interventions (Connan and Treasure, 2000).
- Suggest recording nutritional intake and gradually introduce agreed incremental increases aimed at weight gain of half-a-kilogram per week. (This work is often carried out by a dietician, if available.)
- Agree on regular review dates for discussing progress while also seeking permission to involve carers/parents if appropriate.

It has been suggested, the aligning of professional, carer and sufferer perceptions relating to the course, duration and outcome of the illness process is helpful in improving coping (Treasure *et al.*, 2003). If it becomes apparent that the client is unable to gain control of the symptoms, the professionals involved should start to introduce the idea of hospitalisation. This provides time for adjustment to the idea and allows exploration of any fears involved.

Components of the Inpatient Care Plan

- Dependent on physical concerns some judicious use of restricted movements for a specified limited period that is, reduced exercise, bed-rest, use of wheelchair, supervised showers and toilets where the risk of falls is present.
- Resolution of the feeding issues that is, non-restricted or restricted food choices with only so many forbidden foods, for example, vegetarian, low fat, dairy products etc., energy supplements, and when or if naso-gastric feeding would be considered. Ensuring the availability of the chosen nutrition at the right time through liaison with dieticians and kitchens. This is essential due to the high levels of anxiety involved when confronted with an unexpected food or meal.
- Meal supervision prior to, during and after meals, employment of anxiety management techniques.
- Changes to the care plan should be made only once a week to create a frame in which to reflect and prevent knee-jerk reactions.
- Changes should be agreed and made in the full ward review rather than at any other times to ensure the client and multidisciplinary team are all on board with changes. This allows the most experienced practitioners to take part in any dialogue about change and helps eradicate 'acting out' of unhelpful emotional responses by the clinical team.
- No changes to the care plan until they are documented and communicated effectively with the client and across the team. Consistency is crucial to maintain trust.

Contact with the next referral agency should be made sooner rather than later to allow for any delays in accepting the referral. The sufferer and their carers should have an opportunity to visit the inpatient unit, meet the staff and discuss expectations prior to admission. Patients' perceptions of powerlessness can be lessened by being honest and telling them what to expect (Holyoake and Jenkins, 1998). Notwithstanding this, the potential to encounter resentment and possible frustration is high and helpers must tolerate these feelings without 'acting out' as a response.

Additional Care Planning

Where psychiatric co-morbidity is present then a full mental health assessment must be undertaken by an appropriate professional to consider how this might impact on any intervention.

Documentation

As in other psychiatric conditions there is a need to assess client need using the Care Programme Approach (CPA) to provide a common assessment

Case Example

Jenny was 18-years old and first came to the attention of services when her mother contacted the family GP to express her concern about weight loss. At appointment she described how she was happy with her weight and could not understand what the fuss was about. She described how she had reduced her intake by cutting out 'fatty foods' after she had experienced taunting from peers at college regarding her size and shape. Jenny repeatedly stated there was nothing wrong and it was just that she no longer wanted to eat the same foods as in the past.

She revealed she was exercising daily 'to help keep my weight down'. She denied any purging behaviours. The GP measured her height at 1.73 metres and noted her weight had fallen from 60 to 50 kilograms over a 4-month period. Throughout the appointment her mother expressed her concern and requested Jenny be sent for physical tests. After taking some routine blood tests and failing to find any physical cause the GP suspected an eating disorder and referred Jenny to a practise based community mental health nurse (CMHN).

Outcome

Despite the interventions offered at outpatients, Jenny was unable to prevent further weight loss. Over the next three months she continued to lose weight, dropping to 40 kilograms and a BMI of 13.4, which placed her in a severe category of risk. Her CMHN had established a trusting relationship that allowed her to ask Jenny when she should intervene. This created an opportunity to explore Jenny's relationship with anorexia and consider at what point could they agree Jenny was losing the struggle. During this period the CMHN had spent time with Jenny and her parents discussing their perceptions, fears and expectations.

framework. While this is a useful framework, on its own, it rarely provides the detailed information required to guide intervention for complex eating disorders. In general, the more severe the condition, the more detailed the assessment format used at different points using a 'stepped care' approach. This is appropriate as many conditions are malleable to change with minimal intervention, whereas others will demand detailed psychological and behavioural profiling within specialist settings. At this time there is no universal format for care planning with each service adopting their own system of recording.

Time Frame

The time involved will depend on the goals agreed in the care plan. It is vital all are clear of the expectations regarding intervention. In anorexia this may mean a full restoration of weight or only an agreed increase of a number of BMI points. For outpatient treatment it is usual for an increase of 1/2 a kilogram per week up to target weight. Treatment of this nature will likely be carried out over approximately six months minimum. This will require weekly sessions at first, but this contact will usually decrease as treatment progresses, and follow-up may take place over several months.

Inpatient treatment usually requires a weight gain of one kilogram per week and involves a stay of sufficient length to allow for this. Therapeutic sessions should be sufficiently frequent to capitalise on the increased availability afforded by admission to hospital.

Time needs to be allocated to allow any psychological milestones to be met and this will need to be negotiated in the light of progress made. All interventions should also allow for some discrepancy in progress as recovery rarely follows a smooth path.

Treatment of bulimia may mean a reduction in, rather than total removal of all the target symptoms. This usually involves a time-limited therapy of any number between 4 up to 20 sessions for uncomplicated cases depending on the type of intervention offered. The frequency may range from weekly to monthly again this is dependent on the type of therapy but should be agreed at the outset.

Evidence Base

In the case of anorexia there is little hard evidence on the best methods of treatment (Palmer and Treasure, 1999). Treasure and Kordy (1998) provide an excellent insight into the difficulties involved. Much of what is offered is based on clinical experience rather than randomised control studies (RCTs) or other forms of evidence (Palmer and Treasure, 1999). Some even question the usefulness of RCTs for anorexia (Connan and Treasure, 2000). NICE (2003) guidelines have used a variety of measures to obtain and define what evidence exists. Bulimia has been subjected to considerable research (Wilson *et al.*, 1997) and the use of cognitive behavioural therapy in manual form is widely recognised as helpful in many cases (Fairburn *et al.*, 1993). Some early studies of eating disorders reported similarities in males and females, later studies show some exceptions, therefore some aspects can be generalised to males (Bramon-Bosch *et al.*, 2000).

Dissemination of Information

It is vital efforts are made to avoid the common dynamic of 'splitting' (Palmer, 2000) with the treatment team subsequently 'mirroring' these splits. This can be avoided by ensuring there is clarity of purpose and responsibility of all involved professionals. However the danger in adopting such an open system of communication is that private information can become very public. One way to address this is to provide the client with copies of all assessments made and letters sent to other involved professionals. This approach supports the notion of transparency and enhances trust. Requests to provide partners or relatives with specific information should be explored with the individual to ensure this is helpful to them and not an act of coercion.

Confidentiality should be respected and every effort made to discuss any time when this might not be possible. This is likely where there is considerable risk of serious self-harm, suicide, or where the law requires clinicians to breach confidentiality (child sexual abuse situations where others are still at risk).

Every effort must be made to ensure information gathered is treated with the utmost respect. Any discussion regarding a client should only be conducted in an appropriate environment where it is safe to speak without fear of being overheard by others. Likewise documentation should be held in a safe setting.

Reflective Practice

Consider the impact of nurses' own belief systems relating to body shape, size, eating rituals, healthy diet and fitness. How might this contribute to perceptions of deviance from norms? Consider the dominant societal influences or socioeconomic narratives which impact on females with reference to similarities to males. Consider the concept of a 'therapeutic alliance' while asking if this is likely to exist with all members of a team or only some individuals for some of the time.

From a feminist perspective eating disorders are essentially gendered disorders (Orbach 1979) in response to the problems of sexism, weightism and lookism (Katzman *et al.*, 1994). Some have claimed female therapists are more likely to understand and empathise with another woman (Stockwell and Dolan, 1994). Others question this assumption and suggest that no therapist is value free and conflict can occur in relationships with either sex (Kopp, 1994). It would seem imperative that gender be identified as a possible obstacle with some consideration given as to how this might impact on the relationship. Even where there are no apparent difficulties it may be prudent to seek the help of a colleague of the same gender as the sufferer for supervision purposes (Kopp, 1994).

Speedy (1999) provides a cogent argument for nurses to seek answers to the question of 'why they do what they do'? Speedy (1999, p. 60) contends no alliance exists until the nurse 'understands what makes a particular patient's behaviour seem reasonable given their definition of the situation'.

It is imperative for anyone working in the field to have access to supervision from an experienced clinician if 'acting out' and 'acting into the acting out' of these dynamics are to be avoided. Palmer (2000) has suggested supervision has a number of connotations and may be provided by a number of different professionals each bringing their own expertise. This will require nurses to dismantle their traditional boundaries to supervision where only a nurse can understand what it is to be a nurse. It is likely clinicians will benefit from individual and some types of group and peer supervision. Case presentations in team meetings provide valuable opportunities for inexperienced staff to take part in conversations with the whole treatment team.

Practice Development

Recent guidelines (NICE, 2003) indicate the need for further research and evidence-based practice for all eating disorders. These guidelines will almost certainly lead to a more standardised approach than has been the case to date. Recommendations of this nature will require clinicians to look at the methods of delivering standardised treatments, and ensuring they are administering them in a sufficiently consistent fashion. Given the dearth of high quality evidence available to date, it will be vital for clinicians to understand the strengths and weaknesses in the treatments proposed.

It is probable the future will place services under pressure to deliver outcomes at least comparable to the evidence base. In turn this is likely to result in some standardisation of training for each discipline involved, and will require agreement on the setting of minimum standards. It will be desirable to have some standards rather than the ad hoc approach which has been the norm to date (Palmer, 2000). There are currently no special qualifications needed to work in the field of eating disorders but this may change in the future.

Conclusion

Working in the field of eating disorders is a challenging and yet rewarding experience. This chapter has discussed, explored and detailed a comprehensive overview of the adult services for eating disorders. The treatments and interventions are described and the requirements of the nurse delivering them. The clinical setting is predominantly gender specific, with the overwhelming majority of cases being female. This immediately draws attention to gender and creates an interesting dynamic unnoticed in other areas of mental health. Eating disorders is an arena of specialist practice that offers nurses an opportunity to develop skills and provide care to a unique clientele.

📖 Suggested Further Reading

Garner, D.M., and Garfinkel, P.E. (1997) (eds), *Handbook of Treatment for Eating Disorders*, New York: Guildford Press.

Palmer, R.L. (2000) *Helping People with Eating Disorders: A Clinical Guide to Assessment and Treatment*, Chichester, Wiley.

References

Anderson, A.E., Bowers, W. and Evans, K. (1997) Inpatient treatment of anorexia nervosa, in Garner, D.M., and Garfinkel, P.E. (eds), *Handbook of Treatment for Eating Disorders* (second edn), New York: Guildford Press.

APA (1994) *Diagnostic and Statistical Manual of Mental Disorders* (4th edn), Washington DC: American Psychiatric Association.

Audit Commission (1997) *Higher Purchase: Commissioning Specialised Services in the NHS.* London: Audit Commission.

Berg, K.M., Hurley, D.J., McSherry, J.A. and Strange, N.E. (2002) *Eating Disorders a Patient-centred Approach*, United Kingdom: Radcliffe Medical Press.

Birchall, H. (2002) Management of eating disorders for the generalist, eating disorders, *Psychiatry*, 1, 2: 25–8.

Bramon-Bosch, E., Troop, N.A. and Treasure, J.L. (2000) Eating disorders in males: a comparison with female patients, *European Eating Disorders Review*, 8, 4: 321–8.

Carey, M. (2003) 'A response', *Context*, 69: 10.

Clare, L. and Cuthbertson, G. (1998) Ethical issues in the treatment of women with eating disorders, *Mental Health Nursing*, 18, 1: 15–17.

Connan, F. and Treasure, J. (2000) Working with adults with anorexia nervosa in an outpatient setting, *Advances in Psychiatric Treatment*, 6: 135–44.

Copperman, J. (2000) Eating disorders in the United Kingdom: review Of the provision of health care services for men with eating disorders, Norwich: Eating Disorders Association Publication.

Crisp, A.H. (1997) Anorexia Nervosa as flight from growth: assessment and treatment based on the model, in Garner, D.M. and Garfinkel, P.E. (eds), *Handbook of Treatment for Eating Disorders* (second edn), New York: Guildford Press.

Crisp, A.H., Callender, J.S., Halek, C. and Hsu, L.K.G. (1992) Long term mortality in anorexia nervosa: A 20 year follow-up of the St George's and the Aberdeen cohorts. *British Journal of Psychiatry*, 161: 104–7.

Crisp, A.H., Joughin, N., Halek, C. and Bower, C. (1996) *Anorexia Nervosa: The Wish to Change*. Hove, East Sussex: Psychology Press.

Crisp, A.H., Norton, K.R.S., Jurczak, S. and Bowyer, C. (1985) A treatment approach to Anorexia Nervosa – 25 Years On, *Journal of Psychiatry* 19, 2/3: 393–404.

Department of Health (1999) *A National Service Framework for Mental Health*, London: Stationery Office.

Duran, T.L., Cashion, L.B., Gerber, T.A. and Mendez-Ybanez, G.B. (2000) Social constructionism and eating disorders: relinquishing labels and embracing personal stories, *Journal of Systemic Therapies*, 19, 2: 23–42.

Eating Disorders Association (1995) *Eating Disorders: A Guide to Purchasing and Providing Services*, Norwich: EDA.

Eating Disorders Association (2000) *The Need for Action in 2000 and Beyond*, Norwich: Eating Disorders Publications.

Fairburn C., Cooper, Z. and Shafran, R. (2003) Cognitive Behavioural Therapy for Eating Disorders: a transdiagnostic theory and treatment, *Behaviour Research and Therapy*, 41: 509–28.

Fairburn, C.G., Marcus, M.D. and Wilson, G.T. (1993) Cognitive Behavioural Therapy for binge eating and bulimia nervosa: a comprehensive treatment manual, in Fairburn, C.G. and Wilson, G.T. (eds), *Binge Eating: Nature Assessment and Treatment*, London: Guildford Press.

Garner, D.M. and Garfinkel, P.E. (1979) The Eating Attitudes Test: an index of the symotoms of anorexia nervosa, *Psychological Medicine*, 9: 273–9.

Garner, D.M., Olmsted, M.P., Bohr, Y. and Garfinkel, P.E. (1982) The Eating Attitudes Test: psychometric features and clinical correlates, *Psychological Medicine*, 12: 871–8.

Garner, D.M., Olmsted, M.P. and Polivy, J. (1983) Development and validation of a multidimensional eating disorder inventory for anorexia nervosa and bulimia, *International Journal of Eating Disorders*, 2: 15–34.

Garner, D.M. (1997) Psychoeducational Principles in Treatment, in Garner, D.M., and Garfinkel, P.E. (eds), *Handbook of Treatment for Eating Disorders* (second edn), New York: Guildford Press.

Garner, D.M. and Garfinkel, P.E. (1997) (eds), *Handbook of Treatment for Eating Disorders* (second edn), New York: Guildford Press.

Hepworth, J. (1999) *The Social Construction of Anorexia Nervosa*, London: Sage.

Henderson, M. and Freeman, C.P.L (1987) A self-rating scale for bulimia: the BITE. *British Journal of Psychiatry*, 146: 18–24

Hoek, H.W. (2002) Distribution of eating disorders, in Fairburn, C.G. and Brownell, K.D. (eds), *Eating Disorders and Obesity: A Comprehensive Handbook*, London: Guildford Press.

Holyoake, D.D. and Jenkins, M. (1998) PAT: Advanced Nursing Interventions for Eating Disorders, *Mental Health Nursing*, 7, 10: 596–600.

Hughes, P (1997) The use of the countertransference in the therapy of patients with Anorexia Nervosa, *European Eating Disorders Review*, 5, 4: 258–69.

Katzman, M. A. (1997) 'Getting the difference right: it's power not gender that matters', *European Eating Disorders Review*, 5, 2: 71–4.

Katzman, M.A., Wooley, S.C. and Fallon, P. (1994) Eating Disorders: A gendered disorder. *Eating Disorders Review*, 5, 6: 1–3.

Kayrooz, C. (2001) *A Systemic Treatment of Bulimia Nervosa: Women in Transition*, London: Jessica Kingsley Publishers.

Kopp, W. (1994) Can women with eating disorders benefit from a male therapist, in Dolan, B. and Gitzinger, I. (eds), *Why Women: Gender Issues and Eating Disorders*, London: Athlone Press.

Lacey, H. (1992) Diagnostic issues: clinical features; physical complications; prevalence, St. George's Eating Disorder Conference Proceedings, *Eating Disorders and their Treatment: Anorexia Nervosa and Bulimia Nervosa*, St. George's Medical School: The Priory Hospital Group.

Lawrence, M. (2001) Loving them to death: the anorexic and her objects, The *International Journal of Psycho-Analysis* 82, 43: 43–55.

Miller, W. and Rollnick, S. (2001) *Motivational Interviewing: Preparing People to Change Addictive Behaviour*, New York: Guildford Press.

Morgan, J.F., Reid, F. and Lacey, J.H. (1999) The SCOFF questionnaire: assessment of a new screening tool for eating disorders, *British Medical Journal*, 319: 1467–8.

NICE (2003) Eating Disorders: core interventions in the treatment and management of anorexia nervosa, bulimia nervosa, and related eating disorder, *Draft for Second Consultation*, National Institute for Clinical Excellence, D.O.H.

Orbach, S. (1979) *Fat is a Feminist Issue*, London: Hamlyn.

Palmer, R.L. (2000) *Helping People with Eating Disorders: A Clinical Guide to Assessment and Treatment*, Chichester: Wiley.

Palmer, R.L. and Treasure, J. (1999) 'Providing specialised services for anorexia nervosa, *British Journal of Psychiatry*, 175: 306–9.

Parkin, D. (1995) Interpretations and treatment of anorexia nervosa, *Mental Health Nursing*, 15, 1: 18–20.

Royal College of Psychiatry Eating Disorders Special Interest Group (2000) 'Eating disorders in the UK: policies for service development and training', *Council Report CR87*.

Russell, G. and Marsden, P. (1998) What does the therapist feel? Countertransference with bulimic women with borderline personality disorder, *British Journal of Psychotherapy*, 15, 1: 31–42.

Schmidt, U. (2002) Aetiology of eating disorders, *Psychiatry*, 1, 2: 5–8.

Silverman, J.A. (1995) Something New under the sun: Comments on Gerald Russell's 'Anorexia Nervosa Through Time', in Szmukler, G., Dare, C. and Treasure, J. (eds), *Handbook of Eating Disorders: Theory, Treatment and Research*, Chichester: Wiley.

Silverman, J.A. (1997) Anorexia nervosa: historical perspective on treatment, in Garner, D.M. and Garfinkel, P.E. (eds), *Handbook of Treatment for Eating Disorders* (second edn), New York: Guildford Press.

Solomon, S.M., and Kirby, D.F. (1990) The Refeeding Syndrome: A Review, *Journal of Parenteral and Enteral Nutrition*, 14, 1: 90–7.

Speedy, S. (1999) The therapeutic alliance, in Clinton, M. and Nelson, S. (eds), *Advanced Practice in Mental Health Nursing*, Oxford: Blackwell Science Ltd., pp. 60, 62.

Stockwell, R. and Dolan, B. (1994) Women therapists for women patients, in Dolan, B. and Gitzinger, I. (eds), *Why Women: Gender Issues and Eating Disorders*, London: Athlone Press.

Treasure, J. (1997) *Anorexia Nervosa: A Survival Guide for Families, Friends, and Sufferers*. United Kingdom: Psychology Press Ltd.

Treasure, J. (2002) Treatment of anorexia nervosa, eating disorders, *Psychiatry* 1, 2: 9–12.

Treasure, J. and Kordy, H. (1998) Evidence based care of eating disorders: beware the glitter of the randomised controlled trial, *European Eating Disorders Review*, 6, 2: 85–95.

Treasure, J. and Ward, A. (1997) A practicle guide to the use of motivational interviewing in anorexia nervosa, *European Eating Disorders Review*, 5, 2: 102–14.

Treasure, J., Todd, G. and Szmukler, G. (1998) The inpatient treatment of anorexia nervosa, in Szmukler, G., Dare, C. and Treasure, J. (eds), *Handbook of Eating Disorders: Theory, Treatment and Research*, Chichester: Wiley, p. 278.

Treasure, J., Gavan, K., Todd, G. and Schmidt, U. (2003) Changing the environment in eating disorders: working with carers? Families to improve motivation and facilitate Change, *European Eating Disorders Review*, 11, 1: 25–37.

Waaddegaard, M., Thoning, H. and Petersson, B. (2003) Validation of a screening instrument for identifying risk behaviour related to eating disorders, *European Eating Disorders Review*, 11, 6: 433–55.

White, M. (1995) *Re-authoring Lives: Interviews and Essays*, South Australia: Dulwich Centre Publications.

White, M. and Epston, D. (1991) *Narrative Means to Therapeutic Ends*, New York: W.W. Norton.

Williams, T. (2000) *If the Two Hats Fit Wear Them*, Unpublished, University of Northumbria at Newcastle.

Wilson, G.T., Fairburn, C.G. and Agras, W.S. (1997) Cognitive-Behavioural Therapy for bulimia nervosa, in Garner, D.M. and Garfinkel, P.E. (eds), *Handbook of Treatment for Eating Disorders* (second edn), New York: Guildford Press.

Winston, A.P. (2002) Management of physical aspects and complications of eating disorders, *Psychiatry*, 1, 2: 17–20.

Yager, J. (2002) Management of patients with intractable eating disorders, in Fairburn, C.G. and Brownell, K.D. (eds), *Eating Disorders and Obesity: A Comprehensive Handbook*, London: Guildford Press.

CHAPTER 13

Co-morbidity

Malcolm Watts

Introduction

The terms Co-morbidity and Dual Diagnosis are often used as interchangeable. However, the needs of this client group are complex and include psychiatric, psychological, education, employment and social care (Lehman *et al.*, 1989). Therefore, for the purpose of this chapter, the term co-morbidity is preferred. Co-morbidity is defined as the simultaneous co-existence of a psychiatric disorder and a substance misuse disorder (Weaver, 1999).

There is a clear challenge for mental health nurses and other professions to deal with these conditions in a caring and effective manner. Traditionally substance misuse and mental health services have developed separately (DoH, 2002) and this has often meant that clients were shuttled between services with a loss of continuity and care. Literature has clearly indicated that clients who experience psychosis and have a co-existing substance misuse problem are at risk of falling between two services (Graham, 1998; DoH, 2002). Subsequently many clients have 'slipped through the net' (Gournay and Glorney, 1998) resulting in more severe problems and difficulties in accessing services (DoH, 2002). People with co-morbid problems have complex needs (Hunt and Ashenhurst, 2000) and are expensive to treat, making disproportionate use of legal, health and social services (Watkins *et al.*, 2001). Indeed, Professor Louis Appleby states that,

> Supporting someone with a mental health illness and substance misuse problems – alcohol and/or drugs – is one of the biggest challenges facing frontline mental health services. (DoH, 2002)

Prevalence and Population

There are some difficulties assessing the exact levels of substance misuse in those with mental health problems (DoH, 2002). There has been increasing evidence since the early 1980s that some individuals diagnosed with schizophrenia engage in 'self medication' possibly to reduce unpleasant side effects of their medication (Knudsen and Vilmar, 1984). The co-existence of problems can be described as 'the chicken and egg' predicament. Indeed, people with a diagnosis of severe mental illness assessed in Accident and Emergency (A&E) have a higher degree of substance misuse (Galanter *et al.*, 1988). Conversely, Reiger *et al.* (1988) found that 71 per cent of substance misusers also had a mental disorder.

In the 1990s an increase in the number of population based and epidemiological research studies examining psychiatric disorder identified that some people were using drugs and alcohol harmfully. A number of recognised authorities have indicated that:

- Individuals with mental health problems have an increased risk of developing a substance misuse problem (Gafoor and Rassool, 1998).
- Some 73 per cent of psychiatric admissions are diagnosed with co-morbidity when the person is given a diagnosis of schizophrenia (Smith *et al.*, 1994).
- There is a prevalence rate of 61 per cent lifetime personality disorder among Australian opiate addicts (Drake and Noordsy, 1994).
- A study in Camberwell, London, identified that over 31 per cent of people with psychosis also suffered from substance misuse (Menezes *et al.*, 1996).
- Community Mental Health Teams (CMHTs) have reported that up to 15 per cent of their patients have a co-existing problem of mental illness and substance misuse (DoH, 2002).

Referrals

Primary care services must to be able to assess the needs of those people with mental health problems as is identified in Standard Two of the National Service Framework (DoH, 2002). Therefore referrals to mainstream mental health services, which have the responsibility to address the needs of co-morbid patients (DoH, 2002), will in part be derived from primary care sources. Referrals are also made from secondary level services such as social services, voluntary agencies and inpatient care.

In areas where substance misuse services are set up as part of mental health services these would also receive direct referrals to the responsible consultant psychiatrist direct from primary care. The co-morbidity team may also receive referrals from primary care but in the main they are from mental health services.

Referral to the CMHT with a specialist co-morbidity team Referrals are accepted from a general practitioner (GP), psychiatrist, social services and voluntary sector agencies. The referrals are then discussed at the team meetings and an appropriate practitioner is directed to undertake the initial assessment. The decision regarding the appropriate practitioner is usually governed by the referral letter and usually dependant on the complex nature of the case and that the person being referred is known or not to the service. Should the person not be under the care of mental health services then a psychiatrist will usually conduct the assessment.

Direct referral to a co-morbidity team This team often consists of specialist mental health nurses attached to the main substance misuse or mental health service. Clients are referred from practitioners within the local mental health services. Referrals may differ slightly from the above mentioned in that the request is often for advice and help with a patient who is already receiving care under the mental health service.

It is difficult to provide a 'standard' referral system with the many services throughout the UK. The Dual Diagnosis Good Practice Guide (DoH, 2002) provides a number of useful examples. There are however some common criteria:

- Person must be suffering with a co-morbid problem that includes substance misuse.
- Person must be diagnosed with mental health problems. Some services would specify severe mental illness (e.g. psychosis, bi-polar disorder).
- Other services may accept broader criteria including behavioural disorders, personality disorders, depression and acute/chronic anxiety.
- Some services may accept referrals of those who are misusing substances in order to cope with an acute stress or post-traumatic stress disorder.

Acceptance of a person into the service is not entirely based on their willingness to change, give up or reduce their alcohol or drug use. These problems are often complex and inpatient detoxification is a consideration. Working with this client group is long term, with small but meaningful changes the goal.

Theoretical Framework

There are a number of interventions used in the treatment of co-morbidity (DoH, 2002). This section will discuss two of the major models. One is motivational interviewing as described by Miller and Rollnick (2002). It is a directive, client-centred counselling style for eliciting behaviour change by helping clients to explore and resolve ambivalence. The purpose is to strengthen the client's position on change and avoid confrontation. Key issues include:

(a) Motivation to change is elicited from the client, and not imposed from without.
(b) It is the client's task, not the counsellor's, to articulate and resolve his or her ambivalence.
(c) Direct persuasion is not an effective method for resolving ambivalence.
(d) The counsellor style is generally an eliciting one.
(e) The counsellor is directive in helping the client to examine and resolve ambivalence.

(f) Readiness to change is not a client trait, but a fluctuating product of interpersonal interaction.

(g) The therapeutic relationship is more like a partnership or companionship than expert/recipient roles.

(Adapted from Miller and Rollnick, 2002)

Given that the nature of substance misuse is that of a relapsing condition (DoH, 2002), the second major model is that of Relapse Prevention. Wanigaratne *et al.* (1990) describe a wide range of interventions to prevent relapse in addictive behaviours. It can be used throughout primary, secondary and tertiary levels of intervention. The model covers some eight areas of issues that occur in the development of relapse behaviour and the aim of the therapy is to equip clients with sufficient information and skills in order to deal with situations associated with relapse.

1. Anxiety
2. High-risk situations
3. Thinking errors
4. Psychological traps
5. Assertion
6. Decision-making and problem solving
7. Lifestyle balance
8. Depression.

The Manual of Relapse Prevention also includes a great deal of useful information on starting this therapy, troubleshooting and getting all the above approaches to work in conjunction (Wanigaratne *et al.*, 1990).

Also, this section will discuss the three main models of delivery used in the treatment of co-morbidity. One model will not be favoured over another, but simply explore their effectiveness and difficulties in what is hoped is an unbiased manner. At this time not all areas in the UK have developed specialist co-morbidity services and therefore several models are currently in everyday use. This is also compounded by the nature of NHS services, with individuals almost inevitably referred to one part of the service depending on their major presenting symptomatology.

Serial or consecutive treatment model   This model aims to provide treatment for substance misuse and mental illness in a consecutive manner (Kipping, 1999). It has been identified that the order of treatment depends upon which service the client contacts first, followed by interventions for the other problem by a different service (Baker, 1998). In essence this means that a person contacting mental health services will be treated for their mental illness and then referred on to substance misuse services. However, the issue of non-compliance is often raised by mental health services where the client continues to use substances. In some cases intoxication or the use of alcohol or illicit drugs to deal with stress, hallucinations or the effects of prescribed antipsychotic medication can hinder psychiatric treatment.

Some problems with this model have been identified as:

1. Limited communication between mental health and substance misuse services (Kipping, 1999; DoH, 2002).
2. Poor inter-agency working (Gourney and Glorney, 1998)
3. People with co-morbidity have *complex* needs (Hunt and Ashenhurst, 2000).
4. Coexisting severe mental illness and substance misuse problems are probably mutually interactive (DoH, 2002).

Parallel treatment model This is where the substance misuse and mental health services provide the two services concurrently (Kipping, 1999). This appears to be somewhat better than the Serial Model because the different services work together, although there are a number of weaknesses (Drake and Mercer-McFadden, 1995):

• Liaison between the services, as the services remain separate (Baker, 1998).
• There is incomplete treatment.
• Each service may provide a standard form of treatment but resist modification to deal with the coexisting disorder.

Integrated model The Integrated Model has grown some favour since research indicated that help for individuals diagnosed with a co-morbidity problem needed to be delivered in combination (Drake and Noordsy, 1994). Delivery of this integrated model is the use of concurrent interventions for both mental health and substance misuse provided through one team (Gournay, 1996; Kipping, 1999; DoH, 2002).

An integrated treatment programme has been defined as a programme in which the same clinician (or team of clinicians) provides treatment for both mental illness and substance misuse at the same time. The clinician(s) assumes responsibility for integrating the mental health and substance misuse treatments (Mueser *et al.*, 1998).

Kipping, citing Franey and Quirk (1996), identified that one model will be unable to meet the range of needs expressed by diverse problems of people with coexisting mental health and substance misuse problems (Kipping, 1999).

Principles and Skills

The nature of working with substance misusing clients requires the nurse to be skilled in a number of interventions (Rassool and Gafoor, 1997). Co-morbidity is a complex and complicated problem (Lehman *et al.*, 1989) and requires the nurse to adopt multiple roles in order to achieve a comprehensive level of care (Rassool, 1997).

Practicality A non-judgemental approach is required with a view that treatment will be long term. Progress is often slow and nurses must be able to accept that there is a likelihood of the person undergoing several relapses during the course of treatment. As discussed later a person centred approach is required with a good ability to communicate throughout a range of care services and professions. The nurse must have credibility with the client group and therefore a comprehensive knowledge of mental health, alcohol, illicit and prescribed drugs is required. In addition the nurse must be 'street wise' to what is going on locally in respect to the cost of drugs, quality, strength, variations in supply and some of the local social issues of drug/alcohol users.

Skills As discussed later, the care plan includes a number of different therapies and the nurse must be competent to provide many of these. The essentials will include, a specialist *substance misuse assessment, mental health* and *risk assessment*, the provision of specialist *advice on risk reduction* and *harm minimisation, treatment advice* to other care professionals, a *knowledge of individual* and *group work*, and the ability to *work in a multidisciplinary team*.

In practice it is not possible for nurses to be an expert in all the skills required, however they should have a working knowledge of some. The nurse can become trained to deliver comprehensive drug/alcohol programmes through developing skills in some of the following; *motivational interviewing, addiction counselling, cognitive behavioural therapy, relapse prevention, family therapy* and *brief therapy* (Sussman and Ames, 2001).

Assessment

Approach

The approach used would be in the format of any mental health assessment (refer to Chapters 3 and 6 on Primary Care and Rehabilitation and Recovery). However, for the purposes of this chapter the focus will be on issues related to the assessment of the person's substance misuse. There are five main issues related to a person's pattern of substance use that should be considered in assessment. The approach will incorporate an interview to ascertain:

1. *No substance use/misuse:* includes individuals, who for health, religious or personal reasons do not drink alcohol or use other substances including nicotine. This pattern also includes those individuals who due to past substance use problems are now abstinent. The non-existence of substance misuse would obviate the need for co-morbidity services.
2. *Experimental use:* refers to individuals who have been introduced to various substances and are learning about their effects. Positive and negative reinforcement of their behaviour will play a strong part in their substance use. There may also be 'experimentation' with a variety of substances and

alcoholic beverages. Referral to co-morbidity services would be rare at this level, however some brief advice and information would be helpful at this stage.

3. *Recreational use:* often follows on from experimentation. The substance, for example, cannabis, becomes socially acceptable within the person's peer group and is enjoyed with friends and may become a regular occurrence. Again referral at this stage is rare but there are benefits from advice and information, which could be found in most primary care settings.

4. *Heavy habitual use:* may become the norm for some drinkers and substance users. This may involve regular drunkenness with associated antisocial behaviour. This behaviour could include drunk and disorderly, lateness, absenteeism, drink driving and some physical/psychological problems. Heavy habitual substance misuse may also lead to criminal behaviour to support the cost and to loss of employment and educational opportunities. People with mental health problems may be at this stage while in general mental health care and staff may request help and advice. Most clients would benefit from some brief interventional advice and information but this type of intervention is insufficient in most cases with co-morbidity problems.

5. *Dependence:* on substances may develop from a pattern of heavy habitual use. This will require the specialist intervention of co-morbidity services.

Process

In the process of assessment there are a number of considerations that require addressing within co-morbidity. The information gathered helps both the client and the professional to determine the process of use. Often, it can be the first time the person has spoken about their problems. Therefore, sensitivity is necessary in establishing the nature of their substance use.

Substance Misuse History: It is important to assess what sort of substance has been used/misused, which are seen as problematic and which are not. Taking a retrospective approach, ask about what substances have been used and their level of consumption over the period of time following today backward over the last six months paying particular attention to variations in use.

To build up a picture of the extent of the person's substance use ask about:

- Their age of commencing first drink or/and use of drugs,
- Regular weekend use,
- Regular evening use,
- Regular lunch time use,
- Early morning use.

It is also important to assess any withdrawal symptoms, and other features like tolerance, compulsions/craving, and substance seeking behaviour.

Pattern of use: Ask whether drinking and drug use takes place most days or whether it is in bouts, at weekends or other times, and the time of their first drink or drug use in the day. This should assist in differentiating between recreational, binging and dependent use. It is also important to establish if the person uses substances alone or as part of a group, or both.

Quantity and strength: Ask about the type of alcohol and/or drugs used. Remember it is important to get an accurate picture of the person's substance use. Be specific about the strength of drinks/drugs and quantities. If the person drinks spirits ask how many bottles per day/week. If the person drinks beer/lager ask how many cans per day and what volume and percentage alcohol. Quantities can vary considerably, especially where drinking takes place at home. Ask how much they believe they are spending on alcohol/drugs.

Consequences of alcohol and drug use: Patients should be asked if alcohol and drugs have directly caused them any difficulties or harm (e.g. physical, psychological, behavioural, legal or social problems).

Periods of abstinence or treatment: Asking the person about periods of abstinence or treatment can offer further information on the severity of the problem. It also assists in understanding how the patient views their use of alcohol/drugs and can offer some insight into what treatment the person feels has helped in the past. It can be useful to explore how they managed during periods of abstinence, what helped recovery and what triggered their return to substance use. You will need to know, when, how long, what led to a period of abstinence, what help was used, reasons for relapse.

Getting in touch with previous treatment providers can support the care planning stage and offer possible onward referral points. It is important to know any previous treatment modalities. What was helpful and what was not. Has there been previous inpatient treatment? (e.g. for detoxification), previous attendance at specialist services etc. How long ago was the treatment undertaken and with what outcome?

Forensic history: Are there any past, present or pending charges for any offence and in particular any related to substance misuse?

Role of partner or significant other: If the person has a regular partner, the partner's alcohol/drug use will also be an important factor to consider and their attitude to the client's drinking or drug use.

Other substances: People using alcohol may also be using other substances. Conversely, people using drugs may also drink heavily. The most obvious one is tobacco, but the use of other drugs including prescribed medication and illicit drugs should be explored. Ask when the drug of choice is not alcohol, how much do they drink.

Physical examination is important, for example, gait, skin pallor, irritability, drowsiness, smell on breath, needle track marks, pulse and blood pressure.

Nurses may be concerned about discussing drink or drugs, but the client may also feel uncomfortable discussing their use of these substances. These anxieties need to be taken into consideration throughout the screening and assessment process.

Information Gathering

Most information is gained at the assessment interview(s). Assessment is an on going process and additional information can be gained over time. Various settings can be used for this purpose and include the client's home, the CMHT or a health centre. If laboratory tests are necessary, then a more clinical environment is necessary.

The recording of information would involve an assessment format. This can be 'localised' criteria, but would contain the information required above. The main source of information will be the client. However, other avenues may be sought to enrich the detail elicited. These can involve discussion with carers and partners with permission from the client. It may also entail the perusal of previous documentation, such as medical records, GP notes etc.

Several members of the multidisciplinary team may be involved each contributing some information to the overall level of client understanding. Regular meetings are required between all caregivers to ensure that the information is known to all involved.

Tools Used

There are no specific assessment tools used for co-morbidity. However, the Substance Abuse Assessment Questionnaire (SAAQ) (Ghodse, 1995) is useful and includes medical, psychological substance use and a profile of the substance misuser. It can also be used in conjunction with any mental health assessment tool highlighted in other chapters.

There are also a number of assessment techniques available, including:

- Assessment and Management of Risk of Harm in Dual Diagnosis (Anon., 2002, cited in DoH, 2002).
- The use of AUDIT and the DAST-10 to identify alcohol and drug use among adults with a severe and persistent mental illness (Maisto *et al.*, 2000).
- The Maudsley Addicition Profile (Marsden *et al.*, 1997).

For clearer identification of substance use, various laboratory tests are important in assessing the nature and severity of the alcohol or drug problem. They include:

- Blood alcohol levels (BAL), this is considered more accurate than clinical judgement at indicating those who are intoxicated.

- Urine toxicology (for drugs and alcohol).
- Blood tests for liver function tests, Hepatitis B/C antibodies, HIV.
- Breathalyser. Breath alcohol is considered much more useful in most circumstances.
- Taking a sample of saliva, (the so called '*Gob Swab*') to detect a variety of drugs used.

Risk Priorities

Risk assessment needs to address specific factors relevant to the individual with a co-morbidity diagnosis. The relationship between the severity of substance misuse and the risks associated should be explicitly documented (DoH, 2002). The main concerns explored may incorporate: *possibility of overdose, self-harm and suicide, the likelihood of aggressive, violent or anti-social behaviour, the impact on sexual health and the risk of sexually transmitted diseases.*

Care Planning

How Plan is Determined

A care plan is determined via the assessed needs of the client. They are central to the process of care planning and will help identify and develop the plan. As advocated by DoH (2002) the treatment approach follows four stages:

1. Engagement.
This is concerned with the development and maintenance of a care package. Development of a trusting relationship between nurse and client will help maintain them in the service (Gafoor and Rassool, 1998). A non-confrontational, non-judgmental approach should be adopted. Dealing with the patient's immediate needs (e.g. diet, accommodation and physical health), are more important to the person than making changes to their substance misuse.

2. Encouraging Motivation to Change.
As described above, motivational interviewing is paramount in strengthening a person's motivation to change their behaviour.

3. Introduction of Active Treatment.
At this stage, several months may have passed before the patient is ready to actively engage in treatment for their substance misuse. It may be unrealistic to aim for total abstinence and more appropriate to consider a reduction in substance use. These intermediate goals deal with a reduction in harm. They must be set at a small but achievable level. With attainment of these goals the person's self-esteem and ability will be reinforced.

4. The provision of Relapse Prevention.
Recognising that relapse can and will occur. The focus of this stage will be to identify areas of positive improvement and how the maintenance of change can be achieved.

Practical Application

The main issue is often how to maintain contact with the person despite the fluctuations in their substance use and mental health. Clients often fail to keep regular contact with outpatient clinics or day centres. Protocols that identify discharge following two or three non-attendances, require alignment with the differing needs and care requirements of this client group. The old adage following non-attendance of ...

1. *telephone the person and offer further appointments*
2. *send a letter offering a further appointment*
3. *conduct a home visit'*, ...

is often the strategy that needs to be employed, giving a friendly caring approach and sense of importance (Gafoor, 1997). Increase in substance use and deterioration in mental health can often be rapid. Therefore, minimisation of the need for hospitalisation should always be at the forefront of care planning. It is often wise, based on your knowledge of the person to omit the letter and go from phone call to home visit.

The reduction of both physical and mental harm is also a serious consideration and action must be taken to reduce the consequences of the harm from the patient's substance misuse.

Additional Care Planning

Based on the needs assessment and other information that has been gained, ensuring that the client is central to any plan, there may be several issues that need careful consideration for inclusion. These may include.

- Accommodation
- Education or lack of opportunity
- Employment or lack of it
- Diet
- Social activity, etc.

Documentation

The Care Programme Approach (CPA) for clients in the co-morbidity service is a means of ensuring a specific care pathway that has integration between

Case Example

Community

John is a 28-year-old man concurrently diagnosed with both a psychosis and a heroin addiction. He had been in and out of various mental health services since his teens.

In his mid-teens John had been hospitalised under a section of the Mental Health Act (1983) in an acute ward. It appears that he was difficult to manage resulting in John being heavily sedated. This presentation reoccurred through-out the next few years and it seems that this contributed to the lack of a clear ongoing care plan. John would often fail to attend outpatient appointments, had irregular attendance at day centres, and did not take prescribed medication.

In his late teens John started to experiment with drugs introduced by other patients at the day hospital. He found that cannabis exacerbated his psychotic symptoms and was again hospitalised. Over the next few years John started trying various drugs including heroin. He moved rapidly from weekend use to regular daily use and his consumption increased alarmingly. His consumption increased until he was taking some 5 to 6 bags of heroin per day. He is recorded as stating that 'the heroin keeps the voices in my head away'. However, over a little time there was a marked deterioration in his mental health and his community mental health nurse (CMHN) often had great difficulty contacting or meeting him. A case review decided to refer him to the newly established co-morbidity service.

John was assessed and a person-centred care programme developed which initially included a befriending and socialising approach to encourage John to have more confidence in the health services.

Following several months of careful work, including the introduction of a methadone regime, John's heroin consumption had been reduced to weekend use. John was keen to move on and gave his agreement to move forward to a plan which included, attendance at a day hospital, regular meetings with the specialist CMHN and psychiatrist from the co-morbidity team which included regular drug screening, motivational interviewing and harm reduction strategies.

He was a regular attendee at the day hospital and having provided three clear heroin screens, agreed to a reducing methadone regime. At this time it was considered appropriate to commence a relapse prevention pro-gramme and following agreement with John, to maintain abstinence for the duration of the therapy the programme was commenced.

On completion of the programme John was able to identify key issues regarding his drug using behaviour and adopt appropriate coping strategies. He had developed some recreational interests, which did not involve his old drug using friends and had gained a place on a employment training programme. He continues regular contact with the services but this is now much reduced.

Case Example

Inpatient care

Mary, a 40-year-old lady, was referred to the substance misuse service by her GP for assessment of alcohol problem. Following the unexpected death of her husband two years ago Mary had sort solace in alcohol. Her consumption level was causing concern and she had become a regular visitor to the local Accident & Emergency Department with various minor injuries.

At assessment it was found that Mary was consuming over 120 units of alcohol per week. Her pattern was daily, commencing from late morning. Diet was poor, her home was neglected and her health was deteriorating. She had no relatives living locally and with her history of injury it was decided to offer admission to the inpatient ward for detoxification. She agreed.

The nursing care of Mary's detoxification programme consisted of

- bed rest in a quiet but evenly lit room with two hourly observations reducing to four hourly as the level of severity of withdrawal lessened.
- Administration of the reducing dosage detoxification medication regime.
- Orientation in day, time and place.
- Fluid intake was encouraged of at least three litres per day and a fluid balance chart was maintained. Decaffeinated drinks and fruit juices were chosen.
- A good dietary intake was established following Mary's initial nausea and stomach upset.
- Information and reassurance were given.

Towards the end of Mary's in-patient stay she increased in confidence and her sociability improved. Her antidepressant medication was reviewed and she was introduced to a bereavement counsellor. The post discharge plan included follow-up at the out-patients clinic, access to a group therapy programme, introduction to alcoholics anonymous (A.A.) auricular acupuncture and sessions with the bereavement counsellor.

For specific information on detoxification please refer to Rassool (1998) and Bartu (2000).

mental health needs and those of substance misuse. CPA also ensures the enhanced care of those clients following this model. Because of local differences in definitions in CPA and documentation used, it must be ensured at the outset that agreed definitions between the Substance Misuse Service and Mental Health Services are in place.

Time Frame

It may take several months before the person is prepared to fully engage in the treatment process for their substance use. The initial importance is to agree the treatment goal and to integrate treatment of mental health problems with that of substance use. Any goals must be realistic and achievable. Small steps should be advocated where the person can succeed and they can get a feeling of achievement is most important. The time frame of treatment is not always directly linked to the substance used, more likely to the severity of use and the complexities of the case.

Evidence Base

There are some Clinical Guidelines on the management of substance use available and should be used. These include,

- Drug Misuse and Dependence – Guidelines on Clinical Management (DoH, 1999).
- Dual Diagnosis Good Practice Guide (DoH, 2002).
- Substance Misuse and Mental Health Co-Morbidity (Dual Diagnosis): Standards for Mental Health Services (HAS, 2001).

Dissemination of Information

A major issue with multidisciplinary working across services and agencies is maintaining confidentiality of sensitive client information. It is important that each member of the care team is conversant with current information on the person's condition Regular inter-team meetings can go a long way to solve both these issues. It must have been made clear to the client that some information will be shared with other members of the team (NMC, 2002). Even though there may be at least two distinct teams working with the person, nursing and medical records must be maintained. It is not always possible to do this centrally and therefore letters and reports between each service are regular occurrences. This may lead to duplication but with modern secure methods the risk of loss or misfiling can be kept to a minimum.

In cases where there is a risk of significant harm to the public or client, the police may need to become involved. There is no breach in confidentiality where disclosure is justified in the public interest (NMC, 2002).

Client information may also be required by law or by court order. In some cases, court reports are required by the solicitor acting on behalf of the client, these are usually given with consent. There is occasion when a judge may require a formal report from a nurse in regard to the client's condition. This may be in addition to any medical or social report. In cases of child protection the nurse must at all times act in line with the local protocols and national policies (NMC, 2002).

The client and carer should be provided with information related to the care plan. For example, treatment contracts, handbooks of Relapse Prevention, drink/drug use diaries and several others.

Reflective Practice

The nature of working with substance misusing clients is distressing (Rassool and Gafoor, 1997), and requires multiple skills and concentration for long periods of time. There is often the possibility of verbal abuse, aggression and violence, which are common problems of substance misuse (Sussman and Ames, 2001). The condition of co-morbidity is complex (Lehman *et al.*, 1989) and requires the nurse to adopt multiple roles in order to achieve a comprehensive level of care (Rassool, 1997). There has always been the informal network of support, 'tea and a chat' with a colleague. But, increasingly nurses need to develop their skills, professional competence and need support for stress and to reduce burnout (Rassool, 1998). Clinical Supervision or what is more correctly termed 'Guided Reflective Practice' (Driscoll, 2001) is a requirement for today's practitioners.

Practice Development

As a result of increasing research over the past two decades, government action and the production of the Dual Diagnosis Good Practice Guide (DoH, 2002) it is likely that further co-morbidity services will be developed and established ones expanded. Nurses wishing to work in this demanding field will need to have good all round knowledge of different mental health settings and substances that can be misused.

Conclusion

This chapter has discussed some of the issues of co-morbidity and suggested that the co-existence of substance misuse and a mental illness leads to a complex and complicated condition. The complexity is derived from the multi-faceted combination of psychological, educational, employment, accommodation, social care, and other needs. The complicatedness is due to the fact that these issues are often deep seated, difficult to understand, interventions are not straightforward, the patient is not always open to or accepting of treatment and the condition is one of relapse.

Nurses need to be multi-skilled in order to provide effective interventions in this arena and have a clear challenge to deal with these conditions in a caring and effective manner. This approach will lead to this (often chaotic) client group responding to the services and benefiting from their care.

📖 Suggested Further Reading

Department of Health (2002) *Mental Health Policy Implementation Guide. Dual Diagnosis Good Practice Guide*, London: Department of Health.
Watkins, T.R., Lewellen, A. and Barrett, M.C. (2001) *Dual Diagnosis: An Integrated Approach to Treatment*, London: Sage Publications.

References

Anon. (2002) Assessment and management of risk of harm in Dual Diagnosis clients. London: *Alcohol Concern and Drugscope*, in *Department of Health* (2002) *Dual Diagnosis Good Practice Guide*, London: Department of Health.
Baker I. (1998) Mental illness and Substance Misuse, *Mental Health Review*, 3, x: 6–13.
Bartu, A.E. (2000) Detoxification, in Cooper, D.B. (ed.), *Alcohol Use*, Oxford: Radcliffe Medical Press.
Department of Health (1999) *Drug Misuse and Dependency – Guidelines on Clinical Management*, London. The Stationery Office.
Department of Health (2002) *Dual Diagnosis Good Practice Guide*, London: Department of Health.
Drake, R. and Mercer-McFadden, C. (1995) Assessment of substance use among persons with chronic mental illness, in Lehman, A. and Dixon, L. (eds), *Double Jeopardy: Chronic Mental Illness and Substance Use Disorders*, Switzerland: Harwood Academic.
Drake, R.E. and Noordsy, D. (1994) Case management for people with co-existing severe mental disorder and substance abuse disorder, *Psychiatric Annals*, 24: 427–31.
Driscoll, J. (2001) *Practicing Clinical Supervision: A Reflective Approach*, London: Bailliere Tindall.
Franey, C.and Quirk, A. (1996) *Dual Diagnosis: Executive Summary No 51*, London: Centre for Research on Drugs and Health Behaviour.
Gafoor, M. (1997) Substance misuse and mental health, in Rassool, G.H. and Gafoor, M. (1997) *Addiction Nursing: Perspectives on Professional and Clinical Practice*, Cheltenham: Stanley Thornes Ltd.
Gafoor, M. and Rassool, G.H. (1998) Working with Dual Diagnosis clients, in Rassool, G.H. (ed.), *Substance Use and Misuse*, Oxford: Blackwell Science Ltd.
Galanter, M., Casaneda, R. and Ferman, J. (1988) Substance abuse among general psychiatric patients, *American Journal of Drug and Alcohol Abuse*, 14(2): 211–35.
Ghodse, A.H. (1995) *Drugs and Addictive Behaviour: A Guide to Treatment* (second edn), Oxford: Blackwell Science.
Gournay, K. (1996) Double Bind, *Nursing Times*, 92, 28: 28–9.
Gournay, K. and Glorney, K. (1998) Dual Diagnosis; mental health problems and substance abuse/dependence, *Mental Health Practice*, 2, 3: 28–35. RCN.
Graham, H.L. (1998) The role of dysfunctional beliefs in individuals who experience psychosis and use substances: implications for cognitive therapy and medication adherence, *Behavioural and Cognitive Psychotherapy*, 26: 193–208. UK: Cambridge University Press.

Health Advisory Service (2001) Substance Misuse and Mental Health Co-Morbidity (Dual Diagnosis): Standards for Mental Health Services. London. HAS.

Hunt, N. and Ashenhurst, A. (2000) Drug use, mental health and social exclusion: cause, effect and what can we do about it, *Mental Health and Learning Difficulties Care*, 4, 1: 18–21.

Kipping, C. (1999) Dual Diagnosis: meeting clients needs, *Mental Health Practice*, 3, 3 November. RCN. 10–15.

Knudsen, P. and Vilmar, T. (1984) Cannabis and neuroleptic agents in schizophrenia, *Acta Psychitrica Scandinavian*, 69: 162–74.

Lehman, A.F., Mayers, C.P. and Corty, E.C. (1989) Assessment and classification of patients with psychiatric and substance abuse syndromes, *Hospital and Community Psychiatry*, 40: 1019–30.

Maisto, S., Carey, M., Carey, K. *et al.* (2000) Use of the AUDIT and the DAST-10 to identify alcohol and drug use disorders among adults with a severe and persistent mental illness, *Psychological Assessment*, 12: 186–92.

Marsden, J., Gossop, M., Stewart, D., Best, O., Farrell, M., Lehmann, P., Edwards, C. and Strang, J. (1997) The Maudsley Addiction Profile (MAP): a brief instrument for assessing treatment outcome, *Addiction*, 93: 1857–67

Menezes, P.R., Johnson, S., Thornicroft, G., Marshal, J., Prosser, D., Bebbington, P., and Kuipers, E. (1996) Drug and alcohol problems among people with severe mental illness in south London, *British Journal of Psychiatry*, 168: 612–19.

Miller, W.R. and Rollnick, S. (2002) *Motivational Interviewing: Preparing people for Change* (second edn), New York: Guilford Press.

Mueser, K.T., Drake, R.E. and Noordsy, D.L. (1998) Integrated mental health and substance abuse treatment for severe psychiatric disorders, *Journal of Practical Psychiatry and Behavioural Health*, May 1998.

Nursing and Midwifery Council (2002) *Code of Professional Conduct*, Nursing and Midwifery Council.

Rassool, G.H. (1997) Clinical Supervision, in Rassool,G.H and Gafoor, M. (eds), *Addiction Nursing: Perspectives on Professional and Clinical Practice*, Cheltenham: Stanley Thornes.

Rassool, G.H. (ed.) (1998) *Substance Use and Misuse*, Oxford: Blackwell Science Ltd.

Rassool,G.H and Gafoor, M. (1997) *Addiction Nursing: Perspectives on Professional and Clinical Practice*, Cheltenham: Stanley Thornes.

Reiger, D.A., Boyd, J.H. and Burke, J.D. (1988) One-month prevalence of mental disorders in the United States, *Archives of General Psychiatry*, 41, 11: 977–86

Smith, J., Frazer, S. and Bower, H. (1994) Dual diagnosis in patients, *Hospital and Community Psychiatry*, 92, 28: 28–9.

Sussman, S. and Ames, L. (2001) *The Social Psychology of Drug Abuse*, Buckingham: Open University Press.

Wanigaratne, S., Wallace, W., Pullin, J., Keaney, F. and Farmer, R. (1990) *Relapse Prevention for Addictive Behaviours. A Manual for Therapists*, London: Blackwell Scientific Pubications.

Watkins, T.R., Lewellen, A. and Barrett, M.C. (2001) *Dual Diagnosis: An Integrated Approach to Treatment*, London: Sage Publications.

Weaver, T. (1999) *Dual Diagnosis: The Co-morbidity of Psychotic Mental Illness and Substance Misuse*, Executive Summary. No. 63, The Centre for Research on Drugs and Health Behaviour: Imperial College, London.

CHAPTER 14

Forensic Mental Health Nursing

Michael Coffey

Introduction

Forensic mental health nursing is concerned with the care, treatment and supervision of those service users referred to as mentally disordered offenders. Traditionally this care took place in the large Special Hospitals but in recent times there has been a steady build up of medium and low secure services. With these developments there has been increasing numbers of forensic community mental health nurses working with mentally disordered offenders in the community (Brooker and White, 1997). This changing pattern of service delivery has been prompted by numerous health policy reports but gathered momentum in the aftermath of the Reed Report (DoH, 1992).

Today forensic mental health nursing in the UK takes place in this increased range of sites and now includes police stations, the law courts and prison services. Defining exactly what is forensic mental health nursing is a difficult task given both its origins (Kirby, 2000) and the competing constructions that exist for the term both nationally and internationally (see Whyte, 2000 for a useful discussion). It is increasingly the case however that many mental health nurses working in generic services come into contact with service users with forensic histories. In some cases this is accompanied by some anxiety as to how the nurse will work with the person and the behaviours they might exhibit in the form of offending behaviour.

This chapter aims to offer the reader practical advice set against the background of the existing evidence base. It does this in the frank and open knowledge that there is much work to be done in developing our understanding of forensic mental health services and their delivery, how they are received, their efficacy and the role of forensic mental health nurses. What is absolutely clear is that nursing care plans cannot be constructed in isolation of the other professions involved in the care of mentally disordered offenders and it is preferable that care planning is inclusive, collaborative and multidisciplinary in nature. Moreover care planning must seek to involve service users in the process. Care plans should reflect service user needs to ensure that the process of care is meaningful to those in receipt of it. They should be strengths-focused and seek to establish and sustain recovery while minimising risk behaviours.

Prevalence and Population

There are approximately 1200 detained patients in the three Special Hospitals in England (DoH, 2002) out of a total detained mentally disordered offender population of just over 3000 (Johnson and Taylor, 2002). There are also approximately 1300 court and prison decisions each year using Part 3 of the Mental Health Act 1983 (DoH, 2002). This includes approximately 300 service users on Section 37 with restriction orders (Section 41). Many of these service users will be transferred to medium secure services and it is estimated that about 88 per cent of these are male, predominantly single with half being between the ages of 21–30-years old (Street, 1998).

On average 300 mentally disordered offenders leave hospital each year on conditional discharge (Johnson and Taylor, 2002) and 25 per cent are likely to be recalled to hospital at some point due to concerns about their risk or their mental health (Street, 1998). The majority of those detained on hospital orders are under the category of mental illness although a proportion (between 3 and 5 per cent) are admitted under the category of psychopathic disorder (Johnson and Taylor, 2002). Violence against the person makes up the majority of offences with which mentally disordered offenders are charged or convicted.

Defining the term mentally disordered offender is fraught with problems. For our purposes it includes those who have committed an offence serious enough to attract the attention of the criminal justice system in the form of arrest or arraignment and who suffer from mental distress of a nature that prompts referral to forensic mental health services. This will include those who develop mental health problems while in custody as well as those with established mental health problems that have committed offences. The concern therefore will in most cases be the risk that the person presents to others but this should not become the sole focus of intervention.

The description of the mentally disordered offender above suggests a reasonably defined grouping. There is however at least one other perhaps less defined grouping of mentally disordered offenders that these statistics don't account for and they are an important grouping. These are services users who have never been detained under Part 3 of the Mental Health Act (1983).

They include:

- current and ex-prisoners;
- those on probation orders with conditions of treatment;
- mental health service users admitted to secure services under other parts of the Mental Health Act.

Dvoskin and Steadman (1994) suggest that:

1. These service users will not have learnt compliant behaviours.
2. May be difficult to treat.
3. May be antagonistic towards mental health professionals.

As such they create a particular challenge to mental health services and to nurses wishing to involve them in the care planning process.

Referrals

Access routes to forensic services are primarily through the criminal justice system. In most cases, police, court or prison liaison services identify and assess mentally disordered offenders and determine the threshold for admission into services. Referrals from generic mental health services are not uncommon and are usually prompted by risk behaviours that give cause for concern.

Theoretical Framework

Care planning in forensic mental health nursing has to accommodate a range of competing demands and as such like most care planning activity draws upon a number of theoretical approaches to address health and social care needs. Much focus within forensic services is centred upon the risk the individual presents to others and perhaps less often the risks they present to themselves. As such concepts of risk and its management (Vinestock, 1996; Doyle, 2000; Kelly *et al.*, 2002) dominate approaches to care planning in these services although nurses more generally have been criticised for their failure in this regard (Neilson *et al.*, 1996). Risk is an important concern for the mental health professions more generally but the focus upon it must not be at the expense of a broader consideration of the recovery needs of service users.

Concepts of individual needs assessment (Slade *et al.*, 1999) must be addressed along with seeing as fundamental, the citizenship rights of individuals with a mental illness (Sayce, 1999) regardless of their offending history. Care plans must address the social inclusion needs of service users, aim to maintain and sustain their relationships and social supports, support informal carers and offer individual targeted symptom orientated interventions that increase the persons' opportunities to recover and reintegrate with the wider society. The emphasis here should be upon strengths, goals and aspirations defined by the service user as a basis for developing a comprehensive approach to the provision of care.

Principles and Skills

Watkins (2001, p. 87) informed by the work of Gerard Egan outlines what he sees as the fundamental requirements that will allow mental health nurses to develop lasting collaborative relationships with users of mental health services. These include:

- Meet people with humanity and humility so that the alliance is one of equals.
- Acknowledge that as helpers we are both resourceful and fallible, as is the client.
- Recognise that power can be shared, discovered and generated within the helping alliance.
- Make the helping process participative rather than directive.
- Share our knowledge of the helping process so that people can become more resourceful and self-supporting.

Principles such as these are at the very heart of mental health nursing and it is perhaps telling that such principles need restating.

Frank and Gunderson (1990) have offered evidence that good quality therapeutic alliances predict better clinical outcomes in people with schizophrenia. This suggests that there are real benefits to be gained for the service user by what is considered a fundamental of mental health nursing – that is, interpersonal relationships with therapeutic intent. When working with service users in forensic settings we must strive to facilitate and sustain these therapeutic relationships in the context of the strong legal compulsion which essentially removes choice from the service user and potentially relegates their involvement to that of a mere token.

Assessment

Approach

Care plans should be based upon clinical assessments of service users' strengths and needs. However there is some evidence to suggest that care plans often do not reflect the assessments performed. Perkins and Fisher (1996) concluded as much in an audit of care plans in a rehabilitation service and noted that service user defined problems were relatively neglected. It is therefore worth restating that care planning must be based upon a number of clinical assessments and service user defined need. There is also a concern that assessment must be transferred into care plans and care plans into action (Perkins and Fisher, 1996).

One aspect of the service users' experience that might usefully be assessed is those experiences that lead up to and trigger relapse of their condition (Coffey and Bishop, 2000). The focus here should be to use this assessment to help the service user to develop understanding of and gain control over their illness experience, as an aid to building recovery (Coffey, 2003). As such the assessment of mentally disordered offenders should differ little from anyone who

experiences a mental illness. Once risk behaviours are addressed the requirements are similar (Shepherd, 1993).

Process

Within the initial involvement stage, a number of key issues can be addressed:

- Utilising the principles of engagement described by Onyett (1992).
- The nurse being able to demonstrate their usefulness to the person (Repper
  et al., 1994). In particular, when service users are wary of the case manager/
  nurse.
- Ensuring that the service user has full benefits entitlement.
- Accessing items of clothing and furniture through social services support.
- Helping negotiate a review of medication.
- Providing information to the family regarding illness, medication and the
  potential risk posed to self, partner or children (as in the case example).
- Elicit the partners understanding of the illness and assessing how the family
  interacts, using the Relative Assessment Interview (RAI) (Barrowclough
  and Tarrier, 1992). McKeown and McCann (1995) have developed a version of this instrument for use in secure environments.

Information Gathering

At its most basic, risk assessment involves the collection of information, using
that information in the light of research evidence to formulate an assessment
and then, communicating this assessment in a format which is appropriate to
its intended audience. Information gathering is frequently time consuming
but it is the single most important task in the formulation of comprehensive
risk assessments. Initial assessments will necessarily have to be made without
all the available information but nurses should persevere in seeking out information from key informants and case reports.

There are now some classical examples of mental health services neglecting
to do this and as a consequence failing to establish clear and informed assessments of risks presented by individuals (Ritchie *et al.*, 1994). The aim is to
build a picture of the potential risk behaviours so care planning is informed by
these. Assessment of danger to others must include consideration of a number
of important factors. Detailed accounts of the requirements of such risk assessment practice can be found in Doyle (2000) and Morgan (2000).

Tools Used

There are a number of tools now appearing in practice that are designed to assist
the clinician in achieving some semblance of objectivity in assessments of risk.

For example:

HCR-20: Specific intent to provide clinicians with a standardised measure of risk of violence (Webster *et al.*, 1997).

Behavioural Status Index: A measure to assist clinicians in placing risk behaviours in the context of assessment of other skills such as social skills, insight and communication (Woods *et al.*, 1999).

Other assessment tools include:

Relative Assessment Interview (RAI) (Barrowclough and Tarrier, 1992).

Knowledge About Schizophrenia Interview (KASI) (Barrowclough and Tarrier, 1992).

Whatever the range of tools employed in assessment of service users with mental health problems it must be remembered that tools are just that, something to help you complete a task. They must be used as part of a comprehensive assessment and not instead of it. Formal training in the use of risk assessment tools is often required and ongoing clinical supervision of risk assessment practice is advisable to ensure that assessments are as accurate as possible.

Risk Priorities

Clinical assessments of behaviours that indicate potential harm to self or others may be prioritised. Risk assessment is a notoriously difficult task but some evidence exists to allow us to make certain judgements on assessment that will inform the care planning process. Morgan (2000) provides a very useful, informed and comprehensive approach to risk assessment and its management. For the purposes of this chapter I will focus on just two elements of risk behaviour that is dangerousness and self-harm.

Dangerousness

Work on dangerousness is bedevilled by problems of definition. There is little consensus on what the term means from an objective view point and it might be argued that it has lost any real meaning as a result. Despite this it is a term that features in clinical practice and in the literature on mentally disordered offenders (Chiswick, 1995).

Dangerousness for our purposes is taken to mean the dangerous acts of the person towards other people that have the potential to cause serious harm or fatality. It may include acts which have malevolent intent but not exclusively. The issue of intent is a matter often decided by the courts but intent may be absent in dangerous behaviour or intent may be motivated by irrational beliefs.

We are concerned here with how we first assess risk and second how do we then go about managing that risk in a way which will be professionally competent.

You will notice that I have avoided saying 'remove risk' and this is because it is fundamental to all our daily lives and may be impossible to remove. Grounds (1995) has suggested that clinical risk assessment is not about making accurate predictions but is more about making informed, defensible decisions about the likelihood of harm occurring in terms of social realities and current scientific knowledge.

Self-harm and Suicide

While the focus within forensic services might understandably be centred upon the danger to others of the mentally disordered offender it is important not to let such a focus obscure the daily reality of the mentally ill. This is to acknowledge that the mentally ill are far more likely to be a danger to themselves than to others.

Taylor and Gunn (1999) have indicated as much in their analysis and results from the Confidential Inquiry (DoH, 2001) illustrating that mental health services have some way to go in reducing episodes of suicide among the mental health service user population. For example, approximately 25 per cent of suicides in the UK had been in contact with psychiatric services in the year before death (about 1500 cases per year).

A word of caution must be noted in attempting to predict deliberate self-harm and suicide among those with mental illness. Hawton (1994) suggests that we must be mindful of some limitations in predicting risk of deliberate self-harm;

- Suicide remains relatively rare and predictors poor.
- Research mainly focuses upon completed suicides and it may not be generalisable.
- There is a difference between short-term risk and long-term risk (long-term risk may mean that risk is constant rather than being some way off in the distance).
- Risk factors are variable and not necessarily stable over time.
- Studies tend to focus on group characteristics yet most service users present with unique elements that make them individual.

This is not to invest the process with gloom but to recognise the limitations of our assessments. Despite this, Appleby (1992) provides a useful review, suggesting that at least one aspect of behaviour appears predictive and that is the presence of hopelessness. Measures of hopelessness may therefore be a useful adjunct to the deliberate self-harm assessment process.

The next stage of the nursing risk assessment, assuming that an adequate historical account has been determined, should focus less on known historical risk behaviours, and instead consider the presence of current risk related symptomatology. For example;

- Current delusional beliefs.
- Possession or carrying of weapons.

- Use of illicit substances.
- Potential protective factors such as personal awareness of risk and accepting a responsibility to self-manage.

(Morgan, 2000)

Care Planning

How Plan is Determined

Following the initial assessment interviews described above, a treatment plan is proposed. It is worth noting that given the likely link between mental state and risk behaviours the care plan must address fully those aspects of mental health that are likely to be precursors to the behaviours. This is an essential element of risk management and is important to consider in detail.

Family sessions will follow assessment, concentrating on offering information and education about schizophrenia and the rationale for drug therapy. Once they commence they should continue for at least one year (Kuipers, 1996). Psycho-education will be based on the outcome of the Knowledge about Schizophrenia Interview (KASI) and will aim to address deficits in understanding highlighted therein. Kuipers (1996) also suggests that offering information on the condition has high face validity, helps the family feel more optimistic about the future and helps feelings of mastery and self-esteem. Falloon *et al.* (1985) advocate two sessions of education on the illness and reasons for drug treatment and psychosocial intervention. However, psycho-education by itself will not lead to long-term behaviour change (Lam, 1991). Furthermore, evidence suggests that social skills training alone fails to prevent relapse beyond one year at follow-up (Hogarty *et al.*, 1991).

The care plan also aims to improve communication skills. This may take a number of sessions and may require ground rules such as not interrupting each other and active listening. Indeed, Droogan and Brannigan (1997) noted that concentrating on communication skills can lead to a reduction in expressions of anger and guilt and maintenance of realistic expectations of the patients' performance.

Practical Application

The care plan (see Box 14.1).

One approach to dealing with ambivalence towards medication is Brief Motivational Interviewing (Rollnick *et al.*, 1992). This is based on the premise that it is premature and misdirected to offer advice and persuasion to accept medication, without addressing the issue of potential ambivalence. Indeed, however useful this approach may be, its central respect for the person's autonomy may be undermined by the presence of a conditional discharge order and the possible consequences of disregarding such conditions.

Box 14.1   Features of the care plan

1. Be incremental and include sessions on problem solving and developing coping strategies to reduce environmental stresses (Falloon *et al.*, 1985).
2. Aim to have each family member state, what they perceive as problems and possible solutions to problems.
3. Prioritise problems and negotiate solutions that are agreed to be practised as homework.
4. Emphasise the 'here and now', allowing the family to feel optimistic and successful rather than failures in dealing with their problems (Kuipers, 1996).
5. Directly address ambivalence towards medication.

If medication is shown to help the person control their symptoms and this control leads to a reduction in consequent risk behaviours, then medication management becomes an important element in the risk management plan.

A risk management plan is an integral part of the care plan and risk factors must clearly be indicated. In the case example, this includes the return of sustained false beliefs about others, particularly Yvonne wishing him harm and plotting against him. It will also include default on medication or outpatient appointments, possession and carrying of weapons or plans he has made in this regard for his protection. Should Cliff engage in misuse of substances such as drugs or alcohol this will also be considered an important indicator.

The plan would need to indicate efforts to promote daytime activity by helping Cliff re-enter a vocational training scheme and assist in finding work. Regular reviews of the care plan involving service user, carer and the multi-disciplinary team are essential. This ensures good communication and meets statutory requirements. Facilitating the creation of social support networks may have a positive effect in reducing offending behaviour in some people with mental illness. It also increases level of activity and provides a monitoring network for observing relapse in the patient (Estroff *et al.*, 1994).

Additional Care Planning

In addition to the assessment of potential risk behaviours it is essential to conduct a broader bio-psychosocial assessment of the individual and family. Assessment of symptoms, problems, strengths, social supports and a real attempt at helping the service user to define their current needs should be central to this process.

The following case example illustrates a typical service user seen by a forensic mental health service and some of the elements considered in planning his care. The example is based upon a composite of clinical experiences and any resemblance to specific individuals or events is coincidental.

Case Example

Cliff is a 29-year-old man with a history of paranoid schizophrenia. His early family life was disrupted by the absence of his father and the regular hospitalisation of his mother who also has schizophrenia. He has convictions for a string of petty offences since his teens and has regularly spent time in criminal justice institutions as well as hospital. Cliff's most recent offence involved him becoming increasingly paranoid about his girlfriend whom he was living with at the time.

This culminated in Cliff attacking his girlfriend with a knife and seriously injuring her. He was convicted of attempted murder and placed on a Section 37/41 (Mental Health Act 1983), following hospital assessment. Cliff spent a number of years in a Special Hospital and more recently in medium security. He was conditionally discharged from hospital 6 months ago and remains subject to restrictions.

Cliff has limited insight into his condition and his index offence. He maintains conspiracy beliefs but they are less prominent when he is not acutely unwell. He would like to stop taking his medication and admits that he takes it only because of the threat of recall to hospital. Cliff has recently met a woman with whom he now lives. Yvonne, has two children of school-going age. Neither Cliff nor Yvonne is employed and they spend long periods of time together in the house. Yvonne is concerned about his 'laziness' and his inability to function at the level she has come to expect of a partner. This has caused tension within the family and at times Yvonne becomes very frustrated with Cliff's lack of activity. Yvonne puts his limited functioning down to the medication and would like him to stop taking it. Yvonne has limited knowledge about his previous offending especially his index offence. Yvonne would like information about schizophrenia and about Cliff's index offence. Cliff himself is anxious to maintain the stability of this relationship and it is on this basis he has agreed Yvonne's involvement with the clinical team.

The RAI interview took place in the family home to fit in with family commitments and was divided into separate sessions. Cliff was present at both interviews and these were timed so that the children were at school. This was at Yvonne's suggestion as they are both very young and she felt better able to concentrate when they are not there.

From this assessment it was clear that Yvonne has little understanding about Cliff's diagnosis. His inactivity is a source of constant irritation and frustration for her. She sees his lack of ability to be affectionate towards her as related to his medication. Yvonne has not experienced Cliff being aggressive or violent towards her or the children. However, she acknowledged that Cliff is concerned about plots against him but felt he is being 'stupid'. Yvonne and Cliff are both becoming increasingly isolated which can lead to increased sense of burden (Kuipers, 1996).

Robinson *et al.* (1991) suggest that families will often collude with the service user in an effort to make them appear better than they are. This is especially the case when an element of control exists over the patient's life, as is the case with a Section 41 restriction order. It is therefore incumbent on the nurse to be aware of this and to attempt to determine as far as is possible the veracity of statements.

To help the carer develop an understanding of schizophrenia KASI (Barrowclough and Tarrier, 1992) was used in a later session. Efforts must be made to explain that this interview is not a test but designed to help the nurse give targeted information about schizophrenia.

Brewin *et al.* (1991) note that relatives often blame patients for their behaviour leading to increased tension within the family unit. Sensitive and informed details about the current state of professional knowledge about schizophrenia may help alleviate potentially negative beliefs about the condition.

Yvonne rates Cliff's problems as laziness, poor hygiene and lack of initiative. With some prompting she volunteers concerns about what she calls his strange ideas. She does not feel these are illness related and feels Cliff can control them. She does not think hallucinations are important but begins to think about delusions and makes the connection with Cliff's ideas about plots against him. Yvonne believes that Cliff 'probably doesn't need' medication and that the side effects are Cliff's lack of drive and initiative. Yvonne feels that with strong encouragement he will eventually get up and get things done.

Cliff has a history of developing false beliefs about those close to him and reacting to these beliefs with violence. He is now reluctant to explore in any depth his previous behaviour feeling that he has gone over this enough times and that it is all in the past.

Documentation

All service users seen by forensic services will have their care planned and delivered in accordance with the Care Programme Approach (CPA) (DoH, 1990). One of the essential elements of CPA is that there is a care plan agreed between the relevant professional staff, the service user and his or her carers, and this is recorded in writing. However, Perkins and Fisher (1996) have argued cogently that the mere existence of a care plan is not a sufficient nor necessary condition to the delivery of effective care. Effective nursing care need not be dependent upon a care plan nor indeed does the presence of care plan indicate the quality of care received. However, documented care plans are one way of involving service users in their care and can help provide the comprehensive and co-ordinated care that is so important in working with mentally disordered offenders.

Time Frame

Forensic Community Psychiatric Nurses (FCPN) work can involve both short- and long-term involvement. This of course depends on the nature of the work. Short term (approximately three hours to three sessions) is indicated for roles such as Appropriate Adult or Diversion work in police stations/courts etc. Whereas long-term involvement is a necessity for caseload management, in order to maintain a monitoring stance and develop sufficient relationship with the service user or medium to high security care. There is no defined time scale for this. However, service involvement may be an order of the court.

Evidence Base

Evidence of the use and involvement of forensic mental health nursing has been stated and shared throughout this chapter.

Dissemination of Information

Sharing information in the care plan with close friends and families may help in:

- Monitoring progress or deterioration,
- Preventing recurrence of risk behaviour,
- Sharing responsibility and involvement in the process of care.

However, within the wider context of sharing information this will not always be appropriate. Nurses working within forensic mental health must acknowledge their obligation to maintain confidentiality within the confines of their professional role. Confidentiality has to be balanced between explicit justification for disclosing material and the needs of others to be aware of specific information. This will mainly include carers and families and should involve discussion and agreement (Chaloner, 2000).

Reflective Practice

Forensic mental health nursing is a challenging arena for mental health nurses to practice. The demands on nurses can be daunting and appear excessive. Few mental health nurses receive the type of preparation necessary to practice within this field. Many aspects of practice are acquired through experience and exposure such as familiarity with relevant law and policy, risk assessment procedures and establishing and maintaining nursing expertise within a wider multi-professional field which in many cases will have significant political and clinical power. These aspects of practice can be seen as challenges or opportunities.

The availability of good quality clinical supervision as an arena within which to formally reflect upon aspects of the work is of absolute importance. Learning from and through formal reflection on experience will enhance and consolidate forensic mental health nursing practice. Nurses should endeavour to articulate the need for this level of support and where it is not available to agitate to ensure that it is made available. Various opportunities exist to enhance learning either through one to one clinical supervision, multidisciplinary team meetings, group and peer supervision meetings and the development of journal groups to meet regularly and review relevant evidence pertinent to the particular client group. Assertiveness and creativity in regard to accessing and sustaining clinical support mechanisms for forensic mental health nursing will assist in developing clinical practice, foster a culture of learning and provide an environment for critical thinkers to promote service development.

Practice Development

Services for mentally disordered offenders could be greatly enhanced by incorporating a range of psychosocial interventions into the routine practice of staff working in diverse forensic settings, from community to conditions of high security. In future, there is a strong case for involving families in the full gamut of forensic services, with the potential role as allies in assessment and therapy. Blom-Cooper *et al.* (1995) asserts that there needs to be local development of good practice standards on working with carers.

In forensic mental health, new models of training are required which do not just focus upon changing individual practitioners, but also focus upon organisational change in the setting in which the taught knowledge and skills are to be applied (McKeown and McCann, 2000).

Conclusion

Care planning for forensic service users is much like working with any person with a severe and enduring mental illness. It is however crucial that mental health nurses are mindful that detailed assessment and interventions to address the outcomes of assessment is of utmost importance in managing the risk behaviours the individual presents with. Given the potential for recurrence of these behaviours mental health nurses must document clearly their endeavours so that from a medico-legal standpoint they can be seen to have practised in accordance with the latest evidence. Perhaps however more important than any of this is that mental health nurses establish meaningful collaborative relationships with service users based upon their needs with the ultimate aim of enhancing their recovery and reintegration in the community in which they reside.

📖 Suggested Further Reading

Morgan, S. (2000) *Clinical Risk Management: A Clinical Tool and Practitioner Manual*, London: Sainsbury Centre for Mental Health.

This is an excellent evidence-based practical framework for assessing and managing risk in mental health practice. It is written in an accessible style and avoids the trap of producing long lists of tick box questions or score cards to estimate risk. It is grounded in the realities of risk assessment practice and should be essential material for any nurse engaged in risk assessment and its management.

Watkins, P. (2001) *Mental Health Nursing: The Art of Compassionate Care*, Oxford: Butterworth Heinemann.

An excellent authoritative and informative text that includes a useful section on the importance of establishing, sustaining and ending therapeutic alliances with users of mental health services as a fundamental of mental health nursing.

References

Appleby, L. (1992) Suicide in psychiatric patients: risk and prevention, *British Journal of Psychiatry*, 161: 749–58.

Barrowclough, C. and Tarrier, N. (1992) *Families of Schizophrenic Patients: Cognitive Behavioural Interventions*, London: Chapman and Hall.

Blom-Cooper, L., Hally, H. and Murphy, E. (1995) *The Falling Shadow*, London: Duckworth.

Brewin, C.R., MacCarthy, B., Duda, R. and Vaughn, C.E. (1991) Attribution and expressed emotion in the relatives of patients with schizophrenia, *Journal of Abnormal Psychology*, 100: 546–54.

Brooker, C. and White, E. (1997) *The Fourth Quinquennial National Community Mental Health Nursing Census of England and Wales*, Manchester: The University of Manchester and Keele University.

Chaloner, C. (2000) Ethics and Morality, in Chaloner, C. and Coffey, M. (eds), *Forensic Mental Health Nursing: Current Approaches*, Oxford: Blackwell Science.

Chiswick, D. (1995) Dangerousness, In Chiswick, D. and Cope, R. (eds), *Seminars in Practical Forensic Psychiatry*, London: Gaskell, pp. 210–42.

Coffey, M. (2003) Relapse prevention in psychosis, in Hannigan, B. and Coffey, M. (eds), *The Handbook of Community Mental Health Nursing*, London: Routledge.

Coffey, M. and Bishop, N. (2000) Crisis plans in forensic mental health nursing, *Mental Health Practice*, 4, 4: 22–5.

Department of Health (1990) *The Care Programme Approach*, London: HMSO

Department of Health/Home Office (1992) *Review of Health and Social Services for Mentally Disordered Offenders and others Requiring Similar Services* (The Reed Report), London: HMSO.

Department of Health (2001) *Safety First: 5 year report of the National Confidential Inquiry into Suicide and Homicide by People with Mental Illness*, London: HMSO.

Department of Health (2002) *Inpatients Formally Detained in Hospitals under the Mental Health Act 1983 and other Legislation NHS Trusts, High Security Psychiatric Hospitals and Private Facilities: 2000–2001*, Government Statistical Service, London: HMSO.

Doyle, M. (2000) Risk assessment and Management, in Chaloner, C. and Coffey, M. (eds), *Forensic Mental Health Nursing: Current Approaches*, Oxford: Blackwell Science, pp. 140–70.

Droogan, J. and Brannigan, K. (1997) A review of psychosocial family interventions for schizophrenia, *Nursing Times*, 93, 26: 46–7.

Dvoskin, J.A. and Steadman, H.J. (1994) Using intensive case management to reduce violence by mentally ill persons in the community, *Hospital and Community Psychiatry*, 45, 7: 711–13.

Estroff, S., Zimmer, C., Lachicotte, W. and Benoit, J. (1994) The influence of social networks and social support on violence by persons with serious mental illness, *Hospital and Community Psychiatry*, 45: 669–79.

Falloon, I.R.H., Boyd, J.L., McGill, C.W., Williamson, M., Razani, J., Moss, H.B., Gilderman, A.M. and Simpson, G.M. (1985) Family management in the prevention of morbidity of schizophrenia, *Archives of General Psychiatry*, 42: 887–96.

Frank, A.F. and Gunderson, J.G. (1990) The role of the therapeutic alliance in the treatment of schizophrenia. Relationship to course and outcome, *Archives of General Psychiatry*, 47, 3: 228–36.

Grounds, A. (1995) Risk assessment and management in clinical context, in Crichton, J. (ed.), *Psychiatric Patient Violence: Risk and Response*, London: Duckworth.

Hawton, K. (1994) The assessment of suicidal risk, in Barnes, T.R.E. and Nelson, H.E. (eds), *The Assessment of Psychoses: A Practical Handbook*, London: Chapman Hall, pp. 125–34.

Hogarty, G.E., Anderson, C.M., Reiss, D.J., Kornblith, S.J., Greenwald, D.P., Ulrich, R.F. and Carter, M. (1991) Family psycho-education, social skills training, and maintenance chemotherapy in the aftercare treatment of schizophrenia: Two year effects of a controlled study on relapse and adjustment, *Archives of General Psychiatry*, 48: 340–7.

Johnson, S. and Taylor, R. (2002) *Statistics of Mentally Disordered Offenders 2001: England and Wales*, Home Office Statistical Bulletin 13/02, London: Home Office.

Kelly, T., Simmons, W. and Gregory, E. (2002) Risk assessment and management: A community forensic mental health practice model, *International Journal of Mental Health Nursing*, 11: 206–13.

Kirby, S.D. (2000) History and Development, in Chaloner, C. and Coffey, M. (eds), *Forensic Mental Health Nursing: Current Approaches*, Oxford: Blackwell Science, pp. 288–305.

Kuipers, E. (1996) Interventions with families: dealing with psychosis, in Watkins, M., Hervey, N., Carson, J. and Ritter, S. (eds), *Collaborative Community Mental Health Care*, London: Arnold.

Lam, D.H. (1991) Psychosocial family intervention in schizophrenia: A review of empirical studies, *Psychological Medicine*, 21: 423–41.

McKeown, M. and McCann, G. (1995) A schedule for assessing relatives: the relative assessment interview for schizophrenia in a secure environment (RAISSE), *Psychiatric Care*, 2, 3: 84–8.

McKeown, M. and McCann, G. (2000) Psychosocial Interventions, in Chaloner, C. and Coffey, M. (eds), *Forensic Mental Health Nursing: Current Approaches*, Oxford: Blackwell Science.

Morgan, S. (2000) *Clinical Risk Management: a Clinical Tool and Practitioner Manual*, London: Sainsbury Centre for Mental Health.

Neilson, T., Peet, M., Ledsman, R. and Poole, J. (1996) Does the nursing care plan help in the management of psychiatric risk? *Journal of Advanced Nursing*, 24: 1201–06.

Onyett, S. (1992) *Case Management in Mental Health*, London: Chapman and Hall.

Perkins, R.E. and Fisher, N.R. (1996) Beyond mere existence: the auditing of care plans, *Journal of Mental Health*, 5, 3: 275–86.

Repper, J., Ford, R. and Cooke, A. (1994) How can nurses build trusting relationships with people who have severe and long term mental health problems? Experience of case managers and their clients, *Journal of Advanced Nursing*, 19: 1096–104.

Ritchie, J.H., Dick, D. and Lingham, R. (1994) *The Report of the Inquiry into the Care and Treatment of Christopher Clunis*, London: HMSO.

Robinson, S., Vivian-Byrne, S., Driscoll, R. and Cordess, C. (1991) Family work with victims and offenders in a secure unit, *Journal of Family Therapy*, 13: 105–16.

Rollnick, S., Heather, N. and Bell, A. (1992) Negotiating behaviour change in medical settings: The development of brief motivational interviewing, *Journal of Mental Health*, 1: 25–37.

Sayce, L. (1999) *From Psychiatric Patient to Citizen*, Basingstoke: Palgrave.

Shepherd, G. (1993) Case Management, in Watson, W. and Grounds, A. (eds), *The Mentally Disordered Offender in an Era of Community Care: New Directions in Provision*, Cambridge: Cambridge University Press.

Slade, M., Loftus, L., Phelan, M., Thornicroft, G. and Wykes, T. (1999) *The Camberwell Assessment of Need*, London: Gaskell.

Street, R. (1998) *The Restricted Hospital Order: From Court to the Community*, Home Office Research Study 186, London: Home Office.

Taylor, P.J. and Gunn, J. (1999) Homicides by people with mental illness: myth and reality, *British Journal of Psychiatry*, 174: 9–14.

Vinestock, M. (1996) Risk Assessment. 'A Word to the Wise'? *Advances in Psychiatric Treatment*, 2: 3–10.

Watkins, P. (2001) *Mental Health Nursing: the Art of Compassionate Care*, Oxford: Butterworth Heinemann.

Webster, C.D., Douglas, K.S., Eaves, D. and Hart, S.D. (1997) *HCR-20: Assessing Risk for Violence (Version 2)*. British Columbia: Mental Health, Law and Policy Institute Simon Fraser University.

Whyte, L. (2000) Educational aspect of forensic nursing, in Robinson, D. and Kettles, A. (eds), *Forensic Nursing and Multidisciplinary Care of the Mentally Disordered Offender*, London: Jessica Kingsley Publishers, pp. 13–25.

Woods, P., Reed, V. and Robinson, D. (1999) The Behavioural Status Index: therapeutic assessment of risk, insight, communication and social skills, *Journal of Psychiatric and Mental Health Nursing*, 6, 2: 79–90.

Conclusion

Robert Tummey

Each contributor gives their own informed account of working with people suffering from mental distress. They describe how a professional framework for applying knowledge and skill can achieve the best results with those we work with. As a result, a bridge is created between the contributors' experience from a variety of backgrounds and settings, to reach forward with an offering that binds mental health nurses across the world.

Exploration of the specific chapters from service user and carer perspectives are given. There are lessons to be drawn. Insights that can benefit the development of role in an all-too complex interaction, that is intrinsically human. Each chapter has detailed various scopes for planning care, but each has the presence of creating a bond with clients that is meaningful and fundamental. The need for acceptance and acknowledgement is a theme that has run throughout and will, if processed in a caring and planned way, determine a future hope for those on either side of mental health. Words such as collaboration, communication, partnership and care, all offer a passage of common unity, but it is the 'doing' that is central.

It would be hard to say whether all areas of the UK are in full agreement with each of the theories purported to being used. I suspect that smaller teams, rural units, nurse-led services, inner city provision etc, all provide a variation and further adaptation of the theories or approaches discussed. Indeed, this book has not been intended to be the definitive guide to planning care. It does not cover every blade of grass and has not trampled every inch of charted territory. What it has done is provide an indication and comprehensive overview for the practical application of care in mental health nursing.

The Growth Pursuit

One of the main outcomes from the process of compiling this book is the reassuring validation that mental health nursing is mainly concerned with the process of care for the suffering person. There is generally a lack of emphasis on the nature of illness and a more human embrace for the distress felt by the client. Oscar Wilde stated that 'no life is spoiled but one whose growth is arrested'. The developmental steps taken in each of the services described shows a compassion and empathy that can be owned by nursing. Each of the chapters demonstrates a connectedness and advocate position with the sufferer that promotes growth. A stance that can be enhanced or informed by the advancement of biological science, but nevertheless, not determined by or dictated by it. The essence of involvement that emerges from the pages outlines the purpose of mental health nursing and reaffirms a status in helping, caring and being with the client, pursuits this profession affords and achieves.

Whilst we are charged with the task of assessing, planning care and administering interventions for the benefit of the client, we must not forget the importance of our role as health promoters. At times we may assist in the containment of illness, deliver treatments that reduce symptoms and provide a 'buffer' from the social inadequacies of either the client or the neighbourhood. Ostensibly, we are there with the person. We are in support of their health. We are and should be advocates in the process of health, ensuring the rights of the person are met.

What's in a Name?

The professional status held within mental health nursing and the education undertaken, may be for the protection of the client and the public (NMC, 2002). However, I believe there is some scope in the concept that as mental health nurses at the frontline of provision, the professional standards and theoretical awareness serves as a boundary. It is a protection of the nurse within the complex attendance of caring for someone with mental illness. Some may feel that being a professional carer demeans the right of passage to a detached expert manner. I believe it can allow the achievement of caring in the depths of distress, by getting 'right in there'. For instance, my name is Bob, not Nurse Tummey, yet I maintain a professional involvement at a level that can be quite scary. This is something worthy of note. Wearing a badge with your name on can have symbolic connotations. I felt quite passionate whilst training in a large mental hospital that my name be stated first on my badge, above my 'rank'. As student nurses, we were all issued badges to be worn whilst on duty.

Fortunately my name was stated first, above my status of student nurse and latterly, staff nurse. It is 'I' that will meet you and it is 'I' that will provide the care. The role of nurse enables this to be a consideration and achieved whilst retaining professional identity. I am not ashamed of my profession or feel the need to hide behind it. I announce myself to the service of the client in an open way, safe in the knowledge that I can draw on my education, training and nursing skills to assist the process. I would like to believe that this continued throughout my career.

Also, to retreat to the safe haven of my profession when I require respite, with an awareness of my own needs following an intense encounter within my working week, month or year.

It is this involvement that makes nursing unique and something I feel reassured by.

Owning the Contract

Recently, I accompanied my daughter in purchasing a mobile phone for her birthday. She is still a child and I was buying, but when the shop assistant asked, 'would you like me to put the phone in your name or your daughter's?' I had to think carefully. It is my gift, but I am paying, it is my purchase, but my daughter's phone. I made the decision as a father and placed the phone in my name. However, this could be seen as a metaphor for the experience of writing assessment formats, care plans and contracts. Whose name is the document in? Who has ownership? I believe it is a partnership relationship and contract that should have shared ownership. But effectively, it is the client who is the stakeholder in the venture or the carer.

Stoic Versatility

It is hoped that the information in this book can be used to inform practice and provide a useful guide to the practice of others. Knowledge has been shared. The role, remit and contribution of mental health nursing, covers a wide expanse of care for clients. This should be considered (O'Brien, 2001). Indeed, contained in these pages is a representation of current considered thought. Some have indicated and alluded to the aspiration of nursing care. Some have remained true to a more pragmatic attitude. However, all have captured meaning, ownership of and essence of involvement that transcends a mechanical detachment of delivery. They have incorporated the dignity, humanity and engagement that make nursing so versatile and fluid.

You will see that there is no definition of mental health nursing and no persuasion to forfeit personal distinction within its parameters. Boundaries of role are apparent but not restricting. There is much scope for the use of self and acknowledgement that self is as unique and able as the philosophy of service user empowerment we are beginning to champion. As advocates we adopt our true position alongside the service user. For this is the place change, progress and recovery is achieved.

The Midfielder

Mental health nursing is both challenging and rewarding. There are many ups and downs, with each day never the same. Working with the person in crisis, recovery, whether child, adult or older adult brings the experience of uncertainty. This is also performed against a backdrop of change known as the NHS. Working with colleagues from across the disciplines ensures a smooth process of treatment and care delivery. This has been detailed in all the chapters. Demonstrating a willingness to be a team player is the purpose with which change occurs.

So what of the presence of mental health nursing, acknowledgement of contribution and recognition of achievement? Sometimes this can be an invisible presence through a word here and a discussion there. Not always considered as a priority, but always a necessity. The nurse can be a hidden factor unwilling to seek glory. I can equate this in football terms as the hard-working midfielder who stops the opposing attack and creates the change to progress. Not the striker who gains glory for scoring the goal, or the goal-keeper whose save is remembered, but the player always on the ball and influencing the game.

Conclude the Conclusion

It is hoped that you have gained some benefit from this read and enjoyed the amble through various clinical settings. All from the perspective of the mental health nurse. I believe in valuing the separateness of mental health nursing and its unique input (Tummey, 2000). This may be because I am one myself. However, so are the contributors and I dare say most of the readers. So let's celebrate what we do and what we contribute to the field of mental health.

References

NMC (2002) *Code of Professional Conduct*, London: Nursing and Midwifery Council.
O'Brien, A.J. (2001) The therapeutic relationship: historical development and contemporary significance, *Journal of Psychiatric and Mental Health Nursing*, 8: 129–37.
Tummey, R. (2000) What's in a name? *Mental Health Nursing Journal*, 20, 9: 6–7.

Author Index

Subject Index